THREE IN A BED

Q. Where does a baby sleep?

A. In a cot.

Right?

Not necessarily. Only since Victorian times has it been standard practice for mothers and fathers to send their babies to sleep alone, away from the parental bed – often in another room. After bawling and screaming for up to an hour, the baby eventually cries himself to sleep, only to wake up again the middle of the night, demanding to be fed and then not wanting to be left. His parents snatch a few hours' sleep whenever they can, and get up in the morning feeling as exhausted as when they went to bed.

This book offers an alternative: taking your baby to bed with you. Drawing on startling new evidence, the author shows how babies who sleep with their parents benefit from the increased physical contact, while their parents benefit by getting virtually a full night's sleep.

Three in a Bed explains the advantages of this radical form of babycare, including its invaluable benefits for breastfeeding mothers, reviews the history of babies in the bed and, through interviews with parents, explores current attitutes to the idea. It also contains a new perspective on the tragedy of cot death, as well as practical advice on how to sustain your sex life, hints on safety in the bed and answers to all the commmon objections. Finally, the author deals with the moment when the baby leaves his parents' bed.

If you are a parent, or a parent-to-be, the approach advocated in this book could change your life. After all, one half of our parenting should be done at night.

Deborah Jackson is a freelance journalist who has contributed regularly to, among others, the *Independent*, the *Daily Telegraph*, *Today*, *The Stage*, *She*, *Woman's Own* and *Mother* magazine. She lives in Manchester with her husband, Paul, and their 21-month-old daughter. F

THREE IN A BED

Why you should sleep with your baby

DEBORAH JACKSON

Illustrations by Tom Newton

BLOOMSBURY

First published in Great Britain 1989

This paperback edition published 1990

Bloomsbury Publishing Limited, 2 Soho Square, London W1V 5DE

ISBN 0 7475-1524-7

10 9 8 7 6 5 4 3

Printed and bound in Great Britain by
HarperCollins Manufacturing, Glasgow

TO PAUL AND FRANCES, WITH LOVE

'I'd love to fall asleep and wake up in my mammy's arms'

Samuel Lewis (song title)

ACKNOWLEDGEMENTS

I should like to thank everyone who has helped with and supported me in the preparation of this book. I am indebted to many individuals for their kindness, and to the following organizations for their co-operation:

CRY-SIS
Foundation for the Study of Infant Deaths
Great Ormond Street Children's Hospital, London: Crying Baby
  Clinic
Guy's Hospital, London: Department of Clinical Psychology
Institute of Child Health, Bristol
John Radcliffe Hospital, Oxford: Community Midwives
The Law Commission
London School of Economics: Department of Anthropology
Loughborough University: Sleep Research Laboratory
Manchester University: Law Department
Marriage Research Centre
Museum of Childhood, Bethnal Green, London
National Childbirth Trust
Nottingham City Hospital
Organization for Parents Under Stress
University Hospital of Wales, Cardiff: Sleep Clinic

CONTENTS

PREFACE

Someone once asked me how I would fill a book on the subject of sleeping with babies. If bedsharing were as simple as allowing our children to scramble between the covers with us at night, there would not be much to say. But it is a long time since families slept together in Western society. Most parents regard the practice with suspicion, and commentators tend to dismiss the idea as – at best – eccentric.[1]

This book attempts to put cots in their context. It begins with the moment my own ideas on mothering were changed. It explores the reasons why mother and baby should not be separated for sleep. It looks at the confusion in mothering today, and the centuries of advice that have made mothers struggle against their instincts.

I have supported my arguments for co-sleeping with evidence from many fields: medicine, anthropology, psychology and common sense. The central themes of the book explore the value of touch, the creating of confidence and the answering of infants' physical needs, as well as the benefits for parents. Scientific studies now reveal the importance of bedsharing in an understanding of cot death, and mothers intending to breastfeed will find an entirely new approach in the chapter on sleep-feeding.

The third section of the book answers practical questions about taking a child into bed. It takes a historical and global look at family sleeping, considers how parents maintain a private life and asks when the baby leaves the nest. It tackles the most common objections to having a baby in the bed. Finally, parents relate their experiences of sleeping with their babies and older children.

The title of the book, *Three in a Bed*, refers to the most typical arrangement in Western society. It is not, however, a prescription. Single parents make happy twosomes with their children at night, while large family groups still sleep together, as in the days before central heating. Every home should find the arrangement to suit its needs.

Throughout the book, I have referred to the infant as 'he' and the primary parent as 'she', for clarity. This is not intended to discriminate against men who look after children, or against baby girls – my own daughter included.

Three in a Bed is the first – not the last – word on a very broad subject. I welcome correspondence from parents, childcare professionals and anyone who cares about the future of our children.

INTRODUCTION

It all began in a hospital ward when I was thirty-five weeks pregnant. I had been admitted in something of a panic, when the junior doctor inspecting me thought the baby had stopped growing. They had me in a hospital bed within the hour, muttering things like 'induced labour', and told me not to walk around, other than to answer calls of nature.

This was the first time I had ever been in hospital as a patient. I lay on my back, feeling quite well, and certain that the baby kicking around inside me was not in any danger. Midwives wired me up to a monitor that looked like one of those vibrating machines for reducing flab, and for the first time I could hear the infant heart drumming away.

I lay on my back, excited to hear the rapid 'doof, doof, doof' that accelerated every time the baby jabbed out with a heel or a hand. We were in the antenatal ward, the room heavy with anticlimax, where babies are busy not being born, and everyone is on the look-out for signs of the abnormal. But all around us was evidence of normality. Day and night, the air was filled with the screechings of new lungs. Babies, new-born, crying without end, calling for something they couldn't name and no one seemed able to supply.

At that time it seemed to me that the sound of a baby crying was a happy thing – evidence, at least, that the child was alive. It was just a matter of perspective. A cloud had settled over my own pregnancy, and I would have given anything to be safely on the other side of labour, with a new baby yelling in the cot next to my bed. The screams from the postnatal wards sounded like heavenly wails celebrating birth.

Unable to walk around, and unable to concentrate on work I had smuggled into hospital, I picked up a book someone had lent me a few days before: *The Continuum Concept* by Jean Liedloff – a passionate paperback, telling of the author's travels to the heart of the South American jungle and her life with the remote Yequana Indians.

Her first chapter – 'How My Ideas Were So Radically Changed' – drew me into a strange world. A society where mutual love and respect are the basis for every dealing with others, where work and play are the same thing, where the atmosphere is happy and optimistic. It was a description of a real world, but one that lived up to the expectations of the humans in the group; a world where material greed and wilful destruction were unknown, but where individual expression was encouraged. In this society the children did not throw tantrums, toddlers did not run away from their mothers at the first opportunity, babies did not scream.

I lay in my hospital bed, listening to the contented doof, doof, doof on the fetal heat monitor. Inside the amniotic sac, my baby was in its own kind of Utopia. Constantly fed, warmed, nurtured, all its needs were being perfectly met. Birth would be a rude awakening, however gently it was administered, and the rest of its life would be a series of reminders that the womb was a paradise lost. The nine months of nurture could not be regained.

But perhaps there was another way to start out on life. Given the advances of modern technology, many of the babies born in this large teaching hospital in 1987 could reasonably expect to live another eighty-seven years. Some might even see in the twenty-second century. Was that really something to scream about? Why should we all spend our first few months 'testing out our lungs', as the midwives called it? As my hospital stay stretched into two days, those testing infant cries began to sound like torture.

Of course, things always seem worse in the middle of the night. But when you're eight months pregnant and woken up by an unsubtle blend of trips to the loo and other people's children crying, it's hard to tell where your dreams end and the nightmares begin. I started to have visions of a lifetime of pain and struggle for my unborn child, and began to realize why some friends had said, 'it's just not fair to bring a child into this world.'

After all, what was there to look forward to? Who did I know who was really happy? I struggled to think of someone without hang-ups or bitterness, someone whose life had not been torn apart by divorce or disappointment, someone who was content with his lot, even if that did not include a Barratt home, a BMW or a body like Borg or Bardot. My nightmare turned into a kind of *Apocalypse Now*, ten episodes of *Eastenders* rolled into one, a tragedy of personal torment and atomic horror. I was quite glad when the ward clock struck six, and the tea trolley came rattling into view.

Like the man who read that smoking was bad for your health, I suppose at this point I could have given up reading. But I felt much better the next day, especially when the ultrasound scan showed that my baby was doing very nicely. Her apparent refusal to grow was, according to my consultant, because her head had engaged in the pelvis. Labour was not to be induced, and I could go home that afternoon. I finished Liedloff's book, and left hospital with a new outlook.

The altered approach was quite simple. I explore the reasons for it in the following chapters. It did not take long to persuade my husband Paul that we weren't going to need the beautiful second-hand cot we had just bought. Not for a while, anyway. Our new baby, when it arrived, was going to be sleeping in bed with us.

I suppose, at the time, we thought that would be that. A simple, personal decision that affected no one else, and pleased the two of us. A perfectly 'natural' arrangement, in so far as we understood the word. It fitted in with our views of how we wanted to bring up the baby, and we really did not envisage any problems. We certainly had no idea about the depth of feeling our sleeping arrangements would arouse in others. But it would not have stopped us if we had known.

Three weeks later (10.9.87 – countdown day), Frances Rose was born in a Cardiff hospital. She travelled through the night to be with us, as did her father, who was working in Manchester. She arrived two hours before he did, just in time for breakfast, and two weeks early according to the charts.

That night, I was once again in a hospital bed, worn out but ecstatic. All the visitors had gone, leaving showers of pink carnations, and as the lights went out on the ward, midwives came round volunteering to look after the babies for each weary mother. 'Are you sure you don't want her to go to a nursery?' they asked me. 'You'll need all the strength you can get. We'll wake you up to feed her.' However exhausted I was, I could not see that a night's sleep for me was more important than my little girl's first night in the world. Anyway, I was still running on adrenalin.

The lights went out and I drew the curtains around our bed and plastic cot. I had held Frances all the day – she seemed to want to feed at twenty-minute intervals – and snuggled into bed with her now. In the darkness of the room she opened her eyes wide for the first time, and held out her hand to me. She stuck her tongue out at me, and stared wide-eyed as I stuck my tongue out at her. I could not believe how much beauty and intelligence was wrapped up in this tiny person, only six pounds heavy and ten hours old. I'd had no idea a new baby could be as controlled and calm as this.

I did not sleep much that night, mostly as a result of keeping alert for the night nurses who patrolled every few hours. They would stop at my curtains, peep in and say 'You won't fall asleep with the baby in the bed will you, Mrs Jackson?' 'Oh no,' I promised. Frances slept, fed and quietly played her way through the night – and on and off, I slept, too. It was, without doubt, the happiest night of my life.

I | ALL NIGHT, EVERY NIGHT

It has been a hard day's night. All that pain and yelling and space. Where once there was a warm, enclosing womb, it's gone cold. Nothing to hold you in, no limits to your new world. Perhaps you were drugged, perhaps you struggled fully conscious through the dark passage and out, slippery, into a pair of hands in rubber gloves. Maybe you found the nipple straight away – or did they weigh you first, naked on cold plastic, while you screamed? Were you wrapped in linen and placed in a cot to sleep? Did anyone think of turning off the lights?

I'm not talking about someone else's baby. I'm not talking about your baby, or my baby. This is about you – and me. We all went through it, and like it or not, the experience is still etched somewhere in our subconscious.

Birth is the moment of greatest vulnerability in our lives, and it comes directly after nine months of trouble-free motoring inside the womb. When a child is born, space, light and time are alien to it. The muffled sounds and familiar tastes of the amniotic sac are ripped away. Someone has turned the volume up, and the treble knob, too. Human contact is no longer a constant, but an intermittent delight.

Dr Frédérick Leboyer was one of the first Western doctors to recognize the torment of the baby in modern birthing techniques. As Chef de Clinique at the Faculty of Medicine in Paris, he observed Eastern birthing methods, and saw that intervention was rarely necessary for successful delivery. He also brought controversy to the labour room.

In 1966, Leboyer suggested a new concept: Birth Without Violence. In his book of that name he drew a highly emotional portrait of the baby born in anguish. He believed that much of the infant's suffering could be avoided.

The evidence is there before us.

The tragic expression, those tight-shut eyes, those puzzled
eyebrows ...
That howling mouth, that burrowing desperate head.
Those outstretched hands beseeching; then withdrawn, raised to
the head in the classic gesture of despair.
Those furiously kicking feet, those knees drawn up to protect the
tender bulging stomach.
The whole creature is one jumping, twitching mass.
Far from not speaking, every inch of its body is crying out: 'Don't
touch me!'
And at the same time pleading: 'Don't leave me! Help me!'
Has there ever been a more heart-rending appeal?
And yet this appeal – as old as birth itself – has been
misunderstood, ignored, indeed unheard.
How can this have been? How can this still be?
So can we say that a new-born baby doesn't speak?
No. It is we who do not listen.

The Victorians thought that when a baby cried, he was exercising
his lungs. But now we know babies do not have to cry, either at birth
or afterwards. One explanation for their screaming puts it like this:

Early in infancy, the baby comes fully awake only at times of
crisis, such as hunger. At these times, he is on the verge of what
the adult would call panic; the baby has no time perspective, for
him the crisis drags on interminably, and he is helpless to do
anything about it. If relief is delayed, he becomes even more upset
or exhausts himself with crying; already a tiny seed of distrust
has been planted, and next time the panic is a little closer, the
crisis more exigent.

(Stone and Church, *Childhood and Adolescence*)

When we admire a baby for having a lovely pair of lungs, we are
ignoring nature's most obvious distress call. It is, of course, the signal
to which every mother is programmed to respond.

When we put a new-born infant down, he flails about in search of
human contact. We say he is exercising his legs, but every sound he
makes, every twitch, indicates that he wants to be picked up and
held. In the only way he knows how, the infant is trying to tell the
mother that he needs her.

The principle of separating mother and baby at birth is still common in many hospitals around the world. Sometimes they are separated completely, for up to thirty-six hours, or reunited only for feeds at four-hourly intervals. Many a mix-up has taken place in the time a baby is away from its mother.

But the reasons for allowing a mother to keep her new baby go deeper than this. As midwife Sally Inch explains:

> Unless the baby is in need of the care of a paediatrician and intensive-care nurses, there is no need to remove him from his mother ... Researchers have shown repeatedly that the normal baby is especially alert and receptive after birth, ready to interact with his mother; any rest he needs he will take later, and unless he is in need of specialist observation, or the mother has been given narcotic drugs, there is no one who will 'observe' her baby better or more keenly than she. Moreover, all these necessary procedures can be and are carried out perfectly satisfactorily at home when that is the place of delivery.
>
> (*Birthrights*)

Practices are changing in the West, where a mother is likely to be allowed to keep her baby near her during her stay in hospital. But even in the most enlightened establishments, babies are taken away for weighing and the swift Apgar test, which rates the health of the new-born for heartbeat, breathing attempts, muscle tone and so on.

Yet for a new-born baby, nearness is not enough. An infant lying in his cot does not understand that his mother is just across the room. He also has no sense of time. He cannot know that his mother was with him two minutes ago, or that she will pick him up again in two minutes' time. All he knows is the panic of isolation.

Psychotherapist Jean Liedloff puts into perspective the new-born baby's perception of time:

> Even years later, at the age of five, the promise of a bicycle 'next Christmas' is, in August, approximately as satisfying as no promise at all. At ten, time has pulled itself together in the light of experience to the extent that the child can wait a day more or less comfortably for some things, a week for others and a month for special items; but a year is still quite meaningless when it comes to mitigating want....

Only at the age of forty or fifty do most people have any sort of perspective of a day or a month in the context of a lifetime, while only a few gurus and octogenarians are able to appreciate the relationships of moments or lifetimes to eternity (by fully realizing the irrelevance of the arbitrary concept of time).

(*The Continuum Concept*)

A new-born child has only immediate desire, which consumes him while he is apart from his mother. Yet hospital policy throughout Britain insists that he spend most of his hours tucked up in a plastic cot. Premature babies are even more likely to find themselves mothered by an incubator for their first weeks of life. In most British hospitals, mothers are not even allowed to carry their own babies, for fear of insurance claims should there be an accident.

Hospitals create barriers between mothers and their children, as women wheel their new-born babies around the ward, allow them to cry in the cot at the bottom of the bed, or send them to the nursery. If you sit cuddling your baby all day long, a midwife is likely to advise you to get your rest. As one mother put it:

I have been told off by a midwife for cuddling my one-day-old baby when he couldn't sleep ('You'll have him spoilt rotten before you even get him home.')

(Joy Henderson, Dumfries, *The Independent*, 2 August 1988)

Doctors and midwives do not suggest that cuddling up close to another human being may have a rejuvenating effect, or that continuous body contact is essential for the optimum health of your new child. A mother is encouraged to believe, from the start, that the baby's needs and will are set against her own. So when it comes to lights-out, she listens to the nurses who tell her she'll be better after a good night's sleep, and baby should go to the nursery. In the old days, there would be no choice in the matter. Now they promise to wake you up when he cries. Neither solution is satisfactory, either for mother or for baby.

A new-born child, without experience, and thus without hope, lives in a world of sharp contrasts; either his needs are being met, and all is well – or his needs are not being met, and he is terrified.

The fear babies learn in the first few months does not disappear quickly. A two- or three-year-old may be more aware of his surroundings, but he is still tormented when forced to sleep away from his parents, for reasons he cannot understand. Australian paediatrician Dr Christopher Green describes the panic of a toddler who is left alone to 'cry it out':

> Many health workers tell parents that when their child cries at night they should not go near him, but leave him to cry himself to sleep. This can often take three or four hours; I think it is not only cruel but also an ineffective method of treatment. After ten minutes, most children become hysterical and have no idea why they are crying. They get themselves into a lather, sweat profusely, their hearts pound and they become very frightened. Fear is not a good way of teaching any child good behaviour.
>
> (*Toddler Taming*)

Trying to teach a person something at this stage is akin to torture, because a child cannot comprehend anything but his own panic, or his sense of well-being. The new-born is even more vulnerable. He expects warmth and movement, food and comfort, all of which are supplied at once by his mother's presence, and access to her breasts. Any experience that denies him these things is horrific to him. If his mother (or an equivalent care-giver) is not there, instinct tells him she might as well be dead. If his mother is dead, then he is likely to die, too. These are the meanings of an isolated baby's cries.

Some mothers follow advice that says a baby should never be allowed to cry, but at the same time, they try to educate their babies into sleeping alone at a young age. The net result is that when the babies scream, their mothers come running. This is the beginning of a pattern that will haunt them for the rest of their days.

In order to get the attention and nurture that he seeks, the infant is forced to suffer and convey his suffering to his mother. His mother will suffer, too. She hates to hear her baby cry, but he has to do the thing she hates before she will come to him. As he learns the way of his world, the cries of desperateness will turn to cries of anger, and one day, he will find that being naughty is the best way to get her attention. Or perhaps he gets most love when he falls down and hurts himself – so he becomes accident-prone.

Many mothers have been led to believe that letting the baby cry is the only way to control him – by ignoring his calls for help, she attempts to suppress his will and curb his infant temper. Then a different pattern emerges. The baby displays a syndrome known as 'learned helplessness', a term taken from scientific experiments with animals in the 1960s:

> They divided some dogs into two groups. The first group was given electric shocks from which they could do absolutely nothing to escape. The second group of dogs was placed in identical cages, but given no shocks at all. The same two groups of dogs were then tested in a special box which had two compartments divided by a barrier. In one compartment, the dogs received an electric shock. But by jumping over the barrier, they could escape the shocks. The second group of dogs, which had never had any electric shocks before, very quickly discovered the escape route and jumped over the barrier. But the astounding thing was that the first group of dogs – those which had previously been shocked – did not make any attempt to escape. They just crouched helplessly in the electric shock compartment. Even when the dogs were lifted over the barrier to the safe side, it still made no difference. They had learned from their first experience that nothing they did made any difference, and they were unable to control events.
>
> (Michael Odent, *Primal Health*)

Dr Spock, leading American childcare expert since the 1940s, tells mothers to leave their babies to cry. He describes the state of learned helplessness perfectly, though without believing it does any damage: 'The second night the crying is apt to last only 10 minutes,' he writes, describing the effects of his 'let-them-cry' programme. 'The third night there usually isn't any at all.'[1]

The Spock-trained baby has resigned himself to the hopelessness of his situation. He has learnt life's cruellest lesson: there isn't any point in trying to improve things. Most of these babies will grow into adults who believe the same – suffering is the human condition, and you can't do anything about it.

Whether you leave a baby to cry, or use his tears as an alarm to bring you running, you are interfering with the instinct that makes him tick. If only we knew how not to interfere. We need to rediscover what mothers throughout history have known instinctively – how to offer our children complete security, so that they can grow and develop in confidence.

The prevailing theory runs contrary to this line of thinking. Society presumes that children are anti-social, and that 'pandering' to their needs will 'spoil' them. Moralists believe that education, firmness and discipline are required. Christianity, the major religion of the West, tells us that even new-born infants need to be cleansed of their sins. Doctors, agony aunts and psychologists insist that babies are trouble. Children are wilful, manipulative, and they'll never let you have a moment's peace. We are conditioned to expect the worst.

But let us start from a more positive perspective. The infant human being is a sociable creature. He is equipped with all the faculties he needs for survival. Operating mostly on instincts and reflexes, he does not cry without reason. His communications are urgent, and they relate to his immediate needs.

All the evidence shows us that a baby needs to copy, to follow, to behave as we expect him to. This is the key to his survival. If a child's instinct were programmed to upset the social order, manipulate his mother and be generally obnoxious, the human race would have died out aeons ago. If babies were meant to scream all day and keep us awake at night, our ancestors would simply have chucked the little brats into the river.

A new-born child, motivated by the instinctive will to survive, needs to integrate for his own good. So why do they cry as babies, and manipulate us when they're old enough? Those cries and moans are designed to irritate us as much as possible, so that we change our response. They are certain indications that something is wrong.

The mother who says her baby is a monster is describing the behaviour of a human being looking for comfort. He cries because his needs are not being fully met. A baby who screams is talking to you. At least he feels there is something worth crying for. Pity the child who has withdrawn into a resigned silence.

Babies are not naughty – just needy and utterly helpless. For a long time it puzzled me why a human infant was *so* vulnerable and dependent, when new-born deer can struggle to their feet within hours of birth, when ewes do not have to carry their lambs around everywhere, and kittens can be toilet trained within weeks; why a baby is completely lost without its mother or guardian.

Human babies are born with relatively small brains, although the cranium grows rapidly in the first months after birth. Scientists believe this is because the infant head has to force its way through the narrow maternal birth canal, and a larger brain would risk damage on the way. The new-born baby, operating on a primitive level with a

"We put her down at night and we never hear a thing"

brain that has yet to undergo many complex changes, is completely dependent on his mother for his existence.

Animal-watcher Desmond Morris describes how physical handicap hinders the human infant, while his ancient cousin, the monkey, is swinging from the trees with its parents soon after birth:

> During its waking periods the newborn infant moves comparatively little. Unlike other primate species its musculature is poorly developed. A young monkey can cling tightly to its mother from the moment of birth onwards. It may even clasp on to her fur with its hands while it is still in the process of being born. In our own species, by contrast, the newborn is helpless and can only make trivial movements of its arms and legs.
>
> (*The Naked Ape*)

This seems a massive drawback for human babies who, like monkeys, expect to be carried everywhere by their parents. In the (at least) three to four million years of the evolution of man, the human foetus grew inside the mother's womb while she foraged for food. At birth, the baby was held or bound to the parent's chest, while he or she continued the daily struggle to survive.

Humans, like monkeys, are a 'carrying' species. Other creatures – birds, for instance – work on the 'cache' principle. Their young are kept in nests while the parents look for food. But human babies are not designed to be cosseted in cots while both parents are away.

To feed her baby, the human mother has to guide him to her breast and keep him there. If she wants to carry on with her daily duties, she must learn to do without one arm, or contrive a sling to hold him in place – or put him down. The quality of a human baby's nurturing is completely her responsibility, and the only clues a baby offers are his cries and smiles.

The plight of the new baby is even more puzzling when we consider his potential in contrast with that of other animals. Small-brained or not, surely our superior intelligence ought to aid us to stand, walk, feed and hold things faster than our four-footed friends? We ought to be able to cope with the physical niceties in minutes, leaving us free to talk, invent, explore and create.

Why should mankind have this massive handicap, when he has to compete with lions and gazelles and snakes? How did Neanderthal baby, curled up in the fetal position and unable to wipe his own nose, ever reach adulthood? The answer is, that his parents did not leave him alone. Day and night, he was held next to the skin of his parents and other care-givers. He was not expected to fend for himself.

Within months the human baby makes up for lost time, learning more than a monkey could assimilate in twenty years. By his first birthday, a child may not be able to walk, but he has mastered the necessary vocalizations for language, a skill no monkey can ever match. And something else is going on during the first year of life. A human infant is developing his ego ...

> ... the 'baby' is a very sensitive and knowing human being. He is going through various experiences that are laying down some of the basic, automatic emotional patterns of the personality. He is learning that other human beings can or cannot be trusted. He is learning that they can be kind, reasonable, gentle, dependable and consistent, or that they can be evasive, cruel, loud, capricious and unreasonable. And we know from thousands of observations that what he learns in the first year is not easy to unlearn.
>
> (English and Pearson, *Emotional Problems of Living*)

Helplessness is the vital condition of the human baby, because he needs to be always with his mother. His frailty is her cue to pick him up and hold him. A baby has to sort out his own ego from the muddle he sees around him, and he does that by first identifying with her. He does not initially see a distinction between himself and the breast that feeds him. What he has to learn is not merely how to take control of his legs, his hands and his bowels, but a sense of himself. This is what makes him different from every other animal on earth.

At the beginning, the mother and infant are as one – the rest is a slow struggle towards independence. There is nothing in the struggle that a child cannot cope with, but if we make it more painful or more abrupt for our children than nature intended, then we are creating problems for the future.

Child psychotherapist Dilys Daws makes the connection between infant sleep difficulties and the development of the infant personality:

> Looking at sleeping problems makes us aware of the complexity of the emotions involved in being a parent. We see how subtle is the process by which mothers and babies move from their early closeness to seeing themselves as two separate beings.
>
> (*Journal of Child Psychotherapy*, 1985)

When you put your baby down to sleep in his cradle and tiptoe out of the room, he thinks a part of himself has gone – the part that sustains life and gives him comfort. He does not have the inner resources to cope with this separation. Whether he protests or not, he needs you. It is such an obvious explanation for infant misery that medical handbooks tend to overlook it. Experts keep telling us to put the baby down, because (apparently) it is easier, and mothers should not be subject to the whims of their children. They are missing the point altogether.

All that childcare experts can offer so far is a series of schemes to increase the gap between mother and child. This intervention disturbs the child's development, and reduces the mother's ability to meet her child's needs. The baby suffers and cries. She soon believes the professionals and other mothers who tell her that babies are a bore.

But researchers are tentatively discovering what all mothers used to know instinctively – for instance, the more you hold a baby, the more you want to hold him.

> A great deal of the work done on very early separation has been carried out by the paediatricians Marshall Klaus and John Kennell. In one interesting study of theirs, a group of nine Guatemalan mothers were given their naked babies immediately after they had left the delivery room. A second group of nine mothers and babies were separated according to the usual hospital routine.
>
> The babies in both groups were then sent to the newborn nursery for the next twelve hours and returned to their mothers for their first feed. Observations during this feed of maternal fondling, kissing, gazing into the baby's face, and holding him close showed that the mothers who did much more of all of them were those who had had early contact with their infants.
>
> (Aidan Macfarlane, *The Psychology of Childbirth*)

This is the phenomenon known as 'bonding', which troubles so many mothers today, to judge from the welter of newspaper articles on the subject. 'Mothers who don't love their babies' is the postnatal topic of the 1980s. Could it be that women are simply not being given the chance to relax with their new-born infants in a way that is useful to them? It seems we allow ourselves to be intimidated by professionals from the start. You wouldn't want the waiter in a candle-lit restaurant to engineer your first kiss, so why do we allow midwives to hold baby and nipple at the initial breastfeed?

If mothers are not allowed to follow their instincts when it comes to feeding and nurturing their babies, they will hardly satisfy their own emotional and bodily needs. It seems incredible that parents, in the privacy of their own homes, are afraid to respond to their babies' night-time requirements by taking them into bed.

Critics say that parents who sleep with their babies are succumbing to the infant's whim. Yet nature has designed mother and baby so that their needs are complementary. She to cuddle and feed and nurture her child, he to be cuddled and fed and nurtured.

Many laboratory experiments have been done since the 1960s to discover the effects on animals who are separated from their mothers for extended periods. Monkeys, for instance, display a range of critical physical responses to the lack of maternal contact:

> Studies using telemetry [radiophonic instruments] on a variety of macaque monkey species (bonnet, pigtail and rhesus) indicate that when separated from their mothers, primates as old as four to six months of life ... lose body temperature and can experience disturbances in sleep, with decreased REM [Rapid Eye Movement] sleep periods, changes in EEG [brain] activity, alterations in cellular immune responses, and increases in cardiac arrhythmias [irregular heartbeat]. It has been demonstrated in squirrel monkeys that separation increases their adrenal (stress) secretions and plasma cortisol levels and decreases their ability to combat pathogens [diseases] because of decreases in immuno-globulins ...
>
> (James McKenna, *Medical Anthropology*, 1986)

Human babies deprived of physical affection likewise have a greatly reduced chance of survival. Studies of infants in institutions thirty years ago identified the 'failure to thrive' syndrome, where babies deprived of mother-love lost weight and often died, though they were fed enough to live on.

There are many dimensions to maternal separation for human infants. Psychological and spiritual factors cannot be separated from the physical. Even if he survives his mother's absence, the child is likely to become depressed – listless, unresponsive, sad – and if placed in an institution and deprived of a genuine mother figure, he may well be retarded in comparison with a child reared at home:

> ... two groups of two-year-olds living in the same institution were studied. One group was given very little tenderness, although adequately cared for in every other respect, while in the other a nurse was assigned to each child and there was no lack of tenderness and affection. At the end of half a year the first group was mentally and physically retarded in comparison with the second ... The dramatic and tragic changes in behaviour and feeling which follow separation of a young child from his mother and the beneficient results of restoring him to her are in fact available for all to see, and it is astonishing that so little attention has been given to them hitherto.
>
> (John Bowlby, *Child Care and the Growth of Love*)

Gill Cox and Sheila Dainow, authors of *Making the Most of Loving*, describe the long-lasting psychological effects of separating a baby from its mother:

> Being left completely alone is one of the greatest terrors for human beings. The fear goes back to when, as babies, we realised we were actually separate from our mothers. That realisation created a panic about who would care for us. Each time a baby wakes up and finds itself alone, it cannot know someone is there until it has had enough experiences to provide it with the evidence. By then, the awful fear that aloneness brings is implanted in our experience and can be triggered off at different times in our adult life ...[2]

Psychologists and counsellors take all this as basic theory for the problems their patients suffer every day – but few believe anything can be done about it. Separation anxiety is the root of many common neuroses. Putting baby in a nursery at night is so usual now, that many mothers and doctors cannot envisage any other way of dealing with bedtime. But there *are* ways of changing our mothering practices, so that fewer people end up in the psychiatrist's chair.

Childcare researchers of the 1970s asking the question, 'Are Mothers Really Necessary?'[3] found that we do have our uses, but still they doubted that the mother's presence was crucial to her baby's well-being. The source of their doubt sprang from medical notions of the last century. Victorian doctors believed that the poor classes were inherently weaker of mind and body than the gentry. Experimenters hung on to the notion that depressed, sickly, retarded babies were products of their parents' genes. They argued that since most of the abandoned babies in the studies were offspring of the working class, their slow progress could be explained by hereditary factors.

The only way to eliminate the genetic factor was to study twins. It is difficult to separate and study human twins, without causing a detrimental effect to one of the pair. Instead, one psychologist compared the behaviour of twin goat kids, separating one from its mother for a short spell each day. Leading psychiatrist John Bowlby described the test:

> Except for the daily experimental period of forty minutes, both kids live and feed with their mother. During the experimental period the lights are periodically extinguished, which is known to create anxiety in goats, and this produces very different behaviour in the twins. The one which is with its mother is at ease and moves about freely; the isolated one is 'psychologically frozen' and remains cowed in one corner. In one of the first experiments the isolated kid discontinued suckling from its mother and, the experimenters being unaware of this and so unable to help, it died after a few days. This is ample demonstration of the adverse effects of maternal deprivation on the young of mammals, and disposes finally of the argument that all the observed effects are due to heredity.
>
> (*Child Care and the Growth of Love*)

Scientists were beginning to admit that maternal separation, even if only for regular short spells, could have detrimental effects on infants. The implications for human babies were even more shattering than for other animals, because of the speed of growth of the brain, the formation of the ego, and the breathing changes a baby has to undergo in order to achieve speech.

But it took a long time before the connection was made between infant behaviour and night-time separation. In 1986, when an American, Dr James McKenna, questioned the use of the cot, he had to cross the fields of paediatrics and anthropology to do so. It was controversial ground:

> For other mammal infants, but especially primate infants, short-term separation leads to physiological consequences. This conclusion forces us to consider the possible effects of nocturnal separation on human infants who, in Western and urban societies, regularly sleep apart from their parents in separate rooms.
>
> (*Medical Anthropology*, 1986)

What happens to a human baby who is left in the dark without his mother? Sometimes he cries, sometimes he has nightmares, sometimes he hits his head against the bars of his purpose-built cage. According to the experts, 'Nightmares occur almost universally in children from three to six years of age.'[4] Head-banging is also common, and is usually explained by the child's desire for comfort:

> When we see a baby pushing his head against the bars of his cot or the top of the bed, we tend to pull him down again, thinking that he will be better. It is a waste of time, because this position is voluntary, the baby is looking for a point of contact, he wants to find himself once more enclosed as he was in his mother's womb.
>
> (Laurance Pernoud, *J'élève mon Enfant* – my translation)

Thanks to scientific research, we are now beginning to realize why our babies suffer so. Even when separated from their mothers for a short time, infants undergo a series of physical changes, affecting their temperature, breathing patterns, stress levels and many other factors. Dr James McKenna wrote:

> In order to understand the form and consequences of separation (primarily mother from infant) for the infant, we must know how the infant's body changes physiologically after separation and, thus, how through contact the mother physiologically regulates her infant's temperature, metabolic rate, hormone levels, enzyme production, antibody titer [the strength of antibodies in the infant's system and thus his ability to fight disease], sleep cycle, heart rate, and respiration so as to promote her infant's health

and survival. Together, these data disclose the overall impact of immediate separation and remind us that when human (urban) infants are regularly separated, for example, for nocturnal sleep – which can be regarded as an evolutionarily novel situation – there is no reason to think that their physiological systems are not also affected.

(*Medical Anthropology*, 1986)

These are all measurable, physical reactions of babies separated from their mothers, revealed in laboratory tests with humans and other mammals.

But sometimes observation is enough to tell us that our babies are affected by modern mothering techniques. Anthropologists and field workers in the Third World tell us that babies who are carried all day by their mothers, and who sleep with them at night, develop differently from babies raised according to the Western pattern. The evidence suggests that children suffer in the long term by spending all night, every night alone:

... when the anthropologist Marcelle Geber went to Kenya and Uganda to study the effects of malnutrition on newborn babies and infants, she was astounded to find that these babies were more advanced and smiled more than babies she had seen before in industrialized countries.

She found that around the age of six or seven months the Ugandan baby was able to pick up a toy which was outside its vision. With American and European babies, this is usually possible only at around fifteen months of age. Her test evaluated motor development, and the development of a form of reasoning. One big difference between the two groups was that the Ugandan babies belonged to a culture in which the period of dependence on the mother is not disturbed.

(Michel Odent, *Primal Health*)

Despite the Western tendency to push children, and our emphasis on competition, Ugandan babies are more advanced than our own. The more we interfere with and attempt to train our young, the more we are tampering with things we do not fully understand. We should be fulfilling our babies' expectations of us, not creating our own expectations of them.

Some parents – including members of the La Leche League in America – choose to sleep with their children because they are convinced of the advantages of this arrangement by scientific evidence. Few people in this country, however, have access to the academic discussions that exist mainly in medical journals. Many British parents sleep with their children for purely practical reasons.

Breastfeeding mothers often take their babies to bed for convenience. Some families sleep with their children because of lack of space. Poverty may mean parents cannot afford a cot. Other parents simply follow their instincts in responding to their children's complaints at night. For most parents, the decision to comfort the child in bed is made according to the immediate needs of the infant. Many respond to ill babies by taking them into bed at night, as family doctor David Haslam reports:

> From the moment I entered general practice I could not fail to notice how many children are nursed in their parents' bed when they are sick, not in their own. Both parents and children realise the comfort and security that comes from such an arrangement.
> (*Sleepless Children*)

Others relent to toddlers who will not let them sleep any other way. Sharing a bed with a baby is extremely common in our society, even though prevailing theories warn us against the practice.

Science and common sense are slowly converging to reach the same conclusion: there are many advantages in sleeping with your baby. I shall examine the most compelling reasons in this book, but perhaps all we need to know is that putting an infant in a cot is against the law of nature.

We go to strenuous efforts to separate mother and baby at night, without fully understanding the dangers involved. Now is the time to reunite them.

2 | CRISIS – WHAT CRISIS?

Sticker on the rear windscreen of a car: 'I can handle any crisis. I have children.'

A child is born. No sooner do parents begin to appreciate their little miracle, than the problems begin. Babies cry, they're unsettled, they won't sleep. Mother finds it difficult to carry on with her old life, her career or her relationships. She becomes resentful.

'The expectation is that the birth of the first baby will be an event of joy and happiness,' says marriage counsellor Marian Jackson. 'In fact, this time can be the start of a major rift between many couples.

'The baby has to be attended to because he cries loudest. The mother is often tired – she needs tremendous support. In the nuclear family, she can only look to her partner for this. He, meanwhile, may be feeling jealous and resentful of the baby, who is taking all her attention.

'Because of society's expectations that all should be lovely when the first child comes along, the couple are unlikely to admit these problems. The pressures of the nuclear family are very intense.'

With its emphasis on romantic love and the search for the perfect partner, Western society sets great store by the couple. In countries where strict purdah is practised, women live together in separate quarters, caring for and supporting each other. If we compare the life of a traditional Pakistani mother with that of a modern British mother, it is clear who has the better deal.

In her family village, the Pakistani woman can count on the support of her in-laws and cousins when bringing up her children. Following the birth of a baby, she is exempted from all household duties – other than feeding and caring for her child – for forty days. When her children have children, she will in turn take her part in rearing them and caring for the new parents. (The forty-day 'honeymoon' period for mothers and babies is also a traditional practice in Japan.)

In urban society, where many people live alone, drive to work alone and eat alone, people have to fend for themselves. Yet a selection of headlines from any problem page in a women's weekly magazine reveals how dissatisfied we are with this arrangement. In relationships and out of them, we complain:

'My marriage was a disaster, but I can't bear a future alone.'
'I've lost all confidence in myself as a mother and can't seem to please anyone in the family.'
'Why don't my friends need friendship the way I do?'
'Our relationship's changed, but I feel mean leaving now.'
'Even though I'm only 19 and in love, my life seems to be full of so many worries.'
'The man I love can't bear the thought of being the cause of a marriage break-up.'
'People just don't understand that men can feel hurt and devastated by divorce, too.'

(*Best*, 8 July 1988)

The emphasis is on our capacity to cope as individuals. Women, who have fought for – and won – the rights to vote, work and equal pay, are often expected to rear their children single-handed. While extended families lend all their support to the childbearing woman, the nuclear system means some must survive on their own. The result is that in many 'civilized' countries, the family is in a state of crisis.

Modern marriages and relationships often consist of the smallest of family units: a man and a woman. This may be a stable arrangement, but any change – the loss of a partner, or the arrival of a third party – is bound to bring immense complications and adjustments.

Parents today are aware of the changes babies bring. The Marriage Research Council's survey of sixty-five young wedded couples in the 1980s revealed that people thought it was important to 'be ready' to have children:

The definition of readiness to have children is highly subjective yet founded upon a common image of parenthood which stresses the disadvantages of becoming parents. Descriptions of the impact of children included, 'like having a bomb dropped', 'an extra burden' and 'a strain on the marriage'. Good parenting requires accepting a severely limited social life, constant financial worries, the intrusion of a third person and so on. Above all it demands tolerance, resignation and selflessness.

(Penny Mansfield, *Journal of Sociology and Social Policy*, 1982)

These were the expectations of newly-weds without children. Our society teaches us that, far from enhancing a marriage, children may ruin it. Although one husband in the survey said a child would be 'the cream on the wedding cake', most couples felt the cake wasn't theirs to have to eat:

... for the majority, their chief concern was the preservation of closeness against the intrusion of a third party – the child.

The extended family can take the pressure off a young couple and make mothering less intense. Having plenty of close, practical help enables parents to have time alone within a supportive emotional unit. Parents on their own rarely get time off. Yet grandparents and other useful relatives may not even live in the same town. Recent studies suggest that the absence of grandparents may have a crucial effect on a child's upbringing. Lynn Fairbanks of the University of California has shown that proper development of the African vervet monkey is dependent upon older relatives being around:

Youngsters with grandmothers were brought up in a much more relaxed fashion. They encountered fewer restrictions on their movements, spent less time in the maternal embrace and wandered off on their own more frequently.
By contrast, babies without a grandmother came in for an excess of maternal devotion. Their mothers clung to them, thwarting their attempts to strike out on their own. Maternal caresses were more likely to take the form of a stifling hug than a casual reassuring contact. As a result, they gained their independence at a slower pace.

(Stephen Young, *The Independent*, 16 May 1988)

Even the most casual observer will acknowledge the connection between this behaviour and modern mothering. Whether we are smothering our children with kisses, or screaming at them to 'stop it!' we are undeniably baby-centred. Women with children worry inordinately about their offspring, and when they gather together, tend to talk about nothing else.

After intense mothering, many Western children find it impossible to live alongside their parents. If grandma was excessively protective in her day, she may find that her daughter is still struggling for independence, and shuts her out of life with the new baby. Grandparents are then simply unwelcome, and unable to enjoy the more relaxed role of extended parenting.

Urban mothers try to undo what their parents did to them, but they are unable to call on positive experience to help them in their task. As Brigid McConville outlines in her book, *Mad to be a Mother*, our find-your-own-feet society can be a cruel place for mothers and babies:

> Most venues of the adult world are alien and hostile to her if she is in the company of children. Of course, there are places – like offices – where the majority of people would agree children simply shouldn't be. That consensus is itself rather a sad reflection on the extent to which we have divided the life of home from that of 'work' ...
>
> Most mothers, in the depths of their humility, don't really expect to be welcomed into the places where people without children go. It's probably just as well.

Postnatal illness (depression) affects up to fifty per cent of mothers with young children. Doctors tell suffering mothers that baby blues is a normal reaction after the birth. A potent mixture of hormones, shattered expectations and lack of support might have something to do with it. And as we shall see later, few mothers in 'civilized' countries have the chance to satisfy, or even explore their deep maternal needs. They are encouraged to put the baby down as often as possible, when their instinct tells them to hold him close.

Great and valuable efforts are spent preparing the pregnant woman for the actual Birth Day. For months, women go through their paces, learning the exercises, the breathing, the positions for labour. Some then enjoy giving birth; but few urban women are prepared – emotionally, physically or practically – for the arrival of the babies themselves.

When Frances was small, we attended a weekly mother-and-baby group. Watched by health visitors, the young mothers would sit in a circle and swap horror stories about the traumas of twenty-four-hour parenting. We may all have been capable, independent, sociable beings before our babies were born, but many had since regressed into fearful, overprotective mothers. The lack of confidence in the group was striking – and these were the ones who were bold enough to turn up. One shudders to think of those struggling alone at home.

We all desperately wanted to be good at this new role, but we didn't know how. For some, every attempt was thwarted by an infant who cried and cried and cried. 'I'm sure he does it on purpose,' complained one young mother of her four-month-old son. 'She's got my temper,' said another, talking about a child only ten weeks old. The babies would lie on changing mats in a circle, while their mothers drank coffee and complained. It reminded me of teenage days, dancing round a circle of handbags at a disco. People stared at me because I kept Frances on my knee.

Much as we love them, our children cause us a lot of trouble, and their behaviour doesn't seem to improve with age. To quote one mother who wrote in a family magazine under the headline 'Avoiding GBH':

> There should be some strong warning issued about how the sweetest babies can turn into 18-month-old hooligans: wailing, nattering, disobedient little horrors who know exactly how, where and when to humiliate you. There should be warnings given about the overpowering urge which can overtake one to do something unimaginable – bang their heads together, swing them round the room, heave them through the nearest window ...
>
> The only thing to do is tip the offending offspring into pram, pushchair or wheelbarrow and get them out of the house at once. Pushing them at least keeps your hands off their throats!
>
> (Mrs S. M. of Bridlington, *Family Circle*, 28 November 1984)

This melodramatic, half-humorous style is very common among mothers exchanging baby stories and only thinly disguises the real fears and frustrations going on in most homes. A recent newspaper report told how a desperate mother did throw her two young children out of the window of their high-rise apartment.

Social worker and mother Pam Laurance was surprised by a feeling of anger towards her demanding baby boy. She conducted her own survey of postnatal emotions. 'Most mothers,' she concluded, 'experience chronic feelings of aggression, and harbour aggressive fantasies to do with their very small babies. These are frightening and guilt-inducing.'

Pam's study was entitled 'Excuse Me, I Must Just Go and Strangle The Baby', a sentence once uttered by a friend on the telephone. It elicited this response from one new mother called Claire:

> I felt desperate rather than angry. I felt I was a slave to this tiny demanding human being – as though he was absorbing my whole identity.

Prospects like these result in more and more couples choosing to remain childless. Whether because of friends' disastrous experiences, or fears for our children's future in the nuclear age, it is fashionable to deny all instincts to reproduce. And with a scenario like the one from Bridlington, it is easy to see why. Childcare expert Penelope Leach recalls:

> I had a friend to tea when my daughter was two and she left saying, 'Thank you for letting me come; now I *know* I don't want children.' It had been a good afternoon by toddler standards, too!

> Having children is one of many adult-life options. It is neither a romantic obligation nor a hobby and anybody who can be put off the idea altogether ought to be.

> (*Family Circle*, 28 November 1984)

Yet there are still many pressures to procreate. Biological instinct urges us to conceive, parents long to become grandparents, and the child-centred family remains the advertisers' ideal on television and cereal packets. In the media world, it's mum, dad and the kids – preferably one girl and one boy – who will go on to meet their ideal partners and have more children...

Many of us are keen – some desperate – to have babies. Others see it as a duty. There is even the recent phenomenon of parents planning their quota of kids as close together as possible, 'to get it over with'. In a world that prefers images of perfection to genuine support, babies can be one big interruption to real life.

If mothers used to suffer in silence, they can now turn to many organizations and outlets when baby plays up. OPUS (Organization for Parents Under Stress) has twenty-seven branches in Britain. There is also M.A.M.A. (Meet A Mum Association), The Family Network, CRY-SIS, and Parents Anonymous. Helplines do an invaluable job in keeping harassed parents from harming their own children, but their work is indicative of the scale of the crisis of modern parenting.

The British public in the 1980s has been scandalized by a series of fatal child batterings – apparently preventable incidents in 'at risk' homes which went undetected by social workers. At the same time, hospitals in Cleveland and Manchester reported a rush of suspected sex abuse cases, as a result of which some children were removed unnecessarily from their parents.

In 1987, reports of child abuse rose by twenty per cent in Britain. The NSPCC (National Society for the Prevention of Cruelty to Children) concluded from this that either children were more at risk than ever before, or that the public was only just beginning to admit the extent of the damage.

Society's attempts to care for its children are badly out of line. We reel precariously from abuse to overprotection. In 1988, while British families suffered in the Cleveland crisis, an epidemic of child sex abuse claims was reported in America – this time brought by the parents themselves. The implication was that here was a new bandwagon for unhappy spouses, a sure way of securing divorce.

Lost in all this mess are the children. We are producing babies, toddlers and teenagers who learn to communicate through violence, survive via competition, rebel without a real cause. Depression, destruction and suicide are the legacies of a society that is programmed for negative living. And it all starts, in the smallest of ways, with the patter of tiny feet.

One psychologist has said that family anxieties may be reflected in a baby's sleep problems.[1] Society has a childcare crisis, and so do many families, when parents confront their children over the issue of sleep. It is widely acknowledged that sleep is a problem for babies. One of the first questions visitors ask about your infant is whether or not he sleeps through the night yet. Where there are problems, people believe it is the child who causes the trouble. It is the child who wakes crying, the child who disturbs parents and neighbours in the night. It is the child who must adjust, and learn to sleep soundly like grown-ups. But children are not the only ones with sleep problems. Insomnia – the inability to get to sleep or to sleep as long as society expects[2] – is one of the commonest complaints brought to the family doctor. In 1983, the NHS spent thirty million pounds on sixteen million prescriptions for hypnotic drugs to aid sleep.[3]

Many people suffer bad nights as a matter of course and wake up unrefreshed every morning. Others require laboratory-style conditions for sleep: dim lighting, complete quiet, firm mattress, pillows just so. And few can doze at will in the daytime.

Irritations like these are common in industrialized countries. One is considered lucky to be able to sleep at will – but luck need not come into it. Here is a description of men from the Tauripan tribe, travelling through the South American jungle, with enough wild noises and real animal dangers around them to keep an urbanite awake for a week:

> ... [they had the habit of] telling a joke in the middle of the night, when everyone was asleep. Though some were snoring loudly, all would awaken instantly, laugh and in seconds resume sleep, snoring and all. They did not feel that being awake was more unpleasant than being asleep, and they awoke fully alert, as when a distant pack of dangerous peccary [wild pigs] was heard by all the Indians simultaneously, though they had been asleep, while I, awake and listening to the sound of the surrounding jungle, had noticed nothing.
>
> (Jean Liedloff, *The Continuum Concept*)

Compare this with British surveys which report that less than a third of young-to-middle-aged adults say they wake up in the morning feeling rested and refreshed. Around thirty per cent admit they find it hard to get up in the mornings.[4] We tend to treat sleep like a protected species, a rare creature to be sought out and preserved before we lose it altogether. It serves as an escape from real life. We lay great stress on the standard eight-hours-a-night prescription, complete with a DO NOT DISTURB notice on the door.

It is true that many Westerners, once interrupted from a night's sleep, find it difficult to get back to sleep again, which is why babies can wreak such havoc at unholy hours. Deprived even slightly of our regular due, we cannot function properly in the day. By the time we are adults, the art of sleep has often slipped us by. We are no longer in control of sleep – it controls us.

We are all born with the ability to sleep easily and well, yet by the time we are able to speak, our dreams have turned to nightmares, and we are frightened of sleep's natural element – the dark. The average three-year-old with a talent for telling stories will invent a dozen reasons why he shouldn't go to bed. Parents, at their wits' end, supply twelve equally incredible excuses why he should. It is a war both sides are losing.

The toddler is an old hand at the sleeping game. He has been playing it with his mother since the day he was born. Remember the first few weeks, when he cried for six feeds a night? And that sticky patch at seven months old when you thought he was teething? No teeth appeared, but he always wanted cuddling at five in the morning.

And again after his first birthday, just when you thought he had settled into a nice routine, there he was, rattling his cot at all hours. In fact, when you think about it, there have been as many disturbed nights as peaceful ones since he was born. But all his little friends are exactly the same, so surely there's nothing you can do about it. You've read enough books on the subject to form a library, and none of the experts seem to agree, so what do they know?

Professionals recognize two main problem areas in infant sleeping patterns: a difficulty in settling at bedtime, and regular wakenings throughout the night. Some consider these struggles to be normal phases of development:

> Common sleep problems, such as bedtime struggles and night waking, occur regularly in at least 20% to 30% of children in the first four years of life ... Among some developmental authorities such as Gesell, they are considered nearly universal and transient developmental phenomena in the first two years of life.
>
> (Lozoff, Wolf and Davis, *Pediatrics*, March 1985)

The diagnosis and remedy will vary according to the discipline of the doctor or adviser concerned, but one thing the experts do agree on is the urgency of the sleep crisis in our society. No one disputes the drastic effect of non-sleeping children on a household. Infant sleep problems can tear families apart.

At the Sleep Clinic in the University Hospital of Wales in Cardiff, a team of psychologists and child development advisers deal with hundreds of cases every year. The number of complainants is rising rapidly, as parents realize that their problem is a common one, and there is someone who will listen.

The extent of the infant-sleep problem is now fully appreciated, as clinics and helplines are set up to advise frantic families. Principal clinical psychologist Reetta Bidder, who founded the Cardiff clinic eight years ago, says twenty per cent of children suffer from major sleeping problems – and about one half of British families have regular difficulties getting their children to sleep. Dr David Haslam, author of *Sleepless Children*, says around a quarter of all pre-school children wake during the night. This is a persistent and highly common experience in our society.

While even new-born babies sometimes refuse to sleep, the largest age group seen by the Cardiff Sleep Clinic is in the range of seven months to one year. 'Children should be sleeping through the night by then, and on their own as well,' says Reetta Bidder. 'Lots of families say the child is getting up once or twice a night – for some that is intolerable. Different families have different expectations.

'We see people in dreadful situations. For instance, in one family the mother had moved to sleep in the child's bedroom, and the parents were ready to split up. The father said, "We've come to you just in time." '

Advisers at the Cardiff clinic give each family a chart on which to keep a record of current sleeping problems, and then discuss their lifestyle before looking for solutions to get the child to sleep. Recommendations include moving the older baby to a single bed – his cot may be too small – creating a calming bedtime routine, or offering a late-night supper. The aim, of course, is to get the child to sleep through the night on his own, but on his own, a child may be refreshed by much less than eight hours' sleep. Waking in the early hours, he is ready to play again. As Dr Haslam points out:

> Some children sleep happily through the night, with additional naps of an hour or so during the day, while others only sleep solidly at night for a couple of hours at a time, and rarely seem to need a daytime nap. Despite the differences both types of children will grow up equally healthy, happy and bright. If children could be left to their own devices and did not need the attention of adults, then no one would really be the least concerned about whether they sleep or not.

> (*Sleepless Children*)

Left to his own devices, a baby will drift easily in and out of sleep as his body requires it. But scarcely any child in the West is left to his own devices. The most likely cause of conflict will be the adult's attempts to manage a child's sleeping routine. 'Food and sleep are the big battlegrounds,' says child development adviser Maria Tucker, 'because children know that the parents desperately want them to do things. They know that by seven o'clock the mother is desperate to get them off to bed.'

The usual complaint is that the mother feels her baby is not sleeping enough. It is rare for a mother to moan about a drowsy child:

> It has always struck me as rather odd that in our society we call a baby who doesn't cause any problems a 'good' baby. If he sleeps all night, never throws his food, never hits the cat, never sticks his fingers in the electricity sockets, and never spills his milk all over you, then he is a perfect child ... The rather slow, uninspiring, quiet and apathetic baby is looked at as 'ever so good', and 'not a bit of trouble' ... I always feel very sad when I hear mothers answer the question 'Is he a good baby?', with 'Yes, he's wonderful. I hardly know I've got him.'
>
> (Haslam, *Sleepless Children*)

The trouble is, we expect our babies to be responsive and loving when we want to play with them, but inert and undemanding when we decide it's time for bed.

The 'perfect' child goes directly to sleep when his parents tuck him in. He does not scream in the darkness as soon as you creep out of the nursery. He does not wake again an hour later for a suckle or cereal or – as in the case of my four-year-old friend – to be allowed to sleep on the floor. He sleeps serenely until the morning, when he is woken by neither the dawn chorus, nor the first rays of sunshine filtering on to his cot. He rises just before his parents are due to get up, and plays quietly with the bright plastic amusement arcade they have placed at the foot of his bed. He does not rattle his bars, or yell, or run full pelt into the parents' room calling 'Geronimo!' He smiles sweetly when his mother puts her head round the door, and the day begins with a big hug and a kiss.

We do not expect to have perfect children, but we do tend to treat them as if they were born from the folds of a textbook. We forget that doctors who describe 'normal' infant sleeping patterns use data taken from artificial tests.[5] We only know what is normal for a baby sleeping in a cot in a science laboratory, or alone in his middle-class American nursery. It is forgotten that for millions of years babies slept alongside their parents.

In order to coax a child off to sleep, many parents recreate the conditions of that sleep laboratory: large cot, firm mattress, own room, lights out, door – if necessary – shut. As they grow up, people depend on these conditions for sleep.

One mother told me how a friend of hers locked her two-year-old in her bedroom every night, ignoring her screams, which would go on for up to an hour. When the child did finally submit, exhausted, to sleep, her body would be pressed against the closed bedroom door on which she had been hammering. Her mother would then go and pick her up, and put her back into bed.

'I feel awful listening to it,' said the friend. 'The mother says, "Oh, she'll learn that I won't go up to her and it's useless making that noise." But it's been going on for weeks now, and it doesn't seem to be getting any better.'

This is the kind of child abuse our society tolerates, because it is in the name of socially educating our children. Medical anthropologist James McKenna does not hesitate to question the practice:

It is ironic that the human primate infant – which is born the most immature neurologically, develops the most slowly, and is thus more, rather than less, dependent physiologically on its care giver – is the only primate that, in urban settings, is expected to sleep alone and at a much younger age. Monkey and ape parents would no doubt regard this as a form of child abuse, as do peoples living in preindustrialised societies when told of parent-infant sleeping arrangements in urban settings.

(*Medical Anthropology*, 1986)

Catherine, a French friend, said her four-year-old daughter had asked her: 'Mummy, why do I have to sleep on my own when you sleep with Daddy?' and she could not think of an answer. 'What can I say to her? Why should she have to sleep alone?' Other mothers told her this was an imponderable question, like 'Why has teddy got a yellow nose?' Sleeping separately was just another of life's quirks, not something to be reasoned out, and certainly not to be challenged.

I asked Catherine why she did not allow Stephanie into her bed. 'You know I would love to,' she said, 'but I would never sleep at night. I find it difficult sharing a double bed with my husband as it is. I am a terrible sleeper.'

Catherine's story turned out to be an extreme example of the sleep crisis passing on its effects down the generations. As a small baby, Catherine was brought up by her grandparents, and slept in a cot in their bedroom. At the age of two, she went to live with her father, who put her into a separate room, with the lights off and the door shut. The young girl screamed for nights on end, but no one answered her calls. She was taken to see many specialists for her 'sleep problem', and a doctor finally prescribed tranquilizers. Catherine still remembers the trauma of those years vividly. Any small disturbance – including sometimes the tactile presence of her own husband next to her – is enough to stop her sleeping.

In her clinical work as a child psychotherapist, Dilys Daws deals with many family crises that enter the domain of 'sleep problems'. These vary from the child's nightmares and sleep walking, to violence – or the threat of it – from the parent:

> It can be very confusing for parents to deal with a baby's anger in the night and also to face the anger in themselves at their own need for rest and sleep not being met. Many parents are justifiably afraid of battering their baby in the night.
>
> (*Journal of Child Psychotherapy*, 1986)

If the mother should actually hit her baby, then the problem becomes a matter for public concern – for neighbours, social workers, the NSPCC and newspapers. Few parents are pushed this far, of course, but the thin line between fury and physical violence can seem as nothing in the torment of yet another sleepless night.

Jacquie, a mother from South Wales, recalled the horror of one particularly bad night when her son had cried ceaselessly and she felt she just couldn't take any more: 'The desire to hurt him was overpowering, and I just had to keep telling myself that I couldn't. Eventually we both collapsed on a chair, and I woke up to find us still clasped in each other's arms.'

Advisers at Cardiff's Sleep Clinic recognize that one bad night can obliterate the memory of three good ones for a family. A child who loses sleep is clearly being deprived of his bodily needs – growth hormones are secreted during sleep – while the effects on parents can be shattering in the short and in the long term.

'If you lose a lot of sleep your memory starts faltering,' says Reetta Bidder, 'and that's no fun. With young children you are always on call. I suspect that more accidents happen where the parents have a sleepless child, because human error creeps in. I wouldn't be surprised if there were more accidents on the road.'

Sleep problems can be at the root of many family crises, according to nurse Kathryn Conder:

Almost every survey of child behaviour pinpoints sleeping problems as being of great concern to parents. Families are under stress as yet another sleepless night passes and a vicious circle results with increasing tension. Negative results are all too easy to visualise, with battered children and marriages strained to breaking point.

(*Midwife, HV and Community Nurse*, April 1988)

Dr Haslam also catalogues the dire effects on adults when babies cannot, or will not, sleep:

Happy families need parents who get their sleep. A mother from Manchester made her feelings very clear. 'By the time Thomas was a year old we were obsessed with the idea of sleep. Even our own families found us unbearably dull as we could talk or think of little else. We decided that if this was parenting you could keep it! My husband had a vasectomy before Thomas was two.'

(*Sleepless Children*)

This brings us back to the desire not to procreate. Parenting in the Western world is in a mess, and sleep – essential to our well-being – has turned into a nightmare. In this state of crisis, parents and guardians cling to any passing theory to drag them out of the mire. Reetta Bidder uncovers some incredible stories of parents attempting to put old-school advice into practice: 'I can clearly remember one $2\frac{1}{2}$-year-old who refused to go to bed,' she told me. 'Every night the mother would be holding the nursery door on one side, and the child would be hanging on to the other side, screaming "The monsters are coming to get me!" '

What makes us bar the door to our children? Where did we get the idea that babies should sleep on their own?

3 | THEY'RE ONLY TRYING TO HELP

Childcare is a multi-million-pound industry, with salesmen, specialists, professionals, authors and journalists to inform us of the latest and best ways of mothering. As many mothers in the West have only one or two children – and little other experience of looking after babies – they are keen to seek advice.

Some follow one authority, as, for instance, millions of American and British mothers did with Dr Spock in the 1950s. But today parents are more likely to sample a range of babycare books before choosing the method that suits them. This is the pattern that emerged from a major Marriage Research Council study of British marriage in the 1980s: 'People were aware of all the books written on babycare,' said researcher Penny Mansfield, 'and they wanted to get it right.'

Other parents avoid written matter altogether, but no one in Western society is immune from current trends and ways of thinking. One only has to visit the local shops to see that the done thing is to dress baby up warmly, push him around in a zany coloured push-chair and stop up his mouth with a dummy.

Best-selling books, magazines and television programmes all influence the way we bring up our children. To attempt methods beyond the vision of these fairly conservative authorities is to risk attack. Once a mother takes her baby out into the street she is open to critical comment from anyone passing by. You cannot bring up your child completely on your own.

As a new mother, it is almost impossible to sift useful advice from the dross, especially if the adviser is wearing a uniform. One health visitor told me that Frances, at three weeks old, should no longer be feeding at random. She should be offered the breast every four hours, and I should introduce a dummy. 'Princess Diana,' I was told, 'comforted Prince William by giving him a finger to suck. Dummy is a nasty word, I prefer pacifier. Every baby needs one.'

Not all health visitors are as eager to offer unwanted advice. But when they are, the effect on a young mother can be devastating. I had made no complaint about my feeding arrangements. Frances was gaining weight steadily, and I had had no milk leakage, no cracked or sore nipples, no engorgement – in fact, none of the problems everybody had told me I would encounter in this attempt to nurture my baby. Yet the words of the professional put me off my stride for weeks. It was a long time before I had the confidence to dispel the doubts she had placed in my mind.

It is not uncommon for mothers to read a magazine article saying one thing and a book suggesting the opposite. Relatives offer conflicting advice. Doctors make upsetting comments. A friend does things embarrassingly differently. In today's well-informed society, the new mother is more likely to be over-advised than lacking in help. This can have disastrous effects on her confidence.

Mother and health visitor Jessica Markwell summed up the maternal emotion in her article entitled 'Does Mother Know Best?' She felt full of shame when her baby daughter cried constantly from the moment she was born:

> This sort of thing happened to 'clients' not professionals – didn't it? I turned to family, friends, childcare books – anywhere – for help. The euphoric glow of motherhood faded as I was told I was overfeeding her, underfeeding her, not winding her enough and trying to wind her too hard. Dutifully I fed her less, fed her more, patted her back, didn't pat her back. We both finished each day utterly exhausted and confused ...
>
> Things can't always have been so. When Neolithic Man first put his loving hairy arm around Neolithic Woman and they both gazed enraptured at their little hairy bundle of joy, it must have been something called Instinct which made Mrs Neolith pick up the bundle, and put him to her breast. . . .
>
> (*Practical Parenting*, June 1988)

Giving and accepting childcare advice is the currency of modern mothering. New parents searching out the best way to bring up their children are unlikely to rely on their own experience or to call upon instinct. With so many professionals around, we have simply lost trust in ourselves. But a mother in a primitive tribe would be equally puzzled at the idea of consulting *The Complete Mothercare Manual*.

Women of the remote Yequana tribe in Venezuela, for instance, are in tune with their instinct. They do not need Dr Spock or any other professional to tell them how to behave. As Jean Liedloff said, on her visit to their mountain home:

> I would be ashamed to admit to the Indians that where I come from the women do not feel themselves capable of raising children until they read the instructions written by a strange man.
>
> (*The Continuum Concept*)

Women in urban societies have been reading instructions for many years. In her review of mothering trends through the centuries, Christina Hardyment traces the origins of baby books to the eighteenth century:

> Earlier manuals survive, usually in Latin, and intended for doctors rather than mothers to refer to. The significance of the eighteenth century was that books began to be addressed to 'intelligent Parents as well as the medical World' ... and to be written in English.
>
> (*Dream Babies*)

There was a time when men did not involve themselves at all in matters of birth. This is still so in many primitive cultures, where women are confined to their quarters during labour and sometimes for a set period afterwards.

Ancient peoples considered birth as a process which occurred naturally and spontaneously, unprompted by man's intervention. Women used to be the guardians of dark secrets surrounding the nurturing of children. Even in the highly civilized lives of the Romans and Greeks, medical men kept clear of the traditional 'female' subjects:

> Doctors, who were throughout antiquity with very few exceptions male, concerned themselves only with *diseases*. The normal female functions of menstruation, childbirth, nursing, menopause, were dealt with by women – midwives and wet-nurses. Hence few records exist of normal procedures and reactions.
>
> (Lefkowitz and Fant, *Women's Life in Greece and Rome*)

When doctors first entered the domain of childrearing, it was mainly to describe events, rather than to provide a set of rules. Dr John Ticker Conquest, writing in 1848, observed that 'the bosom of the mother is the natural pillow of her offspring.'[1] The baby slept in his mother's bed.

But observation soon turned to recommendation. Doctors began to take an authoritative stance on breastfeeding and bedtimes. At first they suggested the baby should sleep with the mother for nine months, amending that figure to a few months, then reducing it to six or eight weeks.[2]

Mrs Isabella Beeton, author of the famous cook book, believed that artificial milk was more nutritious for a baby than breast milk.[3] She also recommended that mothers educate their babies to sleep alone:

No-one of experience will hold the opinion that the mother's arms are not the natural shelter for her child, and therefore at first sight it might be supposed that it would be better for the baby to go to sleep there; and if only early infancy was to be considered no-one could object to it. But if allowed at that age, there is a great difficulty in breaking through the habit, and therefore it is better to begin early, at a time when no habits are formed, and when the child really is quite as comfortable in his soft little bed as on his mother or nurse's lap. It is astonishing how soon some children find out the way to obtain what they want, and as all infants instinctively crave for their mother's presence, so they will certainly prefer her lap, and will cry for it at first, in almost all cases. But if, very early after birth, that is, by the second week, they are left to go to sleep in their cots, and allowed to find out that they do not get their way by crying, they become at once reconciled, and after a short time will go to bed even more readily in the cot than on the lap.

(*Manual of Domestic Economy*, 1861)

As Christina Hardyment remarks, 'bedtime was now an opportunity to show who was boss.' There was a new hierarchy: the childcare professional telling the mother what was best for her, and the mother telling the child what was best for him. Oxford community midwife Chloe Fisher, who has researched the origins of her trade, says that the role of the professional kept pace with the expansion of the British Empire:

> At the turn of the century there was much concern about the high infant mortality rate, which was around 160 per thousand live births. This concern arose more from anxiety about the preservation of the race and the need to populate the nearly empty Empire than from consideration for the mothers. Artificial feeding had been recognised as a major cause of mortality and this led to the emergence of many feeding 'experts' who were extremely knowledgeable about cow's milk and how to administer it to babies. These 'experts' then proceeded to have a major influence on breastfeeding management.
>
> (*Oxford Medical School Gazette*, Trinity Term 1982)

Those who controlled the country wanted to control the home, too. And the ordinary person was in need of advice more than ever. As people moved into towns they became isolated. The middle classes built suburbs, valuing the privacy of their new family villas. Mothers no longer nursed together. They had nowhere to meet. They employed nannies to do the job 'properly'.

The poor lived in dark and dirty terraced houses, easy prey to vermin and other carriers of disease. Large families might be crammed into one or two rooms. Poverty often forced the mother to go out to work and fathers laboured long hours. Many who could not find work became thieves and beggars, sometimes the only way to make a living.

Artificial milk for infants was often only a weak mixture of flour and water, or merely watered-down cow's milk. Advertising of bottle milk was as likely to influence a mother as advice from a doctor. There was great ignorance about diet and disease. Undernourished and unclean, the children of Britain were ill and dying, and no product to fight for the Great British Empire.

Professionals believed that mothers had to be taught how to feed and manage their babies. If women could only be educated to be more efficient, cleaner and more disciplined, the high mortality rate might be reduced. No welfare system existed to ease their poverty, no schemes to clean the streets or to provide proper toilet facilities. The responsibility for the future of the nation's children lay entirely with the mother. Her job was to train the child.

New-born infants, who had no self-control and no language other than that piercing cry, must be educated to become little British men (and women) as early as possible. Infant training could begin as early as one liked, and most experts recommended starting from birth, by leaving the baby to cry in his own cot. *Baby*, one of the first mothercare magazines to appear in Britain, recommended just this in 1887:

> Education may, and should, begin from birth, and not only can the senses be trained from the very first, but inherited evils of temper, etc. should be watched for and checked as they rise.

Baby magazine, edited by Ada Ballin, was a vehicle for the expression of the highest authorities on medicine, hygiene and education to reach mothers and 'those who have the care of children'. It carried regular articles on 'Maternal Ignorance', 'Rational Clothing' and 'Infant Feeding, Debility and Mortality'. The general feeling was that if

"But the health visitor says she's safer in her own room"

children could only be educated early enough, a new race of strong, valiant men and gracious, happy mothers could be created.

Mabel Liddiard, writing in her *Mothercraft Manual* which went into twelve editions in the 1920s, illustrates the reasoning behind this early discipline. British babies were neither animals nor uncivilized savages, but budding socialites:

> A baby differs from the suckling animal or from the baby of the uncivilised savage in that, as he grows up, his meal time, sleep-time, play-time and work-time will be determined by social circumstances.

A scientific approach was favoured, calling for many analyses of what was good for baby. Stratagems were devised, and methods of surprising the infant enemy. This was war. Mothers were on a crusade to tame the wild, uncivilized natures of their babies:

> Break their wills betimes; begin this great work before they can run alone, before they can speak plain, or perhaps speak at all. Whatever pain it costs, conquer their stubborness; break the will if you would not damn the child ... let him have nothing he cries for; absolutely nothing, great or small; else you undo your own work.

This was the advice given to Methodist minister John Wesley by his mother Susanna in 1872. Queen Victoria herself had little time for her children or anyone else's, and by the end of her reign, many mothers felt the same about their own offspring.

Two or three generations of women, including the entire sisterhood of nurses, midwives and health visitors, were raised on the idea that babies should be civilized as early as possible. Fashions may have changed in baby management, but a belief in infant training remains the bedrock of modern mothering.

The dos and don'ts of bedtime etiquette certainly come into this domain. But consult an old advice manual for mothers and you will find no section on sleep problems. The Victorian writer did not allow for any difficulties with his method. He assumed that the whims of the wailing child would always be curbed if the parent was strong enough:

It is extremely improper to consider every noise of an infant as a claim upon our assistance, and to intrude either food or drink, with a view to satisfy its supposed wants. By such injudicious conduct, children readily acquire the habit of demanding nutriment at improper times, and without necessity; their digestion becomes impaired; and consequently at this early age, the whole mass of the fluids is gradually corrupted. . . .

We learn from Daily Experience, that children who have been the least indulged, thrive much better, unfold all their faculties quicker, and acquire more muscular strength and vigour of mind, than those who have been constantly favoured, and treated by their parents with the most solicitous attention: bodily weakness and mental imbecility are the usual attributes of the latter.

(*Enquire Within Upon Everything*, 1882)

Abstinence, even for new-born babies, was believed to be character-building. The idea that crying was beneficial to a baby goes back to these early textbooks, in which physiologists concluded that as babies screamed so much, there must be something useful in it:

Instead of being feared, the practice of crying in children in want of muscular exercise is most beneficial in its effects. Sickly and weak children cry a good deal, and but for this, it is almost certain that they could not live long. The very first act which an infant performs at birth is to cry, and many of them continue to do so at an average rate of four to five hours a day during the first years of their existence. It cannot for a moment be imagined that all their cries arise from a feeling of pain. It would be an anomaly in the benevolent working plan of creation and an unmerited infliction of pain on the little innocents, were this the case. Not at all. They cry in default of exercise, or rather, for exercise.

(Samuel Smiles, *Physical Education*, 1838)

Before this, eighteenth-century parents 'had been able to put down the infant's bawls to original sin.'[4] Now crying was considered to be natural and good for the infant, babies could expect to be doing a lot of it, as part of their infant training programme.

The idea that a crying baby is exercising his lungs may belong to the nineteenth century, but it lingers today. The screams of the new-born are still met with admiration from mother, doctor and midwife. 'What a lovely pair of lungs!' they say, as he communicates his terror.

Baby, pioneer of mothercare magazines, offered its own formula for untroubled infant sleep:

> Sleep for the child is even more of a vital need than for an adult, and its sleep will be more natural and healthier if it is not rocked. If accustomed from the first to be laid away in a quiet, darkened, but well-ventilated room, at a certain hour, the baby will form the habit of falling asleep, and will never know any other. A light should not be left burning at night; it vitiates the atmosphere, and sleep is not as sound as in the dark.

Routine, clean air and as little handling as possible was the prescription for the late Victorian baby. It sounds a little old-fashioned, but not absurd, as current professional advice runs along similar lines. What is entirely unexpected in the magazine's description of baby bedtime etiquette is the following remark:

> For the first few weeks animal heat is usually maintained by sleeping with the mother...

Here are the last vestiges of co-sleeping. The writer acknowledges that the parental bed is the proper and usual place for a new-born baby. But the practice must stop there:

> ... on no account should a child of any later age sleep between two persons, as by so doing it must of necessity breathe the emanations from their bodies.

In the 1880s, the fear that the baby would be smothered or spoilt was topped by the belief that bedsharing was unhygienic. Doctors knew that diseases spread through bodily contact, and while they were doing nothing to improve inner-city sanitation, they were keen to prevent intimacy within the home.

A fascinating study of London's poor – though not its poorest – was made between 1909 and 1913 by the Fabian Women's Group. Their aim was to answer the question 'How does a working man's wife bring up a family on twenty shillings a week?' Sleeping accommodation was of particular concern to the well-meaning volunteers who crossed the thresholds of more than sixty tiny Lambeth terraced houses. They were horrified to see babies sleeping in the parents' bed. And in the days before health visitors, the women were there to influence as well as to observe:

> ... some sort of cot was always provided for the little baby. Unfortunately, this is not a universal rule. It appears here because the investigation insisted on the new baby having a cot to itself. Otherwise it would have taken its chance in the family bed.
> (Maud Pember Reeves, *Round About a Pound a Week*, 1913)

The poorer classes were urged, despite their lack of furniture and shortage of space, to bed their babies in banana crates and orange boxes. 'In winter,' wrote Maud Pember Reeves, author of the report, 'the mothers find it very difficult to believe that a new-born baby can be warm enough in a cot of its own. And when one looks at the cotton cot blankets, about 30 inches long, which are all their wildest dreams aspire to, one understands their disbelief.'

Scientists now confirm the fear of the poor London women – a baby alone in a cot cannot be kept as warm as if he were in bed with his parents.[5] But the mothers in the four-year study took the advice gratefully, along with hints on diet and sanitation. Soon the whole nation, rich and poor, was putting its babies into cots.

Between 1915 and 1935, behavioural psychologists added their weight to the argument. They claimed that children should be reared along scientific lines, that a baby – even a new-born – could be trained into sociability. Parents handed over their initiative to a grand circle of child experts, such as leading American behaviourist John B. Watson. He wrote in 1928:

> There is a sensible way of treating children. Treat them as though they were young adults. Dress them, bathe them with care and circumspection. Let your behaviour always be objective and kindly firm. Never hug and kiss them, never let them sit in your lap.
> If you must, kiss them once on the forehead when they say good night. Shake hands with them in the morning. Give them a pat on the head if they have made an extraordinarily good job of a difficult task. Try it out. In a week's time you will find how easy it is to be perfectly objective with your child and at the same time

kindly. You will be utterly ashamed of the mawkish, sentimental way you have been handling it.

(*Psychological Care of Infant and Child*)

It is easy to see why frantic parents, operating against their own feelings and fighting the natural capacities of their children, were unable to sustain this regime. Behaviourism went out of fashion quite rapidly, but its bitter taste continued to sour standard childcare books. In 1935, *The Motherhood Book* advised against carrying a baby from room to room:

> Babies should be trained from their earliest days to sleep regularly and should never be awoken in the night for feeding ... Baby should be given his own quiet bedroom from the very beginning. He should never be brought into the living room at night.

The bedtime routine was an essential part of a mother's day. The more rigid and more regular the pattern, the better she was doing her job. By the 1930s, *The Concise Household Encyclopaedia* had waved goodbye to bedsharing, even for the newest baby. The cot was the in-thing:

> After the bath, the baby has a feed and is put to sleep. He should sleep in his own cot from the beginning as it is both unsafe and unhygienic to sleep with mother or nurse. He should lie on a firm hair mattress.

Officious and unemotional, childcare manuals were still not read by the masses. No doubt many mothers resented their dogmatic style and unsympathetic accounts of how the perfect baby should behave. However, in 1946 childcare advice became as fashionable as nylon stockings when Dr Benjamin Spock published his *Baby and Child Care* book in America.

Spock, unlike most commentators, was prepared to inject some emotion into his advice, and allow that mothers and babies were having problems with the infant training routines. His friendly, understanding style made earlier books sound as dry and unreal as the rules for cricket.

I have a copy of the 1985 edition, which justifiably claims to be 'The Century's Greatest Bestseller'. More than thirty million copies have so far been sold worldwide, and the book is still regularly updated.

Dr Spock was popular with the public because he allowed parents to listen to their children – to some extent – and to supply many of their needs. Nevertheless, his views were attacked by politicians, and critics labelled him 'permissive'. Spock was outraged:

> I don't consider myself permissive and almost all the people who've used this book feel the same way. The people who call me permissive say indignantly that they haven't read it, wouldn't use it. The accusation came for the first time in 1968 – 22 years after the book came out – from several prominent individuals who objected strongly to my opposition to the war in Vietnam.
>
> They said my advice to parents to give 'instant gratification' to their babies and children was what made so many young men who opposed the war 'irresponsible, undisciplined and unpatriotic.' There is no instant gratification in this book.
>
> (Spock and Rothenberg, *Dr Spock's Baby and Child Care*)

Dr Spock certainly does not believe in instant gratification. He refers to babies as tyrants, and, like the old behaviourists, tells parents to let the baby cry himself to sleep. He advises that a child should never be allowed in the parents' bed.

But it was proper that his advice should be scrutinized in the political arena. When thirty million and more mothers abandon their instincts to follow one man's advice, then there will be an effect on generations of children.

It is ironic that the politicians thought Spock was being too liberal in his guidance to young parents. When I first read this passage on 'Chronic resistance to sleep in infancy', it made *me* want to cry:

> A baby shouldn't be able to put adults through a performance like this every night. They know it but don't know what to do about it. Even a baby senses, I think, that she shouldn't be able to get away with such tyranny.
>
> The habit is usually easy to break once the parents realize that it is as bad for the baby as it is for them. The cure is simple: Put the baby to bed at a reasonable hour, say good night affectionately but firmly, walk out of the room, and don't go back.

Most babies who have developed this pattern cry furiously for 20 or 30 minutes the first night, and then when they see that nothing happens, they suddenly fall asleep! The second night the crying is apt to last only 10 minutes. The third night there isn't usually any at all.

(*Dr Spock's Baby and Child Care*)

Nothing at all. Not even a spark of hope. Mission accomplished, as that other Spock, with the long ears and the Starship Enterprise, might have said.

Dr Spock advises setting the kitchen timer to comfort harassed parents who feel as though their child has been crying for hours. He also suggests muffling the dreadful sound with a rug on the nursery floor and a blanket over the window. Oh, and a final suggestion: don't forget to apologize in advance to 'touchy neighbours'.

But neighbours today aren't likely to be that touchy. All children cry at night, don't they? It's 'normal' behaviour, and friends are bound to understand if you say you are following the advice of Dr Benjamin Spock.

Childcare advisers no longer scold mothers or scatter pompous pearls of wisdom before us. Since Spock, their books are often informal and informed, and best-sellers. In France, the popular pae-diatrician is Laurance Pernoud, who revises her book *J'élève mon Enfant* (I Raise My Child) every year. She says one French family in two knows the nightly drama of the child who refuses to go to bed, and offers this solution:

Should you lock the nursery door if your child gets up and wants to come and join you? No ... better to prop open the door with a piece of furniture, so that it is slightly ajar, but the child cannot open it further.

(My translation)

The Victorian barriers are still standing, even if we do not actually send our children to bed with bread and water and turn the key. The aim is to put babies to sleep out of sight, and if possible out of earshot, too. This is what *Good Housekeeping's Baby Book* – popular from the 1940s to the 1970s – recommends:

Some of these small-hour wakers are content to lie and gurgle to themselves, and there is no need to go to them. Indeed, it is foolish from your own point of view to encourage them to expect you. If you are worried about the baby being cold, put him in a sleeping-bag, and if he is a cot-rocker, pad the cot to deaden the sound, then accept the rhythmic thuds as a crude sort of lullaby.

(Jane Vosper)

It is reminiscent of a patient in a lunatic asylum. Bound in his padded cell, so as not to bother the warders when he punishes himself against the walls, the inmate is left to protest unheard. 'You have to know your own child,' says Matron, 'and decide for yourself when good-humoured neglect is the best policy.' You wonder who will be in the better humour at the end of the night: mother, trying to stifle her 'foolish' feelings in the marital bed, or her child, alone in his own nursery.

Jane Vosper, *Good Housekeeping*'s 'Matron', echoed the views of many doctors of the 1960s and 1970s, when she finally suggested giving the baby a sedative to make him sleep. Offering drugs to non-sleeping babies was a common practice in Europe:

I often wish I could prescribe a night nurse under the National Health Service, someone to take charge in the early hours while this awkward phase lasts. Some parents take it in turns for night duty ... But if a weary mother always has to cope on her own, a suitable sedative can be given to the baby for her sake, say for a week at a time.

The idea has filtered through to parents that it is reasonable to administer drugs to babies. The advice on the medicine bottle doesn't tell you that sedating your baby will deprive him of essential Rapid Eye Movement sleep, which he needs for growth, memory and learning:

... of parents asked in a survey published in 1980, 45 per cent found consultation about their sleepless children with doctors and health visitors unhelpful. Significantly, another study published in 1977 showed a group of first-born children as having been given night sedation by the time they were 18 months old. Unofficially, desperate mothers administer cough medicines deliberately to sedate their children.

(Conder, *Midwife, HV and Community Nurse*, April 1988)

Controlling children in the 1980s tends to be more mechanical than chemical. It's a matter of which gadgets to use, rather than which sedatives. Bluff and burlesque are often the styles of writers who do not want to harm their children physically, but joke about feeling like it. Paediatricians admit that they do not have all the answers.

Dr Christopher Green, a consultant paediatrician from Australia, advocates tying the handle of the child's bedroom door, so that (and I quote, otherwise you may not believe me) 'the aperture is just one inch less than the diameter of the offending child's head.'[6]

Dr Green's is the ultimate no-nonsense childcare book, brusquely entitled *Toddler Taming*. It includes a long chapter entitled 'Sleep Problems – At Last, The Cure'. In the final analysis, Dr Green's 'controlled crying technique' is no cure at all. He admits as much himself, when he says that parents 'rapidly getting nowhere' should tame their toddlers with rope across the door ...

> For those who cannot bring themselves to smack their child, but are rapidly getting nowhere, I strongly recommend the 'patent rope trick'. This is one of my better inventions, which came from the drawing-board when I was trying to curb the escape-artist antics of my own children.

Childcare books may be a relatively new invention, but babies have always been brought up according to one set of rules or another. I asked childcare historian Diana Dick whether people were more dogmatic today. 'No,' she said, 'you find people standing on their hind legs in every century, saying "*this* is what you should be doing."'

Of course there will always be people who refuse to accept the given theory, and who speak out against the trend. One such authority was Margaret Ribble, author of the volume *Rights of Infants* published in 1943. Although relatively unknown today, she had a reasonable following then, for her book was reprinted six times in two years. Christina Hardyment summarizes the views of this astounding woman:

> Ribble put forward ideas which were remarkably ahead of her time, although her viewpoint was occasionally idiosyncratic ... Ideally, she felt, babies should not be taken from their mothers and sent to the hospital nursery at birth, under the pretext of

giving mothers a chance to rest. She reasoned from the known fact that lack of oxygen at birth could damage the brain of the newborn child. She extended this principle to the first few months of life, claiming that the baby needed physical stimulus from the presence of its mother's body to keep it inspiring air as fast as it expired it ... Ribble's babies were kept in their mother's beds to boost their oxygen intake. She derided 'the ancient belief, still current that babies who sleep with their mother are in danger of suffocation.' The reverse was effectively true. 'Since the contacts and warmth afforded by the human body are a protection rather than a peril to the infant, he sleeps more safely at his mother's side than in the stimulus-free seclusion of the nursery.'

(*Dream Babies*)

The idea of keeping mother and baby together to promote the infant's oxygen intake could usefully be applied to premature babies. In fact studies presently being carried out in Stockholm, London and San Francisco are testing just this hypothesis.[7]

But with the tide of medical thinking against her, Margaret Ribble's call for prolonged breastfeeding, increased rocking and nightly bed-sharing went largely unheard. Most advice columns continued to advocate putting the child down in a cot on his own, and weaning him early from night feeds.

Modern textbooks still recommend a battle between mother and baby in the attempt to train him to be sociable. Here, for instance, a health visitor and a paediatrician writing in a free magazine sponsored by a manufacturer of disposable nappies, say that a baby should be left alone to cry at night:

The baby may cry longer and louder than previously, but this apparent worsening of the problem prior to improvement is the last hurdle to overcome before the battle for silent nights is won.

(Dick and Pritchard, *Pampers First Years of Life,* 1987)

From the perspective of the professional, the mother and child are at war. The sign of victory is silence. Agony aunts reinforce the imagery with their portraits of 'King Baby', who 'sits firmly in control of his adults' lives ... Suppose,' says one issue of *Woman's Own,* 'you've got a little dictator who won't sleep ...'

The vision of baby as tyrant, king or dictator is designed to spur a mother into attack. Her advisers tell her to engage in combat with this powerful individual before he ruins her life. No one suggests that mother and baby are on the same side.

In a reaction to this strictness, some authorities advocated letting the child have his own way entirely. But so-called 'permissive' advice, the sort which puts the baby's needs before the mother's, can be as divisive as battle talk. Parents fail to anticipate their child's every desire, as his whims become their commands.

Like behaviourism in the 1920s, the permissive approach was unpopular with parents. Mothers felt guilty, an emotion which was no use to anyone. Parents did not want to be at the beck and call of their children all day and they resented the baby-centred world of some theorists. Authors like Libby Purves were quick to redress the balance and restore confidence:

This book is about the way real, fallible mothers *really* get through the day. There are plenty of technical baby manuals on the market: some are excellent, some manage to make bathing a baby sound as complicated as stripping down a MIG fighter engine; nearly all of them are perfectionist in tone. This is an *imperfectionist* book, about the cheerful cutting of corners, without guilt.

(*How Not to be a Perfect Mother*)

Parents could once again feel in charge, if they agreed with Miriam Stoppard:

Having read so many baby books which emphasize looking after the baby's needs, I still feel guilty if I occasionally put my own wishes on par with those of my children. I hope no parent reading this book will suffer any such shame... If, by taking a few short cuts and putting yourself a little higher on your list of priorities, life with your baby is more fun and you are happier, go ahead and do so.

(*Baby Care Book*)

But parents still feel torn between their own desires and those of their children. As marriage researcher Penny Mansfield says, 'there is this dilemma between what we put into our parenting, and what priority we give ourselves and our partners. There has been a swing away from putting the children first.'

While a mother is trying to sort her way through all the theories, there is a powerful new influence which adds to her confusion. Newspapers, magazines and television feed her images and try to sell her things. The sales pitch is often disguised as professional advice. Advertisers know that a sound way to sell a babycare product is to bolster its message with a doctor's approval.

The new mother, vulnerable to suggestions which smack of experience, is persuaded to believe an advert that tells her that a certain brand of soap will help her care for her children, or that if she buys a particular cot she is doing the best for her baby. She is more likely to trust a product if it carries a British Standard kite-mark, or if a scientist recommends it.

Childcare and consumerism are thus a happy team. The shops that offer us designer prams and matching bootees now also market advice on bringing up babies. *The Complete Mothercare Manual 1986* claims to be 'authoritative and completely up-to-date', the perfect combination to persuade a modern mother.

It is understandable that many people prefer solid advice, whatever its source. One woman told me: 'I just keep feeling as if I'm doing something wrong, and I don't know what it is.' Another friend – a midwife – became so bewildered by advice after the birth of her baby, that she became unable to care for the child.

Instinct tells us that something is not well with modern mothering, but we are out of touch with its message. Many mothers are grateful for a firm hand to guide them. Child psychotherapist Dilys Daws recalls playing the part of a stern adviser to a young mother who felt lost:

> One very caring mother of a slightly underweight baby felt she must pick him up every time he cried, which was sometimes hourly through the night. She was sure he needed something, though she was not sure whether this need was emotional, or for more food.
>
> I said sharply that what he needed was a good night's sleep; and so did she. This mother appreciated the matter-of-factness of my comments ...
>
> (*Journal of Child Psychotherapy*, 1985)

My health visitor remarked that most mothers – inexperienced and unable to cope with an apparently troublesome baby – would rather hear one piece of strong advice than read five books on the subject and be left to choose. The irony is that today's parents have more choices than ever before. Not only must they make fundamental decisions such as whether to breast or bottle feed, but they are also offered hundreds of consumer choices. Should they buy a cradle or a baby nest? Which make of pushchair should they get? What colour curtains for the nursery?

But few mothers run to the health visitor because they cannot decide between *Boots* or *Mothercare* brand. These are the kinds of decisions we are educated to make, and we cope well when faced with a dilemma on disposable nappies. Even so, there are books devoted to helping mothers select the best in baby equipment. Prams and pushchairs, car seats, high-chairs, toys, playpens and bouncers are all scrutinized.

'Planning for a new baby does not necessarily mean rushing out and buying everything you see in the baby shops,' says Daphne Metland, author of *Getting Ready for Baby*. Implicit in books of this type, however, is the suggestion that the good mother does her best to afford as much baby gear as she can. The list of bare essentials and useful extras would make an Edwardian mother shrink: 'cot, crib or carrycot, pram or buggy, Moses Basket, baby nest, sheepskin, cot, mattress, sheets, blankets, baby alarm . . .' A new mother today could cure her insomnia by counting sheepskin rugs.

When we don't know what to do with our babies, at least there are a hundred products to explore. And that is what makes it so hard for us to discard the cot. To do without a crib or a cradle is to deprive the nursery of its advertised centrepiece.

We are encouraged to picture our babies lying in their own rooms at night, surrounded by fluffy bunnies and pastel-coloured alphabets. To deny this image is to destroy the whole vision of motherhood for many women in the West. Decking out a nursery is as important as choosing a white wedding dress. Our culture endorses the ritual of the nursery. And if you have a nursery and a cot, you have to have bedtimes and rules, battles and broken hearts.

There is another way, however. No one wants to return to the poverty-ridden squalor of the Victorian slums, or unlearn all we know about health, infant nutrition and public sanitation. But there are some lessons we can learn from mothers who have never read an advice manual.

In 1943, Margaret Ribble described infant marasmus, a wasting disease in children. It struck many babies in better-class Edwardian homes, at the height of the 'do not over-stimulate your babies' craze. It accounted, she says, for one half of the deaths of babies in Britain:

> ... babies in the best homes and hospitals, given the most careful attention, often drifted into this condition of slow dying, while infants in the poorest homes, with a good mother, often overcame the handicaps of poverty and unhygienic surroundings and became bouncing babies. It was found that the element lacking in the sterilized lives of the former class ... was mother love.
>
> (*Rights of Infants*)

Babies need our love and warmth by day and by night. Left alone, every mother is able to provide these things. No amount of well-meant advice should get in her way.

4 | IN TOUCH

'It takes only the most elementary observation to see that a baby
needs its mother even more during the night than during the day,
and even more in the dark than in the daylight. In the dark the
baby's predominant sense – sight – is at rest. Instead the baby
needs to use its sense of touch through skin-to-skin contact, and
its sense of smell.

(Michel Odent, *Primal Health*)

Sight may be the predominant sense in children and adults, but touch
is our first connection with the world. The foetus in the womb and
the new-born infant rely on physical contact for information. A new
baby keeps his eyes closed for much of the time, and whatever patterns
he can distinguish in the early weeks cannot mean very much to him.

Maureen Blackman, a nurse from Scunthorpe, has spent fifteen
years working in special care baby units. During this time, she has
come to realize the importance of human contact for the premature
and ill babies who struggle for life in incubators:

Years ago, parents looked through the glass at their children, and
we told them 'Do not touch, the baby is too ill.' The parents
accepted that, bless them, and knew no better. Now we encourage
mothers to hold their babies, to stay close to them. The babies
respond to this.

I've looked down on those babies over the years, and I think,
how can you know you're alive if no one touches you?

Touch is not in itself a treatment recognized by the National Health
Service, but it is essential to systems of therapy throughout the world.
Massage and faith healing, the Japanese art of Raiki and the latest
Californian Rosen techniques all use touch to promote healing and

a sense of well-being. Touch techniques often benefit patients with whom other therapies have failed:

> ... a Scottish hospital stated that patients who had symptoms of tension and anxiety and who had failed to respond to usual psychiatric or drug therapy were treated by use of reflex stimulation using connective tissue massage. 'All patients showed a significant response to treatment in one or more of the psychophysiological parameters,' said the report. Most who had suffered chronic insomnia, despite massive medication, slept normally after the treatment and maintained this improvement.[1]
>
> (Leon Chaitow, *Here's Health*, May 1988)

The importance of touch in healing and sustaining health has been overlooked by the mainstream of Western medical practitioners, says Norman Autton, author of *Pain: An Exploration:*

> Touch is a medium through which persons repeatedly communicate and it is only through communication that man's greatest need as a human being, the need to love and be loved, is fulfilled ...
>
> Holding hands, putting an arm round the patient, are expressions of affection and friendliness. Kubler-Ross (1969) found that the most expressive relationship during terminal illness was a gentle pressure of the hand in moments of silence. Physical actions symbolize that someone understands, encourages and comforts. Anna Freud (1952) has described how the youngest blitz victims of the Second World War maintained their morale in the midst of rubble and wreckage when they had a living and helping hand to cling to ... For a patient in pain touch helps to locate him in time and space.

As with the sufferer of pain, so it is with a new-born baby. Human touch may be the only stabilizing force in a world that is at once foreign and frightening. Physical contact and movement calm the infant, reassuring him that life is not entirely hostile. Through touch, a child comes to value himself. Psychologists say that an infant reared with the loving caresses of his parents is less likely to suffer aches, pains and illnesses later in life:

One might say that if the baby's body is a joy and a delight in the mother's arms, that same body will become a joy and a delight to its owner later on.

(English and Pearson, *Emotional Problems of Living*)

Parents know for themselves how a child can feel soothed by stroking, patting and cuddling in times of illness or distress.

Martin Muchan, a teacher of the Alexander Technique, manages his son's asthma this way. 'When Marty has an attack, I hold him,' says Martin. 'I tickle his shoulders, chest and back, and keep touching him until the attack wears off. I stroke his hair. It really soothes him. He's now seven, but when he was younger he would sleep with us when he was upset. Touch has been the most valuable medium in our lives.'

Massage expert Gerry Purves believes that Western society is particularly awkward when it comes to touching babies. The all-enclosing womb is replaced by functional contact and quick kisses. These are simply not enough to satisfy our need for physical closeness:

Caring touch is important for an overall sense of mental well-being. Research has shown that people with heart conditions do better if they have tactile contact with even a pet. Babies starved of touch show extreme distress. Yet from the moment of our birth our quota of touch is reduced from the constant massage of the 'in utero' baby to the less frequent cuddles and nappy changing; from the occasional kiss of a grazed knee to embarrassed adolescent encounters. Which leaves us with adult sex as our main source of touch, which, (contrary to public 'hype') I suspect leaves much to be desired in terms of simple loving touch.

(*Cahoots*, Summer 1988)

A ten-year study of 150 middle-aged men in Sweden has shown that those living alone are more likely to die of heart failure than those living with their families.[2] The benefits of keeping in touch with other human beings far outweighed factors such as the consumption of alcohol and cigarettes. Purves advocates a weekly massage as the remedy for the stresses of modern existence. Rubbing shoulders with your loved ones could be saving your life.

Physical therapist Peter Walker has written many books on the art of natural parenting. He teaches parents how to delight their children with touch therapy, massage being the ancient art of 'rubbing better'. He believes touch has untold benefits for the new baby:

> Both the way in which parents hold and touch their children and the frequency with which they do it are known to have considerable effect on the child's general disposition. Observation has shown that children who are deprived of physical contact generally suffer more from anxiety and its related disorders. They are inclined to be clumsy in their physical relationships with their peers and, as adults, may find difficulty in responding to others. By contrast, more loving secure personalities are seen to emerge from families and cultures who touch and embrace one another frequently as an expression of their love and friendship.
>
> (*The Book of Baby Massage*)

Another researcher[3] has demonstrated that rubbing a baby's feet for five minutes every half hour or so reduces irregularities in the infant's breathing. Touch not only has a calming effect, it also plays an important role in maintaining the health of a young child.

A mother carrying her baby provides him with an all-over massage, coupled with the movement he so enjoys. When I went to interview psychotherapist Jean Liedloff to research this book, she had me jogging around her first-floor flat, dodging the potted plants and the cushions, with Frances bouncing along in my arms. This was the way she had seen the primitive Yequana people carrying their children.

'Hold her by one foot,' she said, 'she'll love it.' I tried not to display my fear as I dangled Frances first from her plump ankle, and then from her hand. There were peals of laughter – at last mum, she was saying – at last, you're holding me right.

'Never treat a baby as if he's delicate,' said Jean, 'or he'll grow up believing you.' Children in primitive tribes start carrying their baby brothers and sisters while they are only toddlers themselves. Nobody rushes in telling them to stop, and they do not let the babies fall.

By way of contrast, it is worth mentioning the practice of swaddling a baby, which was once common in many civilizations. Mothers in early eighteenth-century Britain bound their babies tightly and hung them out of the way:

> Its head was wrapped in 'compresses three, four, or five times doubled', pinned to a cap, and further braced by a tight neck

stay. Swaddling was thought to prevent it distorting its supposedly fragile bones by kicking about too much. It also kept babies warm in a draughty age, and was a convenience. While the half-strangled baby hung from a nail, its minder could get on with other tasks. Swaddling slowed down a baby's heartbeat, and encouraged extreme passivity – more sleep, less crying; a swaddled baby made no demands on the adult world around it.

(Hardyment, *Dream Babies*)

Many societies still bind their children today. The tradition is sustained in British hospitals, where new-born babies are wrapped tightly before being presented to their mothers. Nurses in the Eastern bloc handle swaddled new-borns like plates of meat in a restaurant, with the minimum of cuddling.

Swaddled babies are experiencing the close contact they desire, without the benefits of human touch. Societies that practise swaddling have recognized the infant's need for bonding, but they bind the child to itself rather than the mother. It is rather like our assumption earlier in this century, that bottle milk was as good for a baby as the breast, as though nutrition was all a baby received from suckling.

Only in the last twenty years or so have scientists begun to explore the usefulness of rocking, cuddling and holding a baby. The value of rhythmical movement to a child has been known instinctively by parents throughout history, and tests now confirm that babies and other infant animals respond beneficially to a high level of tactile contact.

For instance, one study[4] showed that when kittens were rocked, the movement increased their Rapid Eye Movement (REM) sleep. Loss of REM sleep interferes with memory and the ability to learn.[5] Sleeping tablets reduce our quota of REM sleep.

Other tests have shown that mechanically-breathing teddy bears placed next to babies served to stabilize the infants' breathing patterns. The teddy bears were designed to provide a stimulus similar to the baby sleeping on his parent's chest. An initial study by Dr James McKenna using human subjects confirmed these findings.[6] This discovery may have direct implications on the prevention of Sudden Infant Death Syndrome, as I will explain later.

If teddy bears can be so helpful, imagine the greater rewards of sleeping next to a mother's skin. Babies' motor skills (their ability to co-ordinate themselves in their world) are also honed through body touch and holding.[7]

Another advantage of human contact is the heat exchange between adult and child. Paediatrician Dr Harvey Marcovitch explains why a baby needs special care at night:

> ... while the average baby weighs 1/20th of an adult, his skin surface area is 1/9th of that of an adult, not 1/20th, so he has twice as much skin in proportion to his body size and loses heat much faster.
>
> (*Mother*, February 1988)

A mother often worries that her baby is not warm enough while he sleeps alone in his nursery. Studies now show that however well-wrapped a baby may be, his temperature can never be maintained as satisfactorily as when he has skin-to-skin contact with another human being. Dr James McKenna reports:

> Fardig (1980) found that for 17 mothers and babies, radiant-heated cribs could not maintain the mean skin and core temperature of human newborns placed on their mothers' bare chests for skin-to-skin contact, even when their ambient temperatures were equivalent.
>
> (*Medical Anthropology*, 1986)

One explanation for the loss of heat may be that a baby separated from its mother produces stress hormones, such as cortisol. These cause a drop in body temperature.

Even without the infant's physiological reaction, it is clear that 'a parent-infant huddle reduces the participants' surface-to-volume ratio and thus conserves energy.' (McKenna) Two people together are warmer than two people alone. Constant warmth helps to keep a baby asleep and breathing regularly.[8] It particularly promotes REM sleep.

Parents in pre-central heating days had no problems regulating their babies' night-time temperatures – they simply slept with them. But the modern mother, following observations such as these from Dr Marcovitch, struggles to keep her baby warm at night:

Indoors, babies under three months are happiest when the

temperature is about 75°F (24°C) – above the usual setting for central heating ... These figures are based on the assumption that your baby is in a draught-free room wearing a woollen vest, nappy and a long cotton nightdress or stretch suit covered with a flannelette sheet and two layers of cotton blanket.

Keep your baby in the warmest room overnight and add extra blankets as well as mittens, socks and hat. Calculate that the baby needs two more covers than you yourself would want.

(*Mother*, February 1988)

The arrival of the pram in Victorian Britain added the problem of preserving the baby's warmth in the daytime. Before this, mothers and nannies used to carry their children around – the 'perambulator' was thus a controversial invention. But the editor of *Baby* magazine was all in favour of it:

Senex writes to the *British Medical Journal* protesting against the use of perambulators in cold weather, and maintaining that every child not old enough to walk should be carried in the nurse's arms. I cannot agree with this... If a child is properly wrapped up and protected in the perambulator, there need be no more danger of cold than if it were carried. On very cold days a hot-water bottle may be placed under the infant's cushion, and in very cold or windy weather the little face should be covered with a thick, but not fluffy, veil.

(Ada Ballin, December 1887)

You can wrap up your baby all you like, but he is still going to drop in temperature, like a dinner taken out of the oven. Frances was a winter baby, but I did not have to worry about extra blankets and hot water bottles in the pram. I used to go for walks with her tucked under my coat, on her sling. It seemed incredible, but by the time I returned home she was warmer than when we started out.

Whatever else killed British babies before this century, there was no need for them to suffer in the cold. In the Arctic, the Inuit traditionally slept naked next to their children in their igloos. They did not die of frost-bite. In fact, if hypothermia threatens, there is no better solution:

Experts have different opinions on the best way to treat a cold baby. If he has become cold rapidly then he can be safely rewarmed rapidly. The best place is probably next to his mother's skin under her clothes, and in a hot dry room.

(*Mother*, February 1988)

Actually modern babies, wrapped up in woolly layers with blankets and in centrally-heated rooms, are more likely to overheat than to freeze to death. A survey carried out in the north of England studied babies' bedding and clothing, and found that 'by night there was excess bedding, and many babies had too much, a few of them much too much.'[9]

Overheating is a problem, as this is one factor related to Sudden Infant Death Syndrome. It is clearly not advisable for a baby to get too hot in the night. The baby on his mother's skin takes her temperature, and she his. If it gets too warm under the duvet, she will feel this herself, and respond by throwing off the cover. Sleeping with his mother, the baby remains at his ideal temperature.

The importance of sensory stimulation to the child may never be fully measured and appreciated. But if, as Michel Odent proposes, the brain's thermostat for health is being set during the first few weeks of life, lack of touch at this time could truly be torture of the innocent:

Eastern traditions knew that by stimulating the senses, energy was brought to the brain. Western science is now able to prove that this is so. It is as if the brain needs to be recharged like a battery ... When you stroke a baby's skin it gives energy to the brain at an important stage in its development.

(*Primal Health*)

We do not need to understand the technical reasons for a baby's love of touch in order to fulfil his quite obvious need. And the real beauty of touch-communication is that its benefits are reciprocal. Human contact has a soothing effect on the adult as well as on the child. If it is in the baby's interest to be held throughout infancy, then it makes sense for the pleasure to be mutual. Nature looks after those who serve her needs.

If, rather than separating mother and baby at night, professionals were to encourage the mutual benefits of contact, babycare would become a positive, uniting force. The nervous mother would be reassured by keeping physically in touch with her baby. Bonding, a topic which concerns many writers on childcare would occur naturally and in its own good time. Mother and baby would be able to operate as one, supplying and enjoying each others' needs.

A report in *The Lancet* illustrates the value of body contact in providing security for a young child, and better bonding for the mother or other care-giver:

> Two groups of women were given a baby carrier or a soft seat (bouncing cradle to be placed on the floor) when they left hospital with their newborn babies. The idea was to find out which group of babies seemed more content after just over a year: those who had spent quite a lot of time strapped to their mother's chest ... or those who had been left to bounce gently in a seat ...
> The research, carried out in New York, showed that babies who spent more time close to their mothers were more content to be separated from her at 13 months; they cried and whined less when with a stranger and behaved as if they were more secure.
>
> (Olivia Timbs, *Early Days*, January 1988)

So often we hear that babies need to be left alone to learn independence. The opposite is true. Offer a child security, and he will grow up to be more secure.

There is something magical about holding a baby. It has to do with the beauty of skin-to-skin warmth, the sweet smell of milk-fed breath, and the rare experience of sensuality and innocence wrapped together. Physical contact with a baby is all that it promises to be, because nothing is hidden. A baby lives and communicates through sensation.

It is true that not all babies seem to give themselves easily to our embraces. By the time they are a few months old, some struggle in their parents' arms and refuse to cuddle. This is the result of being put down in prams and cots for much of their early life. A child who is held constantly and allowed human contact throughout the night is always soft and pliant. He becomes so easy to hold, you hardly know he's there.

Mothers who hold their babies from birth find it increasingly easy to do. Outsiders look aghast and say 'Isn't he heavy?', and indeed he is, if you only transport him from the pushchair to the baby bouncer and from the bathroom to the nursery. If you carry a baby constantly, your arms accustom themselves to the weight as it increases imperceptibly over the months. Frances felt lighter to me at eight months, than she did at eight days old.

People who have not held a child in this way, and who have not seen it done, tend not to believe it. A marvellous example of the Western attitude is revealed by Davina Lloyd, editor of *Practical Parenting* magazine:

In America recently, a class of schoolgirls were told to carry a 5lb bag of flour around with them for a whole week and pretend it was a baby. They had to get up in the night to 'feed' it and spend each day 'changing' it and caring for it. The result: the local pregnancy rate dropped dramatically as the girls realised the responsibility.

(*Practical Parenting*, July 1988)

It's a pity babies aren't bags of flour, or our children could be self-raised. It may be useful for a class of teenagers to realize that babies need a lot of looking after – but five pounds of flour will always weigh five pounds; unresponsive and inert in your arms. People who marvel at my carrying Frances must see her in this way: a troublesome, heavy lump. But a real baby bouncing along in your arms is soft and giving, warm and life-lending. On our family walks, the adults beg to be the one to carry the baby.

It is sad that so many people are frightened of holding babies. Once again, this is merely a problem of experience and conditioning. We grow up hearing that infants are precious things. People warn us that we will drop them, so we approach babies with fear and caution. It is a vicious circle, for the baby also learns to be shy of contact with members of his own species.

The circle can be broken. A healthy baby hangs on a sling on his mother's hip in alert contentment, learning all he needs to know in the art of survival. If his mother cannot take him to work, she can insist he is carried by his childminder.

At night physical closeness is preserved with baby and adult cuddling up together. He sleeps easily, secure in the presence of his mother or other guardian, stirring to feed, waking for a second or two and then slumbering on. Bodily contact with a child allows a mother to become more at ease with herself.

The key is to continue with your pre-baby life, and include the child in everything you do. That includes sleep. The value of daily cuddles with a loved one is well known, and the rewards of sleeping next to your baby are even greater.

Mothers who put their children down at every opportunity are creating more work for themselves. As we have seen, the abandoned child undergoes a range of physiological changes – to his metabolic rate, his hormones, enzyme production, temperature, heartbeat, breathing and sleep patterns.[10]

Even if left for a short time, a baby will kick his legs with frustrated energy. He would usually work off this frustration through being held by his mother. That is the method by which human infants, unable to propel themselves, take their exercise. A kicking baby is moving with tense energy, like a bed-bound adult or someone who works at a desk all day. He is not taking genuine exercise, but winding himself up into a frenzy. So when the mother picks her child up again, he is stiffer, colder and less at ease than when he was being held. For the short time she carries him now, his equilibrium is being restored. His temperature picks up, his breathing calms, he begins to relax. Bonded together, the mother and child make up one energy unit, the adult working off the excess energies of the child.

If a mother denies herself the rejuvenating benefits of contact with her child, the times when she does pick him up are a tremendous effort. It's like starting a car over again, rather than keeping the engine running.

Physical contact with our children is a vastly underestimated benefit of being a parent. Peter Tinniswood captured the tonic effect of babies superbly in his comic novel, *A Touch of Daniel*. Daniel is the new baby in the Brandon household. Every day, he is taken to see the two old men who live in the attic at the top of the house, and gives them a kiss. Miraculously, the ailing old fellows begin to radiate good health:

'The funny thing is that they seem to perk up every time I take Daniel to see them,' said Carter Brandon to Pat one evening in the first week of January.

'What's so funny about that?' said Pat. 'I mean to say, the sight of a bonny bouncing baby always acts as a tonic to old folk, doesn't it?'

'Aye, but it's something more than that.'

'What?'

'When Daniel touches them, you can see a sort of red glow comes over their faces.'

'That's happiness.'

'Is it?'

'Like the red glow that comes over me when you kiss me, luv,' said Pat, wrapping her arms around his neck and kissing him on the lips.

The invalid Corporal Parkinson goes on to grow new hair, teeth and a pair of legs, while his companion Uncle Stavely slips the grip of senility to enjoy a fling with the resident nanny. If that's what a daily kiss can do, think of the benefits of being cuddled up with a baby all night. No wonder politicians and old people love babies.

A Touch of Daniel strikes home, because babies are like that. They do transform our lives. Either we resist them, and leave them to kick alone – or we allow ourselves to be touched by their magic.

To sleep with your baby next to you is – as many parents agree – a most wonderful and uplifting feeling. It may also offset the effects of postnatal depression (PND), a reaction so common in the West, that it is considered physiologically 'normal' to suffer from baby blues. Zinc supplements and better social support may help to alleviate PND, but no one has yet considered the nocturnal separation of mother and baby as a possible trigger for maternal depression.

Mothers suffering from severe baby blues are often advised to get away from the baby for a while, and hand him over to someone else. While this may be necessary in emergencies, it is a strategy which decreases the mother's feelings of confidence with the baby. Taking the baby away, at a time when the mother is hormonally-programmed to be with him as part of the natural bonding process, adds to the pain and anti-climax that so many women feel after giving birth.

Could it be that Western women, high on hormones and alive with instincts, are depressed because they are unfulfilled? So many mothers, sitting up in hospital with the baby sleeping in a cot at the end of the bed, feel that something, somehow, is wrong. 'Depressed?' said Brigid McConville, 'It's only "normal" ...':

... at least one school of thought believes that three-quarters of all women in Britain and in America suffer either depression or acute anxiety after childbirth.

(*Mad to be a Mother*)

Ms McConville analyses the social pressures behind long-term maternal depression. Dietary and environmental factors also play a large part in the stresses from which Western mothers suffer. But perhaps there is a biological factor, too. If so, the remedy is not to try to control the baby by strapping him into his pram or cot – but by holding him tight.

Anyone who imagines that having a baby in the bed would be too disruptive should compare the average disturbance caused by a child in the next room with that of a baby in the bed. All babies are prone to night waking, whether or not their parents are aware of it.[11] A baby may stir and resettle many times in the night. But people need to be awake for at least fifteen seconds to realize that they have been disturbed.[12] Neither parent nor child need be bothered by the minimal movements and shifts that the other makes in the night.

Babies are prone to wake more often than adults, as their average sleep cycle (through stages one to four, REM sleep and back again) takes only fifty minutes, compared with a ninety-minute cycle for the mature sleeper.[13]

Every time a person reaches the lightest stage of sleep, he is liable to wake, and may be roused by a light stimulus, or unfavourable conditions. For an infant, such conditions might include hunger, a drop in temperature, or the release of stress hormones because his mother or guardian is not around.

Few mothers realize that when breastfeeding they do not enter the fourth, or deepest, phase of sleep.[14] This phenomenon is governed by hormonal changes during pregnancy. Whether or not the baby is with her, she will be more prone to disturbance than before. With mother and baby both sleeping so lightly, separating them at night is a recipe for disaster.

The infant may wake during any one of the light-sleep periods during the night. He stirs, and if he does not find the comforter he expects, or the company he craves, he may cry. With every second that passes, he becomes more fully awake. The breastfeeding mother will be woken instantly, tuned in, as she is, to her baby's cries. She is destined for many disturbed nights until the baby has been 'trained' to sleep through in his own cot.

If the parents are in deep sleep, (if, perhaps, the baby is bottle-fed) they may take minutes to wake up, and even longer to listen out and decide whether or not to respond to his cry. By the time the parent gets to the nursery, he or she is fully roused (and irritated), while the baby is in complete anguish. No chance for everyone to turn over and doze off to sleep again.

I was once woken in the night by the sound of the doorbell ringing at five in the morning. I dragged myself up to answer it, and when I got back to bed found I was fully awake. Frances, then six months old, had never woken me to that extent, and to my annoyance it took me more than half an hour to get off to sleep again.

Many Western parents experience that degree of disturbance – and much, much worse – for months on end. No wonder they are desperate to persuade their cot-bound children to sleep through the night.

This, by way of comparison, is the night-time pattern of a Yequana baby sleeping with its mother, as described by Jean Liedloff:

> If there is a party while he is asleep, he will be bounced about quite violently while his mother hops and stamps in time to the music. Through daytime sleep, similar adventures befall him. At night his mother sleeps beside him, her skin next to his, as always, while she breathes and moves and sometimes snores a little. She wakes often during the night to tend the fire, holding him close as she rolls out of her hammock and slips to the floor, where he is sandwiched between her thighs and ribs as she rearranges the logs. If he awakens hungry in the night he signals with a soft grunt if he cannot find her breast; she will then give it to him, and again his well-being will be re-established ...
>
> (*The Continuum Concept*)

When you sleep with a small child, it feels easier to be a parent. You are literally in touch with the infant, not at odds with him. The level of satisfaction and contentment rises, and capability increases, along with a sense of doing the 'right' thing. For both parents, there is an increased tenderness which brings them closer to their child.

As Janine Sternberg, a child psychotherapist with three children, described it, 'We slept with our youngest, Sarah, from the first night. My husband Mike was happy about it in terms of all the pleasures of having a baby in the bed, you know how they smell nice and they feel soft... Having the baby there is a tangible expression of our love.' It also gives you a good night's sleep.

The experience of sleeping with a new-born child is strangely comparable with keeping vigil at the bedside of someone who is dying. Rather than easing someone out of life, as many are prepared to do, you are holding the hand of someone slipping into it. Interestingly the Trobrianders, a tribal people of Papua New Guinea, connect the concepts of birth and death in their language:

> Kopoi, the word used when villagers sit and care for a dead person before burial, also means 'to feed' or 'to nurse an infant'. A woman nurses (kopoi) her baby for about a year and a half.
>
> (Annette E. Weiner, *The Trobrianders of Papua New Guinea*)

Birth and death are events that require the support of those who care for us. They are the most vulnerable periods of our lives, and no caring society leaves an individual alone at the beginning or at the end of his time. The adult who shares a bed with a child is giving the proper tenderness for someone newly-born, comparable with the experience of this nurse:

> Something happens to you when you're with patients you feel a lot for. I think it's like a wave of gentleness or tenderness. It sweeps over you when you care. I suppose I show it in my voice and hands. I know that inside I feel warm and soft, I'm sure I do something to express that feeling.
>
> (Davitz and Davitz, *American Journal of Nursing*, 1975)

Carrying a baby, sleeping with a baby and answering its needs, are all in themselves the rewards of mothering. Keep in touch with a child, and his capacity for calm and physical ease enters your body, too. There is less parenting to do, and more time for getting on with other things when the baby comes too.

But social pressure to put baby in a cot is so strong, that parents may not admit that they allow their baby into bed. Many go to great lengths to keep a distance between themselves and their children – even when their instincts prompt them to do otherwise.

Jane Asher, the actress and author, says, 'It's a lovely feeling to have a warm snuggly baby next to you in bed to cuddle,' adding that she has 'no doubt that having the baby next to you is the natural way.' But eventually her baby Alexander was destined to sleep alone:

> I have had to put the crib over the other side of the bedroom so that I am forced to get out of bed each time he wakes – by the

time I reach him I am just about fully awake and strong minded enough not to take him back into bed.

(*Silent Nights*)

Parents prefer to be woken up in the night, rather than be weak-willed about sharing their bed with a baby. Ms Asher's strategy was – incredibly – an attempt to secure 'a certain amount of uninterrupted sleep at night.' No wonder *Mother* magazine carried an article in 1986 about the 'Bedroom Farce' of getting children off to sleep. As one mother wrote:

How cheering to know that I'm not alone in being reduced to ridiculous nightly contortions to escape my reluctantly sleeping child's bedroom.
Of course, we could just close the door and let them play or sob themselves to sleep. But how would we fill our evenings?

(Amanda Ferguson, Cardiff, September 1987)

The cunning we employ to trick our children into dreamland makes a nonsense of our genuine concern for their well-being. We tell ourselves it is vital they get their sleep – but it is apparently more important that they get it on our terms. If we could abandon the social stigma of bedsharing, then we could stop playing these games. Children learn from the beginning that their parents are attempting to lull them into a false sense of security every night.

In our consumer-based society, there are many tempting ways of dealing with our children's needs for tactile stimulation and nocturnal security. Manufacturers mass-produce the cot, they even supply accoutrements to take the place of the mother, who can hardly crawl between the bars to soothe her infant.

Many products are designed specifically as night comforters. Baby sheepskin rugs, warm and cosy, can help the baby to settle. Baby bouncers simulate the wonderful feeling of being jogged around in mother's arms. Baby alarms monitor the infant's breathing while parents are at the other end of the house.

But these products don't really do the trick. No teddy bear or cot-jiggler yet invented can simulate all the benefits of a mother's body. According to Dr McKenna, 'mother's biorhythms physiologically regulate their offspring both prenatally and postnatally.' Babies need their mothers, not machines.

Some of the devices on the market are quite ludicrous. This is what Jane Asher had to say about her two-way baby alarm:

> Some of them have a talk-back switch so that you can comfort the baby by the sound of your voice, but the only time I ever tried to use one Katie nearly leapt out of the cot with shock. I suppose your mother's voice suddenly booming out from a little box must seem a bit strange.
>
> (*Silent Nights*)

Other inventions, equally crude, prove the infant's desperate need for company at night. Nurseries have discovered that a mother's heartbeat, played over a loudspeaker in a hospital nursery, soothes the crying infants. American mothers can buy machines to simulate the noise and movement of a car – well known for its somniferous effects – presumably to save the bother of driving baby round the block.

Hospitals, hooked on new gadgetry, are also experimenting with electronically controlled rocking cots, to soothe colicky babies and premature infants. I talked to Cradlecraft, a company which manufactures a variety of these cribs, for use at home and in hospital. Their automatic crib saves the parent even the trouble of seeing the baby off to sleep. Based on the 'pendulum principle', Cradlecraft's machine[15], which costs £450, will rock the most fretful of babies to contented rest, they say. Salesman Tony Urry told me that paediatricians also believe the invention aids premature babies in tissue accretion.

If an automatic machine can stimulate growth in small babies, think what benefits a premature infant would gain by being kept close to his mother, day and night.

All babies need and expect the kind of contact and comfort that will satisfy them for the rest of their days. If a child has his fill of maternal care – even if it does not come from his actual mother – he will be able to enter adulthood without hang-ups and neuroses. He will be less hooked on money, or drugs, or the many other objects that promise to bring him happiness but never do. He will know that peace of mind comes from within himself, not from external sources.

Psychologist John Bowlby was concerned with the deprivation of institutionalized children when, in 1953, he wrote *Child Care and the Growth of Love*. His words apply with increasing urgency today, as more and more mothers seek to put distance and comfort-giving objects between themselves and their babies:

> It is exactly the kind of care which a mother gives without thinking that *is* the care which they have lacked. All the cuddling and playing, the intimacies of his mother's body, the rituals of washing and dressing by which through her pride and tenderness towards his little limbs he learns the value of his own, all these have been lacking. His mother's love and pleasure in him are his spiritual nourishment ...
>
> It is only when nature's gifts are lacking that science must study what they are in order to make the best shift it can to replace them.

Babies need the soft touch of humans in order to thrive. The life-long benefits of sharing the parental bed are beautifully put in this passage by American novelist William Wharton:

> Ben is stretched out, overlapping his cot by the fire, arms hanging over the sides. He sleeps deeply, calmly, no tossing, no teeth grinding, no startled nightmares, no thumb or finger sucking. We like to think it's because we never let him cry himself to sleep, never left him alone in the dark when he wanted to be with us. Until he was seven, he spent at least half of each night in our bed, usually cuddling with me. I didn't mind, I liked it; I don't think sleeping alone is natural. With our first three we were young and foolish enough, vulnerable to rigid conditioning theories then prevalent, to insist they stay in their own beds, so now each is an erratic sleeper. I myself only became capable of deep, full, refreshing sleep when I was about forty. I can't always manage it, now, even with meditation or Valium, but then things have been hard lately.
>
> (*Tidings*)

Valium is one of the comforters of our adulthood. Jim Horne, director of Loughborough's Sleep Research Laboratory, describes the placebo effect of hypnotic drugs for people who need a psychological support before they can sleep. A well-chewed blanket contains as much medication as these tablets:

All that many sufferers require ... is some form of guarantee that they will have a good night's sleep. Taking the tablet each night sees to that, even though it may not be required. In this respect, the best sleeping tablet may be the one that is never taken but placed by the bedside. Knowing that it is there, ready for use just in case, can be very reassuring.

(*The Practitioner*, October 1985)

Perhaps if we gave more true comfort to our children – the joy of touch, the security of contact at night – then we would begin to satisfy the ancient desires which motivate us all our lives. A child wants nothing but complete acceptance from his parents. When he has had his fill of that, he will move on to other things.

5 | WILL IT BE ALL RIGHT IN THE NIGHT?

Medicine is keeping more babies alive than ever before. A child may be born months before his time, survive a difficult birth, shrug off jaundice, and battle successfully with an infection which ten years ago would have killed him. Improved sanitation and knowledge about nutrition ensure that high infant mortality is no longer a problem in developed countries. But there is still a killer that claims up to 1,500 children a year under the age of two in the United Kingdom.[1] And we don't even know what it is.

Many thousands of pounds are channelled into studying the possible reasons for the Sudden Infant Death Syndrome. SIDS, also known as 'cot death', accounts for up to half the deaths of children in Britain between the ages of one week and two years.[2] Ninety per cent of the babies die before they reach the age of nine months.

Apart from hints that breastfed babies are less likely to die from SIDS, that outdoor deaths are more common in winter and that babies are at greater risk lying face down[3], no one really knows when cot death will strike. It is unlikely that any single factor is responsible for the sudden death syndrome, and there is apparently little a parent can do to prevent it.

Stories of how an otherwise healthy infant suddenly stops breathing, often unnoticed in his cot or pram, add to the fears of new parents. This account in a monthly magazine is typical of the cot death experience. Laura was just three and a half months old:

> The night before she died was much as usual. Early in the morning, at around 4.30, she woke for a cuddle, then Jacqueline put her straight back in her cot which was by the side of our bed.
>
> At 7 we woke up, and immediately wondered why our 'little alarm clock' hadn't gone off at her normal time of 6.30. One look and we knew: she was cold and lifeless. I called the ambulance

and tried to resuscitate her but it was too late. She had been dead for over an hour and there was no hope.

We couldn't believe it was happening to us. We felt angry, guilty, confused ... why, why, why? If we'd been awake, perhaps she wouldn't have died.

(*Practical Parenting*, June 1988)

Guilt and confusion are typical reactions to a death which has no satisfactory explanation. In the experience of child psychotherapist Dilys Daws, many parents with healthy children dwell on the subject to the detriment of their own happiness and that of the family. A mother's fears may in themselves cause infant sleep difficulties:

With sleep problems it seems to me often that what I am doing for the mother is directly containing her anxiety so that she can go back to the baby and contain the baby's anxiety. There is often some real external cause for anxiety in the mother: difficulties in the birth or early weeks that she has not recovered from and not properly absorbed. Mothers worry that their baby may die in the night and this kind of fear is based on reality. Everyone has heard, or read in the newspapers, of such tragic events.

(*Journal of Child Psychotherapy*, 1985)

A mother's fears for her child can grow to horrendous proportions in the night, when the baby is tucked into a cot in the next room, and she is sleeping her light, maternal sleep in the big double bed.

There is a telling scene at the beginning of the film *Terms of Endearment,* when the young mother, played by Shirley Maclaine, tiptoes into the nursery, panicking that her baby is not breathing. She pokes her small, sleeping daugher until she cries. Now the mother is happy. As long as she can hear the screams, she knows her baby is alive.

With all this panic and such little understanding of cot death, it might seem that a nightly vigil is the parents' only option. SIDS is the third most common cause of infant death in many parts of the world, following closely after congenital abnormality and premature birth.[4] Apnoea alarms (breathing monitors) are now on sale, claiming to detect when a baby stops breathing in the cot – but the Foundation for the Study of Infant Deaths warns against these expensive items. Manufacturers, say the FSID, make exaggerated claims of success.

Undoubtedly the most dramatic advance has been the government's Back To Sleep campaign, inspired by research from the Institute of Child Health in Bristol which demonstrated that babies who were laid face down in their cots were more likely to die from SIDS. The FSID has produced leaflets showing parents how to 'Reduce the Risk of Cot Death', which covers factors such as smoking, overheating and placing a baby on its back or side to sleep.

But in the end, SIDS strikes even the most vigilant of homes and the only message the Foundation is able to give bereaved parents is to accept what happened.

> Babies die unexpectedly for many reasons. In some cases the cause is evident at post mortem; but in many others, in whom earlier signs of illness had been absent or trivial, the cause of death is not found ... the tragedy is world-wide.
>
> (*Support for Parents Bereaved by an Unexpected Infant Death*, September 1983)

Worldwide, perhaps, but not universal. Babies continue to die unexpectedly without cause in many parts of the world. But it appears that children in some societies are far less likely to die from the syndrome than others. Recent studies indicate that SIDS is rare in some countries and among certain ethnic groups. This information points us to a revised understanding of the nature of cot death, and may even help to prevent it.

French birth pioneer Michel Odent, travelling in China in 1977, asked medical professionals about the phenomenon of cot death. No one knew what he was talking about. Later, in correspondence with *The Lancet*, Dr Odent reported his findings. Even translators, the most westernized of his hosts, did not recognize his description of a young baby dying suddenly for no apparent reason:

> Nobody understood my questions; the concept of sudden infant death or cot death was apparently unknown among professionals and lay people in such different places as Peking, Hsian, Loyang, Nanking, Shanghai, and Canton. Furthermore I learned that Chinese babies sleep with their mothers, even in the most westernized families, such as the families of interpreters. Ever since then I have held the view that, even if it happens during the day, cot death is a disease of babies who spend their nights in an atmosphere of loneliness and that cot death is a disease of societies

where the nuclear family has taken over.

(*The Lancet*, 25 January 1986)

The 'atmosphere of loneliness' theory is supported by research from Scarborough and Sutton Coldfield. Doctors Stanton and Oakley studied illness in children who subsequently died suddenly and inexplicably. They found that a significant proportion of babies who died from SIDS had earlier been admitted for a long stay in hospital:

> This study suggests that admission to hospital may be an important event for some babies who subsequently die unexpectedly. Although only 16 per cent gave this history, their admission rate was well in excess of that of the control population. They remained in hospital for twice as long and were far more likely to be readmitted on a subsequent occasion. Infection was the commonest diagnosis precipitating admission, but the illnesses were rarely life-threatening.
>
> (*Archives of Diseases in Childhood*, 1983)

The researchers found that babies who died of cot death had often been re-admitted to hospital because parents were unable to cope at home. They ruled out theories that babies were being discharged from hospital too early, or that the deaths were caused by the minor infections which had first brought them into hospital. They concluded:

> A more relevant consequence of the admissions may have been a disturbance of the bonding mechanisms within the family, because of the frequently prolonged separation of the baby from its parents.

Anyone who has spent any time in a childcare ward in hospital will know the extreme suffering that abandoned babies appear to endure. Many infants are admitted without their mother or other guardian, and overworked nurses are unable to offer individual attention as the babies scream in their cots for much of the day and night.

Prolonged hospitalization during the second part of the child's first year is known to have a severely debilitating effect on a baby. Days of crying give way to silent grief and apathy. If the child continues to lack affection from a consistent mother figure over a period of weeks, he adopts grimaces and gestures that resemble those of the adult psychotic. Without the love and attention of a 'mother', a baby can be retarded for life.

Some hospitals create an atmosphere of loneliness for babies. But isolation is only possible where people have space and rooms enough to put babies in. In a high-density city such as Hong Kong, where families are crowded into high-rise apartments, infants are rarely alone. Professor D. P. Davies, a paediatrician working in the Prince of Wales Hospital in Hong Kong, is the author of a study demonstrating that cot death is rare among the Chinese community there. He reports:

> Over the 5 years 1980–84 only 15 cases of cot death were documented by forensic pathologists – an approximate incidence of 0.036 per 1000 live births. If the incidence was similar to that in western countries (2–3 per 1000), 800–1200 cot deaths might have been expected over this period.
>
> (*The Lancet,* 14 December 1985)

Of those fifteen cases, eleven were ethnic Chinese babies, three were British and one Japanese – a higher proportion of Western babies than would be expected from the racial mix on the island (ninety per cent are ethnic Chinese).

The most obvious explanation for the low incidence of SIDS might be that such deaths go unrecorded. Dr Davies does not believe this to be the case. He says that cot death is genuinely rare on the island:

> ... in this small territory with one of the highest population densities anywhere in the world, where closely knit extended families are common, illegal disposal of a dead body is well nigh impossible, and the system of collecting mortality data is highly efficient ...

The findings are surprising because most babies in Hong Kong are bottle-fed, humidity is high and many children suffer from respiratory illness – all factors contributing to SIDS. Professor Davies later turned his attention to the Bangladeshi community living in Cardiff, South Wales, and found that, despite overcrowding, overheated housing and young mothers with many children, Bangladeshi babies were half as likely to die from SIDS as the average Welsh baby.

It is worth comparing Professor Davies's conclusions from Wales with his earlier speculations from Hong Kong. In 1985, he wrote:

> Reflecting further on the living conditions in Hong Kong, I wonder whether there might be some benefit to such high-density living. Babies were left alone much less. Sleep patterns might be different, effecting subtle modulations to physiological responses concerned with ventilatory control. The question 'When can I put baby into his own room?' is virtually never raised. Might closer overall contact with the sleeping baby somehow lessen the risks of sudden death?

In 1993, in his report from the Department of Child Health at the University of Wales, Davies wrote:

> Bangladeshi babies are thought to be vulnerable, and they sleep close to other people both day and night; at night they are either in the mother's bed or in a cot next to it . . . It is not simply a question of space, but of a belief that, as one mother put it, 'I like to wake up in the night and see all my family around me.' He concluded, 'Long periods of lone quiet sleep may be one factor that contributes to a higher rate of sudden deaths in white than in Asian infants.'[5]

Robert Tseng, a paediatrician who has worked both in Britain and Hong Kong, is convinced that something in the Chinese lifestyle makes cot death a rare occurrence. Dr Tseng draws a vivid picture of the nightmare of trying to save a dying baby:

> An infant who has died suddenly and is brought to a casualty department's resuscitation room with its parents is an experience not easily forgotten. I can recall six such episodes over nine months spent as a paediatric senior house officer at a district hospital in Kingston-on-Thames, UK. Over the past 18 months, at a district general hospital in Hong Kong with on-call duties for paediatric resuscitation in the casualty department, I have not once had this traumatic experience . . .
>
> Perhaps there is a holistic answer to the question 'What causes cot death?' which will not readily be found by a vast volume of research in isolated disciplines of medicine

or isolated parts of infants who die of cot death. I echo Dr Odent's view that cot death is largely a disease of societies with certain child rearing cultural practices . . . A closer look into these cultural differences with an open mind might provide better clues.

(*The Lancet*, 1 March 1986)

Medical anthropologist James McKenna of Pomona College, Claremont, leads the field of research into the holistic answer to SIDS. He reports that rates of cot death in non-industrialized countries are notoriously difficult to obtain. Many of these countries do not carry out a thorough post-mortem on infants, or do not record a diagnosis of sudden, unexpected and unexplained death.

Comparisons of urban societies that have standardized their reporting and diagnosis of SIDS are better, but even these can be difficult. For example, SIDS rates are lower in Sweden, the Netherlands, Switzerland, and Israel, where in some segments of society, infants sleep with their parents or in the same room. Moreover, the infant mortality rates in general (rather than just for SIDS) are extremely low in Japan, an urban country in which cosleeping occurs . . .

(*Medical Anthtropology*, 1986)

Asian, Chinese and Malaysian families share many similarities in the raising of their children, including sleeping with them while they are small. As Dr Odent says, sleeping with new-born babies is often the last natural mothering practice to be abandoned, even where bottle feeding and high-tech births have been introduced. Many Asian families in the West live in extremely crowded conditions, and it may be that in this instance, poverty is on their side. Children and babies may have no choice but to share bedspace with the rest of the family.

Despite this wealth of epidemiological evidence, research from New Zealand in 1991 suggested the babies who slept with their parents were at a *greater* risk of cot death. An ITV documentary shown in November that year even recommended that parents should not take their babies into the family bed. Unfortunately, the advice was premature.

It was based on statistics from the Maori population, who still often sleep with their children in the traditional way. Unhappily some not-so-traditional factors have overtaken the Maori lifestyle, including alcoholism and a high incidence of maternal smoking.

In January 1993, the New Zealand researchers came back with a study which corrected their earlier assumption that co-sleeping alone was a factor in cot death. Rather, they conceded, it is the combination of smoking with close-contact nurture which is potentially fatal for the vulnerable baby. (By contrast, smoking was 'very rare' among Bangladeshi mothers in the Cardiff study.[5])

So what, exactly, could be the connection between solitary sleeping and sudden infant death? In his paper, *An Anthropological Perspective on SIDS*, James McKenna gathers a wealth of evidence that supports that where a baby sleeps may be vital. It is important to examine the major points of his academic discussion.

The foetus in its mother's womb begins to breathe rhythmically up to three months before birth. Studies have shown that sensory stimulation (e.g. the rocking of the mother as she walks, and the sounds she makes) keeps the unborn child breathing regularly. All these stimuli are felt and heard by the foetus, who has advanced hearing even in the womb.

At birth, the infant has a natural immunity to cot death. This may be because of a natural gasping reflex, which gets the baby breathing when in danger of suffocation. The reflex is lost after a few weeks, however, as the higher brain takes over and begins to control the child's development. As this happens, the baby 're-engages' with the mother, becoming more dependent on her. The child is vulnerable to errors in brain-controlled functions (such as breathing), especially during the shifts from reflexive behaviour to controlled behaviour.

As one doctor explains, the heartbeat of a normal, healthy baby sleeping alone is notoriously irregular:

> Workers making 24-hour recordings of heart-beat in a large number of normal infants have shown that occasional abnormalities of rhythm are unexpectedly common. It has been suggested that immaturity of heart-beat and breathing regulation may result in arrest of heart or breathing under circumstances which would not normally cause such an event.
>
> (Dr Andrew Evans, *Nursery World*, 31 July 1980)

One of the most important changes a human baby has to make is in the way it breathes, in order to vocalize speech. This is a major difference between humans and other mammals, which do not speak, and are not susceptible to sudden death syndrome.

The baby has to learn how to make purposeful, non-crying noises before he can learn languages. In the first year of life, his breathing slows from 87 to around 47 breaths per minute. And between two and four months of age, the time when a baby is changing his breathing patterns, he is at his most susceptible to SIDS. He is also most responsive at this time to the benefits of touch.[6]

I have already described in the previous chapter how sleeping next to an adult can stimulate regular breathing in a baby. Dr McKenna works on the theory that if a baby is stimulated to breathe by movement in the womb, then a new-born child will be similarly stimulated by the parent at his side. We really are a carrying species, and the infant expects to be always with his mother or guardian.

McKenna demonstrates that vestibular stimulation (e.g. breathing movements of the adult's chest when asleep), rocking, touch and heat exchange all help to promote the health and easy breathing of the infant. Gas exchange may also be an important factor. The baby sleeping next to his parents is likely to breathe in carbon dioxide, a chemical stimulant to take the next breath.

> When parents sleep with or near an infant, it is likely, at least for much of the night, that not only will their body heat be exchanged but also will their expelled carbon dioxide gases. Recently, Sullivan (1984) suggested that during REM sleep, infants can smell carbon dioxide ... If this is so, then in the microenvironment created by its parent [in their bed], the infant could respond to the parent's exhaled carbon dioxide by breathing in some of it. That is, the infant's upper nasal chemo-receptors may receive enough of its parent's CO_2 to increase the chance of a brain stem-inspired inspiration.
>
> (*Medical Anthropology*, 1986)

It is ironic that gas exchange was the very reason why the Victorians felt mother and baby should *not* sleep together. We may recall the words of *Baby* magazine:

> For the first few weeks animal heat is maintained by sleeping with the mother; but on no account should a child of any later age

sleep between two persons, as by so doing it must of necessity breathe the emanations from their bodies.

(*Baby,* 1888)

The author would have the child taken from the bed at precisely the age when he is most dependent on the mother for external stimuli to keep him breathing. The rationale for using a pram was the same:

I think a young child can lie much more at ease in a berceaunette-perambulator than in the arms of a nurse who cramps its movements and causes it to inhale her breath and the exhalations of her clothes.

(*Baby,* December 1887)

It might be that the regular chest movement of the sleeping parent, coupled with the rhythmic flow of air, reminds the vulnerable baby to keep breathing. If there is a problem, author Dr Penny Stanway believes the baby is bound to be safer in his mother's arms than in his own room.

'If you have a baby prone to having its heart simply stop, it's going to start wriggling,' she told me. 'The mother will wake up and feed the baby, which will stimulate the system again. It's far better than relying on cot alarms.'

Dr Stanway also points out that the common night-time feeding position of resting the baby's head in the crook of the arm reduces the chance of the baby choking on his own vomit. Even in terms of basic safety, a baby is better in his parents' bed than out of it.

We know that breastfed babies are statistically less at risk from cot death than bottle-fed infants. Whether or not the milk itself has anything to do with it, a breastfed baby is likely to receive the extra maternal contact he needs to maintain regular breathing, especially at night.

Dr McKenna does not present co-sleeping of baby and parents as a complete solution to cot death, any more than solitary sleeping is the cause of it. But he says that the human baby's dependence on his mother is a compelling reason for not separating them at night. When a baby is at risk of Sudden Infant Death Syndrome, his constitutional weakness may combine with his solitary sleeping habits to make death more likely.

My reasoning is that solitary-sleeping infants will breathe differently (less stably) than will social-sleeping infants, and of course, the parents themselves will be in a better position to respond to changes in their infants, such as serious apneas [interruptions in breathing] or breathing silence.

(Medical Anthropology, 1986)

Dr McKenna has studied the breathing patterns of babies when they sleep with their mothers, and when they sleep alone. Preliminary evidence shows that the baby's breathing – though slower than the mother's – follows hers, and that co-sleeping helps to protect against breathing lapses. This confirmed McKenna's earlier belief that parent and baby were designed to breathe in harmony.

There may be no more fundamental form of parent-infant interactional synchrony than the response of parents and infants to each other's breathing cues which, while cosleeping, may move toward a form of complementary breathing.

(Medical Anthropology, 1986)

Until further studies are made in this field, we can only speculate on the nature and implications of complementary breathing. A full understanding could revolutionize our view of the relationship between mother and baby, and change our assumptions about the level of independence an infant can tolerate. Meanwhile, there is no sign that co-sleeping does any harm. In fact, doctors have noted the benefits for families which fear sudden infant death. Dr Hugh Jolly, for instance, wrote:

Many parents say that they sleep better in a family bed because they are not frightened about what is happening to their young children. One mother told me she could not sleep unless her baby was beside her. Parents who are particularly frightened about 'cot death' have been relieved to have their babies in bed with them.

(Book of Child Care)

Parents who take their babies to bed do not need to worry about whether their child is still alive, as, with bodies touching, they can tangibly feel the life within. If the baby does stop breathing, they are on hand to deal with it in the shortest possible time. Picking up a baby, rocking or feeding him are all known ways of reviving him after apnoea (the cessation of breathing).

Sometimes cot death is confused with mechanical suffocation. People say they are frightened to have a baby in the bed, because they might smother him in the night. There is even an official word – 'overlaying' – which refers to babies who suffocate while in the parental bed.

At the beginning of the century, doctors were on the look-out for any obvious causes of infant death, to halt the high mortality rate. If a baby died suddenly, and happened to sleep in the parents' bed, overlaying was the most usual reason given. Consequently, doctors advised that 'the best safeguard is that the child should be made to occupy a separate bed from its parents.'[7] Overlaying was mistakenly thought to be the cause of sudden, unexpected and otherwise unexplained infant deaths.

Numerous studies have since shown that there is no connection between cot death and overlaying. Dr David Haslam, author of *Sleepless Children* says the idea that parents suffocate their children in bed is 'nonsense'. Dr Hugh Jolly also dismisses the connection between cot death and mechanical suffocation:

> Guilt and misunderstanding are still the penalty of our hazy ideas of the cause of cot deaths, and only now is some light beginning to dawn on this difficult subject. For example, suffocation used to be made the scapegoat for many sudden infant deaths. Parents felt they were at fault for providing the 'wrong' kind of bedding or, worse still, for letting the baby sleep in their bed. At worst, the suspicion of deliberate suffocation arose. Yet at the age when cot deaths are most common – two to six months – a normal baby can lift his head and change his position if he cannot breathe easily.
>
> (*Book of Child Care*)

The BBC TV programme *Tomorrow's World* demonstrated this point in 1978, with a time-lapse film[8] of two adults sleeping with their baby. Each time the baby rolled towards his parents, they moved away in their sleep. A healthy baby is able to shift position in the night, given that he is not tightly swaddled, or that his body is not in a splint.

Any suggestion that breathing is more difficult for the baby while suckling during sleep is quashed by evidence from the John Radcliffe Hospital in Oxford. Dr Paul Johnson, consultant clinical physiologist, reports in FSID's newsletter of August 1986 that the descent of the larynx during early infancy poses no problems for babies:

> The newborn infant is thus able to breathe effectively while swallowing at 3–4 times per second – a reflex act which most adults cannot match.

One prevailing myth about babies is that they are unable to breathe through their mouths, and that this increases their chances of suffocation. Dr Johnson demonstrates that babies are perfectly able to mouth breathe by choice:

> ... the human newborn (in common with most mammals) contrary to the published statements is not an obligate nose breather. This was a popular but unproven view which followed 'tests' in which the noses of babies were obstructed and the infants were observed to attempt to breathe without opening their mouths. However, for ethical rather than physiological reasons the nose was only obstructed for a few breaths. It has now been shown by two independent groups in Belgium and the USA that not only do some newborn babies normally mouth breathe but that they will switch automatically to mouth breathing if their noses are obstructed without waking up.

This is the kind of evidence a mother sees for herself whenever her baby has a cold. He will attempt to nose breathe, but failing this, opens his mouth. Meanwhile, Dr McKenna says that even a one-day-old baby will complain if he has difficulty in breathing:

> Overlying is, of course, possible, but it is not likely, just as strangulation by defective cribs, while known to have happened, also is not common ... soft mattresses, as opposed to hard mats, may change the overall safety picture of parent-infant cosleeping. Nevertheless, even day-old infants will struggle violently and protest vocally in response to obstruction of their air passages.
>
> (*Medical Anthropology*, 1986)

Accidental mechanical suffocation is, in fact, extremely rare. Figures published by the Office of Population, Census and Surveys in 1985 show that the total number of deaths of British babies of less than one year was 6,141. Of these, 1,165 were diagnosed as victims of

SIDS. Only six babies during the year actually suffocated – four in their parents' beds, and two in their own cots.

Apparent instances of smothering tend to reach the national press. A one-year-old child from Wiltshire was suffocated under his parents' duvet after his mother moved him into her room, 'in an effort to get him to sleep'. According to this newspaper report:

> A verdict of accidental death was recorded on Leon Forsey, of Bishops Cannings, Devizes. A spokesman for the Royal Society for the Prevention of Accidents commented afterwards: 'Our advice is that babies are best off in their own cots at that age. We don't recommend they should go into an adult bed alone or with adults.'
>
> (*Daily Telegraph*, 1 October 1988)

Without knowing the exact circumstances, it is impossible to say why a healthy, mobile one-year-old was unable to wriggle free from his parents' duvet during the night. But a baby at risk in his mother's bed would be even more at risk in his own cot, where he might suffocate under his quilt without anyone there to notice his struggles. Incidents of this sort make the headlines precisely because they are so rare, while cot death goes largely unreported. Unfortunate exceptions to the general rule are no reason to leave babies alone at night.

The Foundation for Infant Deaths has itself recently reported cases of babies dying of cot death while sleeping with their parents – a rare but possible occurrence. From data available to the Foundation, information officer Tracy Curds confirmed that 'of the very few babies who were found dead in their parents' beds (and registered as SIDS) there was NO evidence of overlaying.'[9]

Interestingly, the same researchers found that SIDS families had moved house almost twice as often before the infant's death as had control families. This further corroborates the idea that disruption and separation – likely consequences of the trauma of moving house – are critical in a baby's life.

If a baby is to sleep with his parents, there are a few very simple precautions to take. The baby should feel free to move. The co-sleepers (adults or children) should all be well. They should not be drunk, or drugged, or excessively overweight. No one should smoke in the bed, or near the baby. Water beds should be avoided, and pillows arranged so that they cannot fall and smother the child.

Modern parents tend to be overprotective of their babies, not careless. These essential preparations will seem obvious and common sense. In poor households at the end of the century, not all parents took as much care. More babies suffocated in their parents' bed at weekends – presumably when mother or father came home drunk.

Since 1908 there has been a law in Britain to safeguard against parents' going to bed drunk with their children. The Children's Act provision was incorporated into the Children and Young Persons Act of 1933, and is still in force today. It reads:

> ... where it is proved that the death of an infant under three years of age was caused by suffocation (not being suffocation caused by disease or the presence of any foreign body in the throat or air passages of the infant) while the infant was in bed with some other person who has attained the age of sixteen years, that other person shall, if he was, when he went to bed, under the influence of drink, be deemed to have neglected the infant in a manner likely to cause injury to its health.[10]

In his own investigations, Dr Hugh Jolly found that all deaths of infants sleeping with their parents could be explained by drink, drugs, obesity or illness. The annual rate of mechanical suffocation, on the other hand, is negligible. It is some 200 times less likely to occur than SIDS. It is also completely avoidable, which cot death is not.

Researchers from Zimbabwe go further: 'Sudden infant death may result from trivial embarrassments, upper respiratory tract infections ... and so on. It may begin with remarkable episodes of distress, which, if they had been witnessed, might have been simply attended to and though little of.'[10]

Making our babies sleep alone at night may be a risk we cannot afford to take.

6 | THE MIDNIGHT FEAST

When my grandmother wanted to breastfeed, the midwife told her: 'You wouldn't want to eat a beef steak in the middle of the night, so why should your baby want milk?' She followed the advice, feeding her baby only during the day, at the prescribed four-hourly intervals. Within a few weeks, her daughter was losing weight, and my grandmother gave up. Like most mothers of her time, she was told she did not have enough milk for her baby. The fault, apparently, was hers.

Thousands of British women tell similar stories today. Childcare books imply that breastfeeding is a specialized art, which is difficult to perfect. Friends say it is a struggle which they did not enjoy. Many give up because they have insufficient milk. Meanwhile, rather than support the breastfeeding woman, food companies promote artificial feeds and encourage early weaning on to solids.

A recent report by the government Committee on Medical Aspects of Food Policy found that breastfeeding was the best nutrition for babies, and that it should be provided for at least a year. But the Committee also accepted that most babies in Britain are likely to be bottle-fed by the age of four weeks.[1] Whatever the experts tell us about the benefits of breastfeeding, fashion still favours the bottle.

It should be no surprise to learn that for millions of years all babies were breastfed, whether by their mothers' milk or by that of a wet nurse. Some tribes and cultures, including our own, believed that the pre-milk, colostrum, was bad or dirty, and so separated the baby from its mother in the first few days. Colostrum was known as 'witch milk', until the English doctor, William Cadogan, pronounced its virtues in the mid-eighteenth century. Cadogan was an advocate of unrestricted feeding:

Nature, if she be not interrupted, will do the whole business perfectly well; and there seems to be nothing left for a Nurse to do, but to keep the child sweet and clean, and to tumble and toss it about a good deal, play with it, and keep it in good Humour.

(*Essay on the Nursing and Management of Children*, 1748)

Mothers' milk was the obvious nourishment for a child, and without it, a baby would probably starve.

By the middle of the nineteenth century, however, alternatives to mothers' milk were being sold alongside the cures for baldness and linctuses in the classified ads. Babies could now be spoon-fed, or reared from bottles with leather teats. In 1882, the edition of *Enquire Within Upon Everything* made these suggestions:

Children who are brought up by hand, that is to say, who are not nursed by mother or wet nurse, require an occasional change of diet, and thin gruel affords a wholesome alternation to milk. When cow's milk is used it should be obtained, if possible, from one and the same cow, and diluted with boiled water. Swiss milk is recommended by some medical men. The Aylesbury Dairy Company furnish a speciality for young children under the name of 'Artificial Human Milk', which is recommended.

It was around this time that doctors and other experts began to prescribe the best methods and formulas for feeding infants. At first, their recommendations were merely an attempt to bring order to the apparently *ad hoc* way in which most mothers fed their babies. Constant feeding in the day and at night was seen as a messy (and unmedical) way of doing things:

The time of taking food is not a matter of indifference; very young infants made an exception; for as their consumption of vital power is more rapid, they may be more frequently indulged with aliment.

It is, however, advisable to accustom even them to a certain regularity, so as to allow them their victuals at stated periods of the day; for it has been observed that those children which are fed indiscriminately through the whole day, are subject to debility and disease.

(*Enquire Within Upon Everything*, 1882)

The 'discriminating' mother introduced a system to her breastfeeding technique. The laws of mothering were no longer to follow the mood of mother and child – rules were made by the doctors, equipped with new, scientific theories on nutrition.

Community midwife Chloe Fisher has pored over many early textbooks in an attempt to discover where we lost the art of successful breastfeeding. She found that doctors imposed several types of restriction on lactating mothers: (1) an insistence on regular feeding times; (2) control of the frequency of feeding; (3) a limit on initial sucking at the breast; (4) limits on the total duration of each feed; and finally, (5) a complete ban on night feeding.[2]

To this list we might now add the social pressure to wean as early as possible. The trend in Britain is to introduce new foods to the baby at three months – or even earlier, if the baby seems especially hungry and constantly at the nipple. It is fashionable to express distaste at seeing toddlers breastfed, and most women who do breast-feed stop after a few months. The most common reasons for weaning are lack of maternal milk, discomfort, social pressure and the return to work – not rejection of the breast by baby.

In the 1920s, pioneers such as New Zealander Truby King were to influence a whole generation of medical professionals throughout the English-speaking dominions. While King's intentions (to rear well-nourished babies and educate women on matters of hygiene) were honourable, his recommendations created a breastfeeding timetable of the most rigorous kind.

Victorian doctors said new-born babies should be fed every one and a half hours. This was more or less an observation based on common practice. As doctors revised their opinions, the gaps between feeds widened. Edmund Owen, writing in the 1880s, suggested:

For the first month a baby should be fed every two hours, and if he be a good sleeper he may be woke up for his meals, at any rate he should not be allowed to pass the third hour without food. If he be allowed to sleep on, he wakes up at last so desperately hungry that he overfeeds, and, by an attack of vomiting, much of his meal is wasted ... Regular and frequent feeding is a great thing for little children.

(*Baby*, 1888)

But Truby King and his disciples of the 1920s believed the new-born to be made of sterner stuff. They introduced the four-hourly feeding rule. Mabel Liddiard, an English woman and a devoted fan of King, wrote:

> Public opinion has changed very rapidly on this subject – not many years ago the mother was asked to feed two-hourly, night and day. What wonder that breast-feeding went out of fashion! Then the three-hourly interval was recognised as best, while now the four-hourly has been approved.
>
> (*The Mothercraft Manual* (1924–1948))

The horrors of breastfeeding were to be found in every manual on mothering. The words of the Victorian authority, Mrs Jane Ellen Panton, set the tone for a hundred years of breastfeeding advice: 'Let no mother condemn herself to be a common or ordinary "cow" unless she has a real desire to nurse . . .'[3]

The message to mothers and midwives was clear – breastfeeding was an unpleasant task. It was not realized at this time that one of the greatest reasons for the unpleasantness was that the baby was limited in his feeding. The truth belies the theory. The long gaps now usual between feeds, are the times when engorgement and potential damage set in. Intermittent snacking by a baby held constantly at the breast does no damage to mother or child – the breast does not need a rest.

Ms Liddiard's methods still apply in most modern hospitals, where most breastfeeding begins. According to *Mother* magazine, the average new-born baby has six feeds a day – which means that four-hourly feeding is the current practice.

Frances weighed 6 lb 1½ oz when she was born. As she was on the border of being a 'tiny' baby, I was instructed to feed her at three-hourly intervals, rather than every four hours.

Although I chose to feed her almost constantly instead, I did keep a record of the gaps between feeds for a while, until I tired of writing down '20 mins', '10 mins', '30 mins' and so on. One young trainee midwife mentioned that the reason I did not suffer from cracked nipples, engorgement, blisters or soreness was the constant feeding. But that was not part of the standard advice.

There was a slight problem when it came to weighing Frances before going home. I was supposed to wait for at least an hour after a 'feed' to put her on the scales, but as I always held her in my arms, and as she suckled frequently from the breast, no such interval conveniently arose. We went home regardless. Three weeks later, she had gained a rapid two and a half pounds in weight.

Recent evidence from Thailand shows that test-weighing of babies in the night interferes with their intake of breast milk.[5] (This is when babies sleep with their mothers.) The practice of weighing a baby in the first few days when the milk comes in, is in itself a disruption to the establishment of breastfeeding.

But there are many other reasons why women fail to feed their own offspring. In the first place, the new mother may not expect to succeed. All around her is evidence that others have failed.

From those early hours, when the midwife forces the baby's mouth on to the nipple, to the final act three weeks later, when the woman, battered and sore, finally says 'I've given up', our breastfeeding experiences are a shambles. Those women who do go on to enjoy and succeed in this mysterious art are seen as weird, earthy types, clinging to their babies in an 'unhealthy' way.

In the relatively poor valleys of South Wales, social stigma is the greatest bar to breastfeeding. Having a night-life is important to most young women – and that means going to pubs and clubs, not pacing the landing with an unsettled baby.

Midwife Gail Pritchard from the Rhondda Valley in South Wales, slept with and breastfed her two daughters, and gives talks on the subject. Her toughest audience is a class of teenage valley schoolgirls: 'In the Rhondda,' she says, 'only one in a hundred women breastfeed. It is absolutely unheard of to suckle a baby past four months old. None of the fourteen and fifteen-year-olds I talk to want to breastfeed, because it means they can't go out at night.'

The same objection was presented to me in Manchester, by the young doctor who came to treat me for a flu bug. He was amazed that I was still breastfeeding a ten-month-old child, as his wife was tired of feeding their new baby after ten days. When he heard that I fed Frances without limitation, he quizzed me on the scientific evidence for my method, and then said 'So you were housebound for six months?' I told him that from Frances' earliest days, we had gone to the theatre, out to meals and even abroad, with as little fuss as if the bundle in the corduroy sling were a cabbage patch doll.

'Engorgement is normal, isn't it?' the doctor hazarded, echoing the words of Dr Hugh Jolly in his *Book of Child Care*:

Some aspects of breastfeeding that might cause problems if

misunderstood [are] after-pains and engorement, which are really normal stages in the establishment of feeding.

My doctor had no idea that it was possible to escape the discomfort of swollen breasts, cracked nipples and the pain of the infant gums clamping down over the areola. Luckily, I was able to show him the draft copy of a new publication, *Successful Breastfeeding*, produced by a team of midwives and health visitors (no doctors) for the Royal College of Midwives. Many childcare professionals prefer to see the scientific evidence in a medical journal, rather than trust the experience of a mother.

Successful Breastfeeding is a practical guide distributed free to the 32,000 members of the Royal College of Midwives. 'In future,' said Chloe Fisher, one of the document's co-authors, 'midwives who are not practising the methods shown in this book will have to justify themselves.'

The book is not so much a list of rules for mothers and midwives, as an untangling of the mess which constitutes modern breastfeeding advice. It debunks many of the myths about restricted feeding. For instance on engorement, the commonest problem in early feeding, it says:

Milk production continues as efficiently at night as by day, and if the milk is not removed as it is formed (as regulated by baby's needs to go to the breast) the volume of milk in the breast will rapidly exceed the capacity of the alveoli [milk-producing sacs inside the breast]. The consequent engorement is not only uncomfortable for the mother, but it will begin the process of lactation suppression. Feeding the baby at night will minimise or prevent the potential problem of engorement.

My doctor left vowing to persuade his wife to take their little boy into bed to feed.

Professionals seem to be at as much of a loss as mothers themselves. Deprived of successful examples, even doctors do not know for sure what is the normal experience of the breastfeeding mother and baby. Chloe Fisher believes our ideas of normality are severely impaired. Two generations of women have witnessed a universal failure to breastfeed and the apparent success of bottle-feeding. She says this is why mothers and midwives mistakenly treat the nipple like a plastic teat when teaching a baby to suck.

Neo-natal weight loss and excessive weight gain are always a cause of worry for the professionals, who are on the look-out for signs of illness or crisis when they examine babies. As all mothers know, it is easy to become weight-obsessed, both with your own figure and that of your child. Every trip to the clinic revolves around a pair of scales. ('He hasn't gained today, Mrs Jones,' – exit one mother with 'failure' tattooed on her heart.)

One friend with a bonny breastfed baby was reprimanded by the health visitors because his weight was off the top of their chart. They wanted her five-month-old son to go on a diet, ignoring the fact that a staple diet of breast milk was his best insurance against being an overweight adult.

I, too, was often accused of 'overfeeding' my child, though she was never force-fed. Sometimes it felt as though the word meant 'overmothering' or 'mollycoddling'. It is a sentiment that harks back once more to the beginning of the century:

> The intervention of imposing a limitation on the ultimate duration of a feed when lactation has become established originally occurred because of a fear, widespread in the medical profession at that time, of a condition which they labelled 'overfeeding' and which was said to cause such serious problems as failure to thrive and diarrhoea. A French doctor wrote 'nothing is further from my thoughts than the advocacy of overfeeding.' He then describes how mothers fed their babies frequently, and that by test weighing he discovered that the baby was taking '... far too much. We are forced to keep them apart from their mothers.' (Budin, 1907)
>
> (Chloe Fisher, *Midwifery*, vol. 1, 1985)

By contrast, Jean Liedloff told me that the babies of the Yequana tribe in South America were far fatter and softer than the average British baby. They feed constantly, and are never far from the breast, night or day. Overfeeding is not possible when the baby is on breast milk alone.

Successful breastfeeding is not unknown around the world, especially in regions untouched by Western culture. But armies, missionaries and multi-national companies have done their best over the years to impose westernized methods on the impressionable Third World. Not content with ruining the relationship between mother and child in this country, we have exported our restrictive suckling practices, often with disastrous results.

A friend who worked in Malawi in central Africa told me how the women there scrape together precious coins to pay for bottle milk, because it is the Western, and therefore the modern, thing to do. In the 1970s, when the slogan 'Coke is good for you' was broadcast worldwide, African mothers actually put cola in bottles and fed it to their infants. Health workers are still trying desperately to undo the damage caused by the methods and messages of the sophisticated, industrialized world.

In India, where only thirteen per cent of homes have a continuous water supply, many babies fall ill and die from complications in bottle-feeding. Chloe Fisher bitterly regrets the British part in spreading unreliable advice:

> In the developed world, slavish adherence to the earlier theories probably did as much harm to human lactation as did the promotion of artificial feeds. But that we should have been guilty of taking these ideas to the developing countries, where artificial feeding can cause gross malnutrition, if not death, should make us pause for serious thought.
>
> (*Oxford Medical School Gazette*, 1982)

Chloe Fisher delivered a paper to the International Conference of Midwives, in which she quoted a textbook for Nigerian student midwives. It was written by Victoria Ajayi, a Nigerian midwife trained in Britain:

> 'First day – 2 min at each breast.
> Second day – 5 min at each breast.
> Third day – 7 min at each breast.
> Fourth day – 10 min at each breast making 20 min feeding time.
> Twenty minutes altogether is the maximum time from then on.'
>
> These instructions contain three of the commonest interventions which still exist; to limit very severely the duration of the early feeds, to restrict the ultimate duration of the feed, and requiring that both breasts are used at each feed. In practice this can result in the baby and the breast being out of phase and engorgement occurring, with the mother believing that she does not have enough milk, and the baby being denied the high fat hind milk.
>
> (*Midwifery*, 1985)

The baby allowed to suckle as he wants will feed for an average total of three hours in the twenty-four[6] – that is, if he sleeps with his mother at night. Immediate access to the breast has many benefits for mother and baby, as we shall see later.

But midwives continue to recommend that mothers put their babies in the nursery overnight. Other hospital practices – such as the administering of drugs during labour – may have short-term effects on the baby's ability to suck, yet we know that the first few days are crucial to establishing a feeding pattern, and for allowing the baby to drink the maximum amount of colostrum.

Sally Inch, author of *Birthrights,* examines the problems which sometimes arise after the use of pethidine during labour. (Its use is extremely common in British hospitals):

> It may also make the baby dopy, sleepy and slow to breathe, and the effects on sucking may last for up to two weeks.
>
> Pethidine delays the development of the ability to habituate for at least two months and the overall effect of pethidine on the newborn may be the unfortunately familiar sight in some maternity hospitals of the baby who is at the same time jumpy and sleepy and a poor feeder in addition!

My Manchester doctor complained that his baby slept so much he never seemed to want to feed. He could not, therefore, understand what I meant by unlimited feeding, or how 'demand feeding' could be put into practice. The baby who cries a lot is a better communicator than the baby who sleeps a lot in such a case. At least the mother of the crying child knows she can soothe him by carrying him and allowing him to suckle frequently. My doctor's new baby was hardly making any demands at all.

The answer is to keep mother and baby together, day and night. The baby who sleeps near the breast will suckle in his sleep. During REM sleep, he will move his jaw as if feeding – every mother will have seen her baby doing this. If the baby is on the breast, this action stimulates milk to come through and the baby receives nourishment without waking. He will therefore relieve the breast of heaviness between more serious feeds, and stimulate the breast into constant and long-lasting milk production.

Unlimited feeding is not merely a matter of 'demand' (waiting for the baby to wake and cry), but of symbiosis – the 'association of two different organisms living attached to each other to their mutual advantage.'[7] Clearly, the presence of the mother at night is crucial to the success of the symbiotic relationship. Such freedom was far from the minds of the educators of the Victorian age:

> It is improper and pernicious to keep infants continually at the breast; and it would be less hurtful, nay even judicious, to let them cry for a few nights, rather than to fill them incessantly with milk, which readily turns sour on the stomach, weakens the digestive organs, and ultimately generates scrofulus affections [forms of tuberculosis].
>
> (*Enquire Within Upon Everything*, 1882)

We now know that sour milk in the stomach is not the cause of TB. The ban on night-feeding was an essential part of the restrictions placed on breastfeeding mothers. If frequent feeding in the day was a nuisance, then how much more demanding was the baby who cried at night. Now that there were larger homes, with airy nurseries, babies could sleep well away from their parents, and be trained to 'sleep through'.

Children can be conditioned to sleep through the night, but it is rare for a baby to take a regular ten hours or so of slumber throughout infancy. The only way to avoid disturbance is for the breastfeeding child to sleep with the mother. Not only does this create the minimum of noise and fuss, but it may, according to new evidence, allow the mother to get a better night's sleep:

> The quality of sleep the newly-delivered mother experiences may be improved by breastfeeding at night. Although there is no direct experimental evidence to suggest a role for oxytocin in the control of cortical [brain] activity, there is a suggestion that dopamine receptors in the brain mediate sedation and sleep, and that dopamine may be involved in the mechanism of oxytocin release. If this is the case, it may account for the often reported and observed sleepiness that many women experience when they breastfeed, which facilitates a rapid return to sleep at night.
>
> (*Successful Breastfeeding*)

It is this natural drowsiness that results in many babies sleeping in the big bed. Although the mother may not have originally intended it, she falls asleep on the job.

Child psychotherapist Janine Sternberg slept with her first two children on and off this way, until she realized – with the birth of her third child – that it was not worth dragging herself out of bed at night: 'So often at night you'd feed the baby and it would appear to fall asleep sucking and you'd very gently get up, and just as you put it in the crib, it would wake up again.

'Eventually it dawned on me – why bother? Sometimes the baby would just stay with us by default, or out of sheer exhaustion. You'd be feeding, and the next thing you know you'd find you'd been asleep, and had woken up and that the baby was asleep next to you all the time.'

More childcare professionals, like Chloe Fisher and her colleagues at the John Radcliffe Hospital in Oxford, are beginning to encourage co-sleeping. The late Dr Hugh Jolly, for instance, changed his mind when he saw the practice at first hand. Babies were permitted to sleep with their mothers at Charing Cross Hospital where Dr Jolly was consultant paediatrician:

> I always used to advise parents against bringing their children into bed with them but I have now changed.... Everything is much simpler if [the baby] is allowed to 'sleep-feed', meaning that he sleeps alongside you in bed and feeds when he wants, often without waking you. This is a controversial practice both in the United Kingdom and the United States, but it is perfectly safe provided the mother has not had a sedative. In the hospital where I work we have practised this method for years without problems. Many mothers have told me they cannot sleep if their baby is not in the bed. Many others have had their babies in their beds for years but felt guilty until recently when they were told it is safe.
>
> (*Book of Child Care*, revised edition, 1985)

On night-feeding itself, Dr Jolly remarks:

> Because you have slept beforehand and are warm and relaxed, it is likely to be a satisfying feed for the baby ...

In other words, sleep-feeding may be a cosier and less stressful experience than day-feeding, especially for the new and nervous mother. Rather than insisting that the new-born sleeps in a cot, hospital midwives might consider leaving him in his mother's arms, from where, in the unpressurized quiet of the night, he will naturally take to the breast.

Mike Woolridge, a lactation physiologist at Bristol University, develops the idea that night-time feeds are often happier for mother and baby than day-time sessions. He writes:

> Intriguingly, for many mothers who attend the breastfeeding clinic, and who are having difficulties feeding (e.g. breast refusal at day-time feeds) the night-time may be the only ones which go well.
>
> (Woolridge and Jones, *Bristol NCT newsletter,* June 1988)

A friend of mine who was careful – on advice from the experts – never to take her baby into bed, breastfed in agony for four months until her milk supply finally dried up. Her first experiences of breast-feeding were in a bright and noisy hospital ward, as unlike home as possible, with two midwives cramming the baby's jaws around the nipple at feeding time. The baby screamed, and she felt like doing the same. She never enjoyed the feeds, nor felt relaxed enough to lie down or walk around while feeding, and always associated the event with that first, raw bite of the baby's gums against her breast. Had she been able to breastfeed in the drowsy domain of the bed; had she fed and held her baby constantly, the pain, embarrassment and feelings of failure may never have dogged her determined efforts. Even at the end, she bitterly regretted not being able to carry on.

One has to admire the selfless way in which many Western women tackle breastfeeding, which they believe to be best for their babies. But if they had better counselling and support in the first place, their suffering would be unnecessary.

One mother wrote to a national newspaper:

> The saddest thing of all is that if only you can learn to do it properly, breastfeeding can be very pleasant for both the mother and the baby. Nobody who switches to bottle-feeding because they can't stand the pain should feel guilty: it's the people who should be showing them how to do it who ought to take the blame.
>
> (Patricia Finney, London, *The Independent,* 2 August 1988)

It is unnecessary and intrusive for a midwife to stand over the uninitiated couple (mother and baby), positioning the infant jaw around the nipple. Only if there is an acknowledged failure to feed need she offer her expertise, and even then her role should be one of helping the mother to relax, rather than engineering the mechanics of the first bite.

Ironically, the latest debates on breastfeeding have concentrated on preparing the nipples, a preliminary which is unnecessary when mother and baby are constantly together. Patricia Finney writes:

> Most babies, given the chance, would like to suckle all day and night and the effect on the mother's nipples can be like suddenly walking thirty miles in bare feet.

Remedies such as massaging the nipples with surgical spirit, or tucking cabbage leaves inside your bra, leave many women wincing – and rightly so. Breasts do not need to be toughened up for feeding. Constant suckling, especially at night, keeps the areola moist and supple; and a baby who is offered the breast as often as he wants is unlikely to approach the scene like Jaws Junior, ready for the kill.

Many mothers complain about the ferocity of their baby's bite. This may be the result of the long gaps they are imposing between feeds. As Edmund Owen said back in the 1880s, the new-born is ravenously hungry after three hours without food.[8] The unwitting child thinks that if he chomps harder, he'll get more milk out – especially if he knows he is going to be whisked off the breast before he has properly finished.

Chloe Fisher advises all mothers to let the baby choose when he comes off the breast, however long that takes. A baby eventually stops suckling of his own accord.

Current advice leads the mother into a downward spiral: her breasts become engorged, baby cannot fix properly on the areola, her nipples become cracked, feeding is painful, mother limits feeds even more to avoid pain, baby bites even harder next time ...

It would have helped, for instance, if the midwives attending my friend had read this paragraph about allowing mother and baby to feed and sleep together:

... the mother needs to be able to put the baby to the breast at night, not only to stimulate her breasts, but to *'practice'* attaching the baby to the breast while it is still soft, in preparation for effective milk removal. Furthermore a woman delivered in hospital needs to have experienced her baby's feeding patterns *'round the clock'* (which is something that women delivered at home will do automatically), so that she does not feel that there are any confidence-sapping gaps in her knowledge when she goes home.

(*Successful Breastfeeding*)

The immediate effects of constant suckling from the first few hours and in the first few days further reveal the symbiosis of mother and baby. I returned to shape within a week of giving birth, and my uterus contracted in a rapid two days – which the doctors could hardly believe. Frances received the maximum amount of the valuable pre-milk (colostrum), so rich in protein and anti-bodies.

A mother's milk will still come in, even if her baby does not suck at the breast for twenty-four hours after the birth,[9] but this does not mean the first days are of no value for breastfeeding. They allow the mother and baby to establish a rhythm that will set them up for months of painful or pleasant suckling.

Engorgement often sets in by the end of the first week, when babies have not been allowed to suckle freely. Swollen, painful breasts are a sign of insufficient feeding, and this is one step towards running down the mother's milk supply. Mothers who are allowed to feed their babies unrestrictedly from the beginning are the ones least likely to suffer with breastfeeding problems later on. The early 'colostrum days' are their chance to get a pattern going before the milk flows.

Dr Michel Odent believes that if there is no interruption in the early phase of feeding, babies may gain weight from the outset. He questions the assumption that a new-born baby 'normally' loses weight immediately after the birth. His findings are based on studies of the women he has assisted at home births in Britain over the last three years, ninety per cent of whom sleep with their babies.

According to Dr Odent, an instinctive approach to feeding, coupled with the relaxed atmosphere of a home delivery, enables women to satisfy their babies' needs. Hospitals, he says, including his own at Pithiviers near Paris, cannot completely capture the calming effect of giving birth at home. His neo-natal weight charts for home-delivered babies who feed without limitation night and day do not dip as you might expect, but rise steadily from birth.

An American study conducted in the 1970s further suggests the importance of bringing mother and baby together at the very beginning:

> ... two groups of mothers had expressed a desire to breast-feed. One group were given their babies to suckle shortly after birth, and the other had no contact with theirs till some sixteen hours later. No mother in either group had to stop breast-feeding for physical reasons. However, two months later, those mothers who had had their infants to suckle immediately after birth were still all breastfeeding, while of the others five out of six had stopped.
>
> (Aidan Macfarlane, *The Psychology of Childbirth*)

Jacque, a mother from South Wales who wanted to breastfeed, had a particularly long and difficult labour in hospital. An hour after the birth, she fed her son and was then left to rest. She slept off the effects of two painful nights and an epidural. Eight hours later, a midwife came to see her, asking 'When was this child last fed?'

Nobody had suggested to her that the baby needed to feed, or that she needed to relieve her engorged breasts. Jacque had read books about breastfeeding that told her that the milk didn't come in for three days, and that the baby would not be hungry for twenty-four hours in any case. She suffered terribly from cracked nipples and severe engorgement, and it was only her own perseverence that enabled her finally to breastfeed her baby.

Once a breastfeeding pattern has been established, a mother and baby need each other to maintain the rhythm of symbiotic suckling. It makes sense that a baby should be able to stimulate the optimum amount of food for himself at night as well as during the day:

> Once lactation is established, night feeds provide the infant with a substantial proportion of his 24 hour intake. The younger the baby, the more likely he is to consume the same volume of milk during the 12 hours from 5 pm and 5 am as between 5 am and 5 pm; i.e. 50 per cent on average. It is therefore to be expected that the baby will be hungry at night ...
>
> (*Successful Breastfeeding*)

Frances took as much as she needed, and stimulated my breasts to manufacture just the required amount – no more, no less. I was not blighted by the problem my mother, my mother-in-law, my grandmother and my friends had had – insufficient milk. Nor was I over-producing.

Before Frances was born, I had invested in a large pack of breast pads, to mop up the leaks, also a set of plastic breast shells to catch the drips of milk to store them in bottles to freeze, for those 'essential' nights off. When, in the first week, I clearly had enough milk for my baby, the community midwife was very excited, as she wanted me to send any spare milk to the hospital's bottle bank. But I only ever dripped a few measly drops, and these ceased to flow within two weeks.

Frances suckled a lot at first, though not constantly. She did not need a dummy, nor did she suck her thumb, except briefly in the early days as a sign that she wanted the breast. Feeding at all times, both night and day, meant that Frances and I were attuned to each other.

The baby who gets his fill of the breast will not need to suck on anything else. This is good news for his tender gums.

Presumably our teeth were meant to fit into our mouths in a reasonable fashion, without the aid of dental apparatus and metal braces. A baby sucking furiously on something hard is paving the way for a lifetime of dental problems. The human breast is the only sucking device guaranteed not to deform the shape of a baby's gums. It is soft and yielding, and does no damage.

Feeding Frances at night was my own way of meeting her needs, unprompted by professional advice or scientific evidence. Many other mothers sleep-feed their babies in the same way. A year after my baby was born, *Successful Breastfeeding* confirmed our experience and gave new reasons for taking the baby into bed. Not only does night-feeding keep the baby satisfied, it also releases a higher level of prolactin, which sustains breast-milk production in the long term:

> A recent study has demonstrated that prolactin release in response to night-time suckling is greater than during the day; thus milk production may get its greatest '*boost*' when the baby feeds at night.
>
> (*Successful Breastfeeding*)

Long-term lactation is not achieved by four-hourly feeding routines. The areola needs frequent and regular stimulation. If this is provided, almost any woman can breastfeed a baby, even if she has never given birth. Many experts[10] quote examples of women who have breastfed adopted babies.

The women of the Pitjandjara, a desert people from Australia, breastfeed their babies for at least two years. Their adult women are milk-producing throughout their fertile lives, and are able to breastfeed each other's children.[11] A grandmother may breastfeed an infant of the third generation, when mother falls ill or is absent.

Another value of night-feeding is its role in suppressing ovulation. Round-the-clock suckling is invaluable to women relying on the contraceptive qualities of breastfeeding. According to birth campaigner Sheila Kitzinger:

> Breast-feeding tends to reduce fertility but it is not an effective contraceptive unless you are suckling the baby intermittently right through the 24 hours and are giving him or her no other food or fluid at all.
>
> (*Pregnancy and Childbirth*)

Successful Breastfeeding makes a connection between a woman's fertility and the milk-release hormone, prolactin:

> The frequent suckling, which results in elevated prolactin levels, also suppresses ovulation – although the exact mechanism is not yet clear. The contraceptive effect of breastfeeding, although not 100 per cent reliable, may be of great importance to those who for personal or religious reasons do not wish to use conventional (western) methods, and it is therefore vital that these women are not subjected to any restrictions on feeds, especially at night.

We should consider the effects of modern breastfeeding management on millions of families across the non-industrialized world. Many people, dependent on natural family spacing, have found their families unexpectedly enlarged because fertility returned too soon. If left to feed unhindered, a women may go for a year or more before the return of her monthly period.

In fact, most women in the West feed their new-born babies according to such strict routines that their periods return almost immediately, and accidental pregnancies leave mothers with babies only nine or ten months apart. The swift onset of menstruation is directly linked to our universal failure to breastfeed for any length of time.

A study carried out in Scotland[12] has demonstrated that supplementing breast milk with other feeds, and reducing the amount of time allowed for suckling, have a direct effect on the monthly cycle. Researchers say that no mothers in their study ovulated during unsupplemented breastfeeding, although the women were well nourished.

It is little wonder that Western women, having few children and little respite from periods, tend to be anaemic. Even more worrying are studies which show that the monthly drag on the reproductive system, for years on end, may make women more prone to degenerative diseases, such as cancer. Night-feeds would help to stem menstruation for many months.

When a mother sleeps with her baby, she is truly demand-feeding, because the infant takes exactly what he needs. Even if feeds are initiated by the mother during the day, by night they are baby-led. And as he and his mother are asleep, there is no emotional pressure for him to feed for shorter, or longer, periods than he wants to.

A baby who is allowed to suckle in the bed takes consistently the same amount of milk every night for twelve months, the crucial period highlighted by the Government's report published in 1988. Night-feeding provides an opportunity for nature to take control:

> Data show that nocturnal breast feeding was not restricted at any age. As weaning foods were introduced, 'day' time breast feeding was reduced, but night time feeding remained unaffected, and thus made up a higher proportion of 24 hour milk intake in older infants.
>
> ... the amount of breast milk consumed at 'night' was not related to infant age and remained constant over the first year of life.
>
> (Imong et al., Proc. 5th Asian Congress of Nutrition, October 1987)

Once the breastfeeding pattern is established to include night-feeds, it is hard to destroy. But there was one occasion in the early days, when I almost upset the rhythm between Frances and myself.

A friend lent me a breast pump to express milk for storage, as she had done. I spent half an hour pumping away with pitifully little result. The nipple rapidly became sore, and two days later the breast started to over-produce. Just one intervention meant a lot of work to regain our symmetry.

I soon realized that I could go out in the evening with my tiny baby anyway, and that 'nights off' were no longer the attraction they had once seemed. The odd occasions I left Frances with someone else during those first months did not fill me with relief, but with longing to have her back in my arms.

One nationwide survey[13] showed that forty per cent of British mothers chose to breastfeed their babies because it was 'convenient'. And so it is, offering simplicity – an easy way of carrying the perfect infant food, stored at a perfect temperature, everywhere you and your baby go. But society conspires to make things difficult.

The breastfeeding mother is not encouraged to suckle her baby in public, and other women are often her worst critics for this. (Edwardian mothers could buy an 'anti-embarrassment device', which fed baby via a tube concealed in her clothing.) In private, the 'norm' is to try to breastfeed at night camping in separate rooms.

While the baby in the cot cries into the night and learns either the futility of expressing his needs, or how to make his parents come running, the baby in the bed is learning the value of hope. The breast is always there. He sucks on it, and at first nothing happens, but he knows that if he keeps sucking, *through his own endeavours,* the milk will come through.

He does not need to scream, or become angry, or ruin anyone else's sleep. And he is rewarded with just as much milk as he needs and wants – because in the early days, need and desire are the same. The analogy with a beef steak in the middle of the night does not hold. The foetus in the womb is on constant tap to nourishment via the placenta, and a new-born baby must be weaned gradually from this uninterrupted flow. He certainly does not differentiate between night and day in his feeding requirements.

We are nearing the end of the twentieth century with a vastly improved knowledge of nutrition and obstetrics. We can see the foetus floating in the womb, and we can keep tiny premature babies alive – yet we are so far from restoring confidence in women, that thousands are still unable to feed their own young.

An alarming report, published by the British Government in July 1988, confirmed the worst: breastfeeding is declining in popularity. A survey of 7,000 mothers carried out between 1980 and 1985 showed that only half breastfed for two weeks or more, and that just twenty-five per cent suckled their infants for more than four months. A newspaper report at the time quoted Jean Robinson, a member of the General Medical Council: 'Women are consistently saying that they are not getting enough support in hospital, and that they are often given inadequate advice.'[14]

Lone voices throughout the century have questioned the medical management of breastfeeding. They have gone largely unheeded. In 1953, one writer proclaimed the virtues of instinct-led feeding:

> When this regime becomes universally adopted, as surely it will, so the last chapter on the history of infant feeding will be concluded.
>
> (I. G. Wickes, *A History of Infant Feeding*)

Some of us feel the last chapter is taking a long time to write.

7 | NOMADS AND NANNIES

It's time we put ourselves into perspective. Babies who scream in the night, breasts that blister from misuse and electronic cot alarms are the trappings of modern mothering in the developed world. History and anthropology show us that not all societies suffer like this with their children.

It would be wrong to assume that every non-industrialized culture has child-rearing methods that are superior to our own. This glance across centuries and continents is not intended to be a brochure of beautiful babycare ideas. It may, however, be useful to be aware of what other people are doing, if only to reassure ourselves that yet another 'difficult' phase of civilization is likely to pass.

Many of the habits of primitive man (or of people without a written language) are still practised by the hunter-gatherer tribes which roam every continent. Such groups are often labelled as outcasts in their own lands, and find their traditional lifestyle open to attack. Governments want to pin people down, missionaries want to convert them, roving camera crews want to record the last glimpses of uncivilized man in his environment.

The hostility of our own society towards the gypsy community is a typical example of our impulse to socialize others according to our own rules. In the words of an anthropologist from Granada Television:

> . . . nomads are feared and despised by those who govern them. People who cannot be confined to one place throughout the year are difficult to control for purposes of education, health and, most important of all, taxation.
>
> (André Singer, *Disappearing World*)

Despite the difficulties, some nomadic tribes survive. The G/wi, a people numbering around 2,000, wander in bands through the Kalahari Desert in southern Africa. Theirs is an egalitarian and loose-structured society, where men and women work together in all but a few tasks (men hunt, women prepare the food). Most marriages are stable; spouses are chosen on the wishes of the couple as well as of other family members. Mutual affection tends to be warm but not showy.

Anthropologist George B. Silberbauer explains how the G/wi bushmen raise their children:

> A baby is never left alone, but is carried everywhere on its mother's hip or slung in her cloak. If the child cries, it is given the breast immediately. When the mother is sitting in a group, the baby is passed around and rocked in the arms of anybody old enough to do so without dropping it. Men and boys show the same fondness for babies as do women and girls. Babies are not parted from their mothers at night, but sleep held in their mothers' arms... A baby thus spends its first years in the secure affection of attentive band colleagues.
>
> (*Hunters and Gatherers Today*)

A similar pattern is found among the Paliyans of southern India, who move in groups through the rain shadow of the Palni and Anaimalais mountain ranges. The Paliyans value individuality and personal independence above all else. Equality is so important to them that individuals always share their good fortune with others in the group, but other co-operation between group members is rare. Minimal assistance is offered to the weakest among them, and men strive to avoid violence or competition. Husband and wife have an equal say in all matters relating to their marriage. This is how they treat their children for the first two years of life – a view by anthropologist Peter M. Gardner:

> The child spends most of its sleeping and waking hours in direct physical contact with its mother's body. In the daytime, it rests on her left hip in a sling formed from a swath of her upper sari cloth. At night, it sleeps by her side. The mother gives her breast to the child at the slightest whimper, as often as four or five times an hour; denial even at night would be inconceivable, because, as they put it, the child's throat would become dry. Infants over a year regularly ask for these night feeds. There is a great deal of

maternal warmth during the first two years, and much concern is expressed for the infant. Unless a child is ill, prolonged crying is unlikely. Outbursts of anger are rare; they are averted or appeased quickly, if possible.

(*Hunters and Gatherers Today*)

A third example comes from Africa:

Night sleep was quantified in a study of infants of the Kipsigis, a Kenyan people. They slept beside their mothers, awakened often, and suckled during the night. They slept less in 24 hours than did a comparison group of American infants.

(Elias, Nicolson, Bora and Johnston, *Paediatrics*, March 1986)

Pat Gray, co-founder of CRY-SIS, a British support group for the mothers of crying children, told me about her travels on the Indian continent.'I went to Sri Lanka,' she said, 'where the people live in simple houses, made of mud with dried cow dung on the floor and palm leaves for a roof. They sleep on rush mats made out of coconut fibre, and the babies sleep on the floor near their parents.'

Parents belonging to non-industrial cultures are far more likely to sleep with their infants than not. One survey[1] shows that co-sleeping is or may be practised in seventy-one out of ninety societies. McKenna's table of co-sleeping cultures (opposite) illustrates a variety of ways in which parents sleep alongside their young children.

The Copper Eskimo and the Dogrib Indian, the Guayaki of Paraguay and the Walmadjeri bushmen of Australia all sleep with their children. The anthropologists who write about these tribes never fail to mention the apparent 'indulgence' of parents towards their offspring. But not all primitive tribes are so generous. Not all sleep with their babies.

The Nootka, an Indian tribe on the north-west coast of India, are known for their aggression. Within the group, violence rarely goes beyond swearing and hair-pulling, but tribal warfare is a regular and savage occurrence. Their practice is to raid other tribes during the night, or during a ceremony, with the aim of beheading as many men as possible and bringing home the women and children as slaves. Victorious warriors return home singing, with the heads of the slain on poles. They publicly torture and humiliate any prisoner chief before killing him.

Culture	HRAF ID	Where Do They Sleep?	Upon What Do They Sleep?	Comments
Ganda	FK7	Infant with parents	Bed, with bark cloth, laced with cowhide thongs	Teenagers & single adults in same-sex groups
Flores	OF9	Infant with parents	Bamboo sleeping bench (hale-hale)	Children with friends in same-sex group
Lau	OQ6	Infant with owner & wife	Pile of mats; Tongan tapa as covers; bed called palang	At 7 to 10 years, boys move to other huts
Maori	OZ4	Families sleep together, several to a hut	Special sleeping huts for summer & for winter	Winter huts have sunken floors & are heaped over with dirt for warmth
Bushmen	FX10	Infant with parents	Scooped-out area in hut, in grass	At 7, girls sleep with grandparents or relative
Yap	OR22	Infant with parents until 2 or 3, sometimes in hanging basket		At 5, child moves from parents' room
Garo	AR5	Infant with parents	Mats from bark of trees	Bachelor quarters
Katab	FF38	Mothers with infants, husband, siblings	Mattress of rags	Bachelor & maiden co-sleep dorms; sleep during times of scarcity
Mauri	MS12	Infant with parents	Sleeping mat. Kathari mattress of rags	
Tiwi	O120	Children with parents	Mats of paper bark (melaleuca)	
Cuna	SB5	Infant with mother in same room; father in same hammock	Handmats – cotton of ciba tree covered with plantain leaves	
Tzeltal	NV9	Youngest infants on parents' mats (patates)		At 5, sleep with same-sex sibling
Bhil	AW25	Infant with mother		Sisters & brothers separated past childhood

(Table of co-sleeping practices, *Medical Anthropology*, 1986)

The Nootkan baby is separated from his mother at birth, so that his head can be elongated according to the group's ideals of beauty. (A neighbouring tribe flatten the heads of their new-born for the same reason.) This is how a baby spends his first months:

During these four days following the delivery, the woman placed and kept the baby in a temporary cradle consisting of a mat suspended on either side between a pair of poles, with a crossbar to hold up the neck, bark mats for bedding, and a head-pressing device of cedar bark running over the forehead plus bark pads on either side of the head ...

After four days in the temporary cradle the baby was moved to a one-piece wooden one, hollowed like a canoe, with a projecting headpiece and a footpiece flush with the sides. The baby was bound into this cradle, which was carried vertically. A girl baby's cradle had three holes bored in the footboard for urine to leak through, but a boy baby's cradle did not; he was left with his penis exposed.

(Carleton S. Coon, *The Hunting Peoples*)

An interesting comparison may be made between the habits of two tribes from the South Seas – the New Guinea Arapesh and the Mundugumor. While the Arapesh, an extremely gentle people, nurse their children on demand and sleep with them at night, the Mundugumor are 'exactly the opposite':

They despise the pregnant woman. When a child is born, he is placed in a hard, uncomfortable basket. He is nursed only when he simply will not stop crying. His mother stands while she nurses him, and as soon as he stops sucking, if only for a second, the baby is put down. Instead of letting the child wean when he is ready, the security-seeking child is pushed away from his mother. She forces him to wean long before he is ready, but at a time when he can survive on other foods.

These people lack all trust in one another. Until the government outlawed it, they actively practiced head-hunting. They are hateful and distrustful. Sexual foreplay is performed with biting and scratching one's partner to the point of bleeding.

(Tine Thevenin, *The Family Bed*)

For good or for bad, the traditions of isolated tribes are fast disappearing. Peoples who for centuries shared bedspace with their children have been urged to abandon the practice, and to adopt Western ways.

The Mistassini Cree are one of the groups of big hunters living on the Labrador Peninsula, on the remote east coast of Canada. They have had contact with Europeans for three hundred years, although this was limited until prospectors built a railroad in the 1950s.

Today most Mistassini have converted to Christianity and are registered as Anglicans, but as each member of the group is free to choose his own religion, ancient shamanism is still practised. Mothering techniques are similarly a mixture of old and new: babies are breastfed on demand for at least a year, but these days they are expected to sleep alone:

> Bedding is derived from European sources and consists mostly of woollen blankets and occasionally sleeping bags ... Infants are placed in moss sacks and sleep in hammocks. The latter are most likely a European inspiration. Cradle boards are known and said to be occasionally used ...
>
> (*The Hunting Peoples*)

The modern Japanese family may no longer take its children to bed as is still the tradition in rural parts; mothers on the Indian continent are persuaded to try the cot along with the bottle; the Inuit who used to sleep naked together in their Arctic igloos now tend to cover up their babies and put them in cradles.

It is now considered normal in many societies to separate mother and baby at birth. But why depart from nature's needs at all? Why should any civilization, at any time, decide that mother and baby should sleep in separate beds?

Natural-childbirth pioneer Michel Odent is fascinated by the question. He travelled to China to observe mothering practices there, and was amazed by what he saw.

'I was studying the conditions of birth,' he says, 'and found that Chinese hospitals tried to copy the West by having delivery tables, with stirrups and so on. They were very proud of their modern equipment. But something they had forgotten to copy was to separate the mother from her baby.

'I found this out quite by chance. We were in a village visiting a house, and I asked who slept in the bedroom. The woman said, "I sleep here with my baby because he is just six months old."'

Many cultures consider bedsharing, hammock- or mat-sharing with their children to be normal behaviour. Of the societies for whom the practice is anti-social, the United States and the Soviet Union are the prime examples. North American theorists and psychologists lead the field in Western childcare, but Communist countries also separate mother and baby with regimental efficiency from birth.

'In Russia, Czechoslovakia and East Germany, it's worse,' says Odent. 'In one maternity unit, I saw a huge nursery, with babies wrapped like parcels. At feeding time, the baby is brought to the mother, and then taken straight back to the cot. This applies to hospitals throughout the Communist bloc, and that is a great part of humanity.'

Dr Odent has his own theory as to why certain societies choose to separate mother and child at night: 'The only cultures we can study are those which have survived, and which have eliminated the others,' he says. 'So even the most primitive societies surviving today are likely to be the most aggressive ones.

'Perhaps to separate mother and baby at birth is to create an aggressive civilization. And if we look at the two most successful and aggressive cultures of all – Russia and America – we can see that there mother and baby are kept apart.'

Studies have shown that when babies are deprived of physical contact, they are more likely to grow into aggressive adults. One survey[2] of primitive cultures illustrates that lack of touch in infancy produces individuals disposed towards violence. A warring tribe will harden its offspring by separating babies from their mothers for the first few days, or at night-time. It may not be coincidence that American and Russian babies are also kept in cots.

Despite the spread of 'modern' practices, sleeping next to babies is still taken for granted by many social groups. Paediatrician Betsy Lozoff begins her study on sleep-management in North American families with this point:

> Pediatric health professionals often advise parents not to sleep with their children ... This approach to sleep is different from the practices that one of the authors (B.L.) observed in Latin America and Asia while conducting medical and anthropologic research projects. Infants were generally not expected to go to bed

by themselves at a regular time or place or to sleep alone during the night. Instead, they were held until asleep and slept with their parents or other family members. Bedtime struggles and crying in the night were not apparent. These observations led to a search of the anthropologic literature, which confirmed that the practices currently recommended by pediatricians differ from those generally found in other cultures. In addition, in one sample of more than 100 societies, the American middle class was 'unique in putting the baby to sleep in a room of his own.'

(Lozoff, Wolf and Davis, *Pediatrics*)

For 'American', read British, European, or any country which encourages competition and harbours aggression. The separation of mother and baby at night is supported by taboo in some primitive cultures and by medical say-so in ours, but the effect is the same.

Societies which attempt to wean, train or otherwise mould the baby (sometimes in physical ways, like the Nootkan Indians), tend towards violence. This in turn leads to 'success' in world terms. We did not get where we are today by showing indulgence to our children.

Throughout history civilizations have sometimes favoured, sometimes banned co-sleeping. A letter from one mother to another in the third or second century BC offers childcare advice based on the Pythagorean theories of which the Greeks were so proud. This emphasized balance and measure in all things:

Myia to Phyllis, greetings. Here is my advice to you now that you have become a mother. Choose a proper and clean wet-nurse, a modest woman who is inclined neither to drowsiness nor to drunkenness ...

The nurse will give him the nipple and breast not at whim, but after due consideration. In this way she will encourage the baby's health. She will not succumb to sleep when *she* is tired, but when the newborn wants to rest. She will offer the child no small relief ...

It is best, if the baby is put down to sleep when it is well fed with milk. Such rest is sweet for little ones and such feeding most effective. ... Moreover his water should not be too hard nor too soft, nor his bed too rough – rather, it should fall comfortably on his skin. In each of these areas, Nature desires what is rightfully hers, not luxuries.

(Lefkowitz and Fant, *Women's Life in Greece and Rome*)

Whereas Myia implies that a baby has its own bed or cradle, a second letter – from a first-century Roman household – indicates that a wet-nurse was expected to sleep with her charge:

> The wet-nurse should be self-controlled so as to abstain from coitus, drinking, lewdness, and any other such pleasure and incontinence ...
> In regard to drinking, first the wet-nurse is harmed in soul as well as in body and for this reason the milk is also spoiled. Secondly, seized by a sleep from which she is hard to awaken, she leaves the newborn untended or even falls down upon it in a dangerous way ...
>
> (*Women's Life in Greece and Rome*)

Fears of smothering the child were always paramount. Historian Diana Dick believes this is why co-sleeping with babies was considered 'a grievous sin' by the Church in the ninth century. 'I think there was the worry about overlaying the child,' she said, 'although you must remember that babies were swaddled in those days. They would only have their eyes and nose free – so the baby would be unable to move if he was being smothered.'

The French dauphin, Louis XIII, was tucked in at night with official 'bedfellows'. On his first night, so the story goes, the young prince disgraced himself by wetting the bed. This may be another reason why rich folk in civilized societies, cultivated in personal cleanliness and outward neatness, would not always tolerate having a baby in the bed. The modern nappy does away with this particular objection.

But if well-to-do European parents were reluctant to sleep with their babies, they did not expect them to sleep alone.

American mother Tine Thevenin charts the history of bedsharing, which often meant couples, children or servants sleeping together. In the days before central heating and electric lights, neither adult nor child was expected to pass the night alone in a separate bedroom:

> During the sixteenth century in England, the so-called Trinity bed was developed. It consisted of a large bed upon which the immediate family slept. Two smaller beds, often referred to as trundle beds, rolled out from underneath the large bed. The older children, servants, or relatives slept on this.

In the seventeenth century, perhaps the largest of all beds was designed by John Fosbrooke for the royal family. It could sleep 102 persons! Obviously the 'luxury' of separate beds and bedrooms of which we boast today was not at all considered to be a sign of wealth or prosperity at that time.

(The Family Bed)

With the rise of the middle classes and the creation of the concept of childhood – previously children were considered to be little adults and not given any special treatment – the practice of co-sleeping began to wane. Christian moralists of the eighteenth century urged people not to share beds unless married, and children of the opposite sex were taught to hide their bodies from each other. All manner of touching and sexual exploration by children was to be discouraged.

In the late eighteenth century, the idea of independence training was put forward: children must learn early self-reliance. This meant toilet-training from three weeks, and sleeping alone at a few weeks old.

Cleanliness being next to godliness, it was not long before hygiene was peddled as a reason for sleeping apart. Sanitary conditions in the poorest part of London were a disgrace, as this extract from Dr Wilan, a late eighteenth-century observer, reveals. There was a lot for the doctors to worry about:

> It will scarcely appear credible, though it is precisely true, that persons of the lowest class do not put clean sheets on their beds three times a year; that even where no sheets are used they never wash or scour their blankets or coverlets, nor renew them until they are no longer tenable ... that from three to eight individuals of different ages often sleep in the same bed; there being in general but one room and one bed for each family ... The room occupied is either a deep cellar, almost inaccessible to the light, and admitting no change of air; or a garret with a low roof and small windows, the passage to which is close, kept dark, and filled not only with bad air, but with putrid excremental effluvia from a vault at the bottom of the staircase. Washing of linen, or some other disagreeable business, is carried on, while infants are left dozing and children more advanced kept at play whole days on the tainted bed ...
>
> (*Diseases in London*, 1801)[3]

Sickness and disease were killing the poorest inner-city dwellers, a situation which worsened in the Victorian and Edwardian eras, before the introduction of the Welfare State. What was needed was a major spending programme to prevent London from becoming a sewer. Instead the people were warned against the dangers of sharing a bed.

The middle classes, who were increasing in number, were able to follow the professionals' advice. Now that they could afford it, they were being sold the newly valuable commodity of privacy – privacy from one's neighbours, and privacy within each house from the servants and from the children. In your clean-air suburb, you could have a villa with separate bedrooms (a vast improvement on the traditional curtained-off bed which dominated the living room a hundred years earlier).

> The greatly increased number of bedrooms in Victorian as compared to Georgian houses of the same class is eloquent testimony to the value placed on privacy within the family. The *Builder* in 1864 was quite smug on this point: '... When we reflect

upon the scanty supply of sleeping apartments which it was usual to construct in an ordinary London house of the annual value of from £80 to £120 a year, at the time when Regent Street was built, and which scarcely ever exceeded in number two principal bedrooms and three or four attics, it becomes difficult to conceive how the last generation bestowed themselves in their sleeping arrangements.

'... our present ideas on the subject render increased accommodation in this respect absolutely necessary.' Smaller houses had smaller rooms, but nearly as many of them.

(Olsen, *The Growth of Victorian London*)

The late Victorians separated even man and wife in the search for wholesome living:

In 1893, *Scribner's Magazine* carried what was probably the first twin-bed advertisement to appear in the United States. It read 'Our English cousins are now sleeping in separate beds. The reason is: *never breathe the breath of another*.'

(*The Family Bed*)

The Edwardians took separation of mother and child to its limits. A baby's life in middle- and upper-class Britain was by now one of solitary confinement. Nanny took charge of all the children, allowing them plenty of fresh air, but not much else in the way of live entertainment. The young Queen Victoria, besotted with Albert, but not a great fan of babies, introduced the perambulator to fashionable society, and soon everyone was wheeling their infants around in mini carriages. Older children were sent away to boarding schools and military academies. Parents delegated most of the upbringing and education of their offspring to professionals. When babies cried, mothers and nannies were encouraged to ignore the screams until the child fell off to sleep. According to Jessica Markwell:

Crying babies were less intrusive than they are today, because the fashion then was to leave them in their prams for long periods, well out of earshot.

(*Practical Parenting*, June 1988)

In 1882, *Enquire Within Upon Everything* described the perfect nursery. It could not be less like the squalid conditions of inner-city slums.

> A Bedroom or Night Nursery ought to be spacious and lofty, dry, airy, and not inhabited through the day. No servants, if possible, should be suffered to sleep in the same room, and no linen or washed clothes should ever be hung there to dry, as they contaminate the air in which so considerable a portion of infantile life must be spent.

You can imagine the difficulties the majority of people would have encountered following this prescription. Townsfolk and villagers throughout Britain were still crammed into undersized accommodation. The poorest families had just one room. Only the rich could afford the luxury of an airing room, a nursery, a schoolroom and a playroom, not to mention the servants' quarters.

Britain's poor were the last to sleep with their babies on a full-time basis. The following describes the typical arrangement in a pre-war inner-city household:

> Besides Mother and Father there were five sons and five daughters. Our parents had the top front bedroom, sharing this with the baby and the next youngest child. The girls had the top back bedroom and the boys the ground-floor bedroom. It was mostly two at the top and two at the bottom of a double bed and the odd one in a little truckle bed, the 'iron' bed we called that ...
> Mother had her priorities right, children must have love and food, food for their growing bodies and love to make them secure ...
>
> (Scannell, *Mother Knew Best – An East End Childhood*)

It was thought that order, cleanliness and moral exactitude would alter the face of Britain. But the separation of infants at night did not bring harmony to all homes. If anything, the frustrations of parents and children created new problems.

The temper tantrum is a phenomenon that is not mentioned in medical literature before 1800. Children were now depicted as wilful, rebellious and in need of severe punishment. 'Spare the rod and spoil the child' – a saying taken from the Bible – was often invoked. For the first time the generation gap revealed the unsavoury truth about

Victorian society – the more children were treated as if they were naughty, the naughtier they became. The puritan ethic did not stem behavioural problems; rather it created them.

Children themselves had few rights. Child abuse often went unrecognized, and until the establishment of the NSPCC in 1884, doctors were likely to blame babies' broken bones on congenital disease. Nobody admitted that children were being battered, especially in the nicer homes. In the words of an early NSPCC annual report:

> The average age of victims shows that cruelty is chiefly practised on little children; small babies come in for a large share.
>
> Cruelty is not confined to wretched dwellings. Pianos and bric-a-brac may be in the drawing rooms of people who behave like brute beasts to their offspring.[4]

In 1885, a certain Mrs Montague locked her child in a cupboard as a punishment. The child suffocated. In court, her lawyer argued that parents had absolute rights over their children, and that therefore Mrs Montague was beyond criticism.

The era of the despotic parent, starched-apron nanny and distant child is over. But in Britain today, an increasing number of women work full time, leaving their children in care. It is good that women are returning to work in large numbers, but when the mother comes home at night, she does not take the child into her bed to enjoy his tactile company. Instead, she gets embroiled in the recommended bedtime routine, with a song, a bath, a story and a firm good-night.

Baby may or may not respond to this treatment, but I would envisage a new and dangerous generation gap emerging as a result of our mothering practices. If working women could drop the formalities and take their babies into bed, they would be more in touch with their children. There could be a crisis looming, as children grow up more closely bonded to their minders than to their parents.

The idea of taking a baby into bed all night, every night, as a matter of course, is new to most mothers I know. It is not recommended in any of the childcare manuals, and so it does not occur to them. It might not have occurred to me, had I not spent those few pre-natal nights in hospital. Yet, for every woman who says she would never try it, there is another who 'confesses' to sharing bedspace with her children occasionally. I would estimate that about three-quarters of the parents I spoke to during my research said they slept with their children at some time or other. Many opt for a bedside vigil with their babies, rather than actually getting into bed with them. Parents are getting as close as they can to their children without breaking society's rules about bedsharing. This is how one mother coped with her three-and-a-half-year-old's reluctance to sleep alone:

'She asked me why Mummies and Daddies slept together as they were big people,' said Penny. 'When I tried to explain that all her friends' Mummies and Daddies slept together, she simply declared that there must be lots of lonely children about. I found it hard to argue with that, so for the last 18 months, we've been sitting by her beside till she drops off.

'Yes it is tedious, but my doctor agreed that it would be very cruel to let her get worked up every night.'

(*Mother*, June 1988)

No wonder many parents choose the more practical solution, and sleep with their children. A fascinating study made in the US by Betsy Lozoff and her team[5] reveals that many people bedshare on a temporary basis. It is a cross-cultural report, which shows a marked difference between white and black families in their attitudes to bedsharing.

Ms Lozoff found that, contrary to the advice of Dr Spock and other childcare experts, thirty-five per cent of white families and seventy per cent of black families routinely took their children into bed. While white families tended to allow bedsharing at times of stress, or when the children had sleep problems, black parents were more likely to sleep with their children as a matter of course (see table opposite).

More than half (fifty-six per cent) of white children who came into their parents' bed were rated as having overall disruptive sleep problems. 'Among black children,' however, 'there was no association between co-sleeping and stress, maternal ambivalence, or sleep problems.'[5]

It is impossible to say whether the white children's sleep problems were caused by being taken into bed, or whether white parents were sleeping with their children because of the problems. But as co-sleeping was far less likely to occur in the cases of parents who were educated and highly trained, it could be concluded that white middle-class families do attempt to follow the advice of the childcare books. Only when this advice does not work do parents respond to the needs of the children by taking them into bed.

In another report by Americans Hanks and Rebelsky[6], it was shown that only eighteen per cent of middle-class mothers who slept with their children actually admitted the fact to their doctors. The modern mother who sleeps with her child knows she is going against the trend, and is unlikely to admit to her 'unacceptable' behaviour.

Many mothers who told me that they took their babies into bed also expressed their relief at talking to someone who did not condemn them for it, yet said it was hard to throw off feelings of guilt. Nurse Maureen Blackman said, 'My daughter Hannah is two. We call her Hannah the horrible. A couple of nights a week she'll howl at three

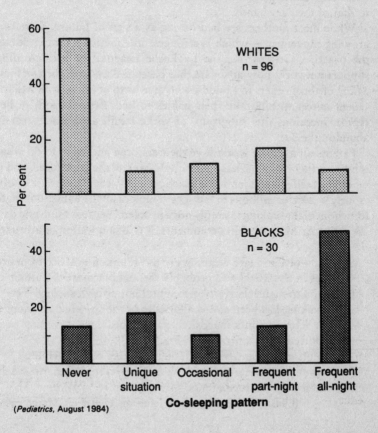

(*Pediatrics*, August 1984)

a.m. I'm afraid we have given up as parents and taken her into bed. She sleeps beautifully with us.'

It is an enormous self-condemnation to say you have given up as a parent, especially when it's for something that is obviously working for you and for your family. But this is how parents are made to feel in our society when they sleep with their children. Co-sleeping is recognized as a sign of failure, not of success.

Maureen Blackman added another explanation for her guilt: 'Bed has such nasty sexual connotations,' she said. 'The media has done it. Parents are afraid to admit that children are in bed with them, because health visitors may think "aha".'

It comforted Maureen to think that Elvis Presley slept with his mother until he was fourteen – apparently the done thing in parts of Kentucky.[7] Girls there may graduate straight from their parents' bed to that of their husbands.

While most mothers see bedsharing as a sign of failure, there is a growing movement – which is strongest in America – that endorses the practice. Groups like the La Leche League, the breastfeeding support network, now advocate that parents sleep with their babies. Many of the mothers in London who give birth at home with Michel Odent automatically take their babies to bed. Betsy Lozoff, in her report, mentions the 'subgroup' of white families who deliberately abandon the cot.

Parents all over the world love their children and want to do what is best for them. No one has a monopoly over all the good ideas, and it would be facile to condemn the practice of co-sleeping when it so obviously works for millions of families. Think of all the babies out there for whom night-waking is simply not a problem, because mum and dad are there. As Marjorie Elias comments, it is all a question of attitude:

Sharing a bed and late weaning are the common practice of many societies in the world and probably throughout most of human history, although relatively uncommon in our own society. Yet, night waking has been called a 'disease of the so-called developed world'. Where infants share their parents beds, night waking is not reported to be a problem.

It seems ironic that, although night waking is so much less frequent in infants cared for in Western style, it presents so much more of a problem for parents.

(Elias, Nicolson, Bora and Johnston, *Pediatrics*, March 1986)

For whatever reasons, civilized or not, babies need comfort and company at night; and some parents are determined not to let social conditioning get in the way.

8 | NOT IN FRONT OF THE CHILDREN

TURNED OFF SEX

Since my little girl caught my husband and I making love, I freeze every time he touches me. We have three children and the youngest, who's three, has to share our bedroom.

She is a poor sleeper and most nights she gets into our bed. When she gets in, my husband usually goes to sleep in her bed.

We cope with that, but one night she woke as we were making love, and said out loud, 'Mummy, why are you wriggling about?'

It's put me right off sex. My husband thinks I'm making excuses but I'm not, as I like sex very much and enjoy making love with him. I just can't respond for fear of her waking.

(Letter to the agony column of *The Sun* newspaper, 25 July 1988)

Sex after childbirth is complicated enough, without the extra dimension of babies in the bed. For many parents, the prospect of children interrupting their sex life is enough to put them off the idea of bedsharing. Even those who are genuinely interested in the idea take me to one side, whispering, 'How do you do *it*?'

Others worry that bedsharing may be connected in some way with sex abuse, a headline topic in Britain in the 1980s. In the late 1970s, the NSPCC knew of only a few sexually abused children, but 7,119 cases were registered in 1987. A MORI poll in 1988 suggested that one in twelve British children suffers this kind of abuse.[1]

The sudden rise in these figures may be partly explained by our growing awareness of the existence and dangers of child sex abuse. If the problem is not new, public outrage is. The present climate makes it all the more difficult to discuss sleeping with our children as many people associate sex with the bed.

If we examine Western attitudes to sex, we find a tendency to confuse it with intimacy of other types. Men cannot hold hands in public without being considered homosexual; 'going to bed' with someone means much more than sleeping with them. This was not always so. As Tine Thevenin describes, 200 years ago casual household guests might be invited to bed-down for the night:

> ... before the steady decline of co-family sleeping gained full momentum, it enjoyed one final triumph. The custom of bundling came nearest to being a world-wide custom, including its practice in America, during the period from 1750–1780. The usual definition of bundling is a man and woman lying on the same bed with their clothes on. They may be either conversing or sleeping. Usually, they were covered with a blanket or a quilt.
> This practice was even accepted among the sex-conscious Puritans, who would never have allowed such a practice to prevail had it proven to be a subtle cover-up for sex.
>
> (*The Family Bed*)

Sexual repression is usually the product of a civilized society. Primitive groups are too busy trying to procreate and survive to stop people expressing their physical needs. Our own history shows swings from the liberalism of the Middle Ages to the repression of the Puritans, the libertinism of the Restoration era to the sober strictness of the Victorians. Every age reacts against the attitudes of the previous generation.

We can thank the Victorians for our particular range of hang-ups. Trying to deal with the AIDS (Acquired Immune Deficiency Syndrome) crisis has been particularly awkward in Britain, where campaigners have found that words like 'condom' and 'climax' are more likely to offend than to inform. Sex is the butt of our adult humour, and the filling of our tabloid newspapers.

After the birth of a baby, sex becomes even more problematic. Once the act of intercourse has achieved its procreative purpose, couples are expected to muddle through with the remains of their sex life. A recent survey in *Mother* magazine[2] tackled the taboo subject of 'sex after birth'. An analysis of the responses by clinical psychologist Dr Maurice Yaffe and his team from Guy's Hospital, London, showed couples were likely to have less sex after the birth of a baby than they had before his arrival.

Only fifty per cent of the mothers who responded to the survey said they were still interested in sex after the baby arrived. Fewer (forty-five per cent) said they often had orgasms when they did make love. Fifteen per cent said they made love once a month after the baby was born. Breastfeeding made no apparent difference to desire, nor to the frequency of sexual activity after the birth.

The first few months of a baby's life can bring enormous tension to the nuclear family, which may have been quite stable previously. The mother devotes most of her energies to caring for the baby, and sex may take a low priority, even if she is in a physically fit state for it. The only advice and solace a woman finds at this point is a cursory six-weekly check-up by a doctor who pronounces her – usually – sexually available once more.

With so little relief from her soreness, support for her tiredness, and understanding of her emotional upheaval, a new mother might feel quite panicky about her first postnatal sexual encounter.[3] And so might her partner.

Michel Odent says that thirty per cent of men experience some form of impotence immediately after childbirth, especially if they have been a witness to the birth. The arrival of the baby possibly signals a time for parents to take a short natural break from sexual activity, helped by hormonal and other biological interference. The satisfaction a breastfeeding mother experiences may in itself be a mechanism that relieves her desire for sexual intercourse.

But our society does not allow for this settling-in period. Partners may be impatient to return to their usual pattern of sexual intercourse soon after the baby has arrived. While many primitive groups have built-in taboos for sex after the birth of a baby[4], nothing interrupts our media's flow of romantic and sexual imagery. No one says it's OK to wait a while.

Penny Mansfield, deputy director of the Marriage Research Council, says that whatever the individual reactions of the couple to sex, this is likely to be a time of tension. She conducted a survey in which forty-nine couples were interviewed after six years of marriage, comparing their responses with their eve-of-wedding hopes.

'A group of men found the waiting quite difficult. Wives tended to go off sex during pregnancy, and things did not get better with the arrival of the baby. What's more, women found their husbands unsatisfying in terms of emotional reward, and they would find more affection and emotion from the baby.'

Couples who were unable to talk about their different needs were those most likely to be heading for difficulty or divorce.

Sex immediately after the arrival of the new-born is not nature's priority, whether we sleep with our babies or not. But if couples think love-making will be easier with the baby in a cot, away from the bed, they could be mistaken.

The tiredness and the headaches that go with it are probably the greatest dampeners of the sexual libido. Trying to train a baby to sleep through the night on his own can be an exhausting experience. And if the baby is crying in the next room, it can be hard to concentrate on feeling sexy.

The couple that brings a baby to bed addresses all these problems head-on. There is evidence that sleeping with your baby is more likely to promote intimacy and desire – and sexual activity, if it is wanted.

A baby is an extremely sensual being, and both parents can enjoy the innocent thrill of holding their new baby at night, cuddling up close to the warm skin. When the child wakes in the morning, it is with a stretch and a smile, teasing the parents slowly out of their sleep – not a rude awakening three or four times in the night, and again at five in the morning.

When parents want to be alone together, they do not have to banish the child from the room. When the baby is asleep near by, there is nothing whatsoever to prevent intimacy. There is no need to whisper unless you want to, because a baby is used to sleeping through noise in the womb.

The mother, biologically tuned-in to her child, is more likely to relax when she can see he is safely by her side. Actress Jane Asher, who slept with her baby Alexander from his birth, writes:

> There is the common worry that a couple's sex life will suffer, but in practice this is rarely a problem – a deeply sleeping baby is pretty oblivious to everything going on around him, and in the words of the song 'love will find a way!'
>
> (*Silent Nights*)

Parents in many cultures[5] make love when their babies are awake alongside them, a practice which – contrary to Western belief – does not scar them for life, and makes a nonsense of our embarrassment over sexual education. Jean Liedloff writes:

> There is concern, too, about the infant being present when his parents make love. Among the Yequana, his presence is taken as

a matter of course, and must have been so as well during the hundreds of millennia before us.

It may even be that in *not* being present he is missing an important psycho-biological link with his parents, which leaves him with a sense of longing for it that turns later into a repressed, guilt-laden Oedipus (or Electra) wish to make love to the parent of the opposite sex, when in fact he really wanted the infant's passive role in the first place ...

(*The Continuum Concept*)

Perhaps this is why sex is something that brings out the child in us. Instead of forming a part of our growing experience, love-making has always been pushed aside, something we have had to discover for ourselves. It is diffiult to take a mature attitude about something which our parents treated with secrecy. Jealousy of the parents is something child psychotherapist Dilys Daws has encountered in her work with babies and young children who refuse to sleep. The child senses his exclusion from the couple's intimacy and interrupts them:

... the meaning of the baby or child's not sleeping seems to be in a non-resolution of Oedipal feelings: that is, where the reason for not sleeping seems to be an anxiety about the parents being together and excluding the child. Often the taking up of the parents' evening together can be as detrimental to a marriage as intrusion into their night.

(*Sleep Problems in Babies and Young Children*)

The child who is always welcome in his parents' company will not need to play the intruder. To be put in a cot the second he goes off to sleep may incite even quite a young child into rebellion. It would be better to allow your child to sleep near you in the night.

If you do not want your children to be the only ones in their class to have a natural sex education, then find a cozy space for love-making near where he sleeps in the evening or afternoon. Children's daytime snoozes provide ample opportunity for parents to catch a few private moments together.

Daphne, a mother from Leeds, told me the wonderful story of her toddler announcing to his grandparents that 'mummy and daddy were playing gee-gees in bed last night'. You may feel this is the kind of intimate experience our society isn't quite ready for. So hold your horses, if you prefer, and wait until the little ones are slumbering – and invest in a squeak-free, non-bouncy bed.

Once the baby is asleep, the only limits to time and place are in the parents' imagination. Many couples rediscover the excitement of their early relationship, as they enjoy cuddles by the fire, and make secret rendezvous around the house.

All studies show that the most important indicator for a happy relationship is the level of communication between the couple. No two couples will have the same needs or desires, and no amount of sex will repair what is otherwise an uncommunicative relationship.

Rather than banishing sex to one corner of our lives, we need to admit our need for sensuality in many ways. In our touch-starved lives, sex takes on an inflated importance. The more we suppress it, the more it nags us. However,

> Sex, like breastfeeding, is ninety per cent mental attitude and ten per cent technique.
>
> (*The Womanly Art of Breastfeeding*)

The success of our sex lives is mainly in our minds. If what you are doing – or not doing – feels right, then it probably is.

Doctors Andrew and Penny Stanway show how blurred the lines between sexuality and sensuality have become and how reluctant we are to admit our desires. They even put the act of giving birth into a sexual context, reporting on birthing centres in America where parents are encouraged to make love (though not have full sexual intercourse), during labour. Afterwards:

> The couple then cuddle together with their baby. Left to their own devices, they will soon sleep with their baby between them, especially if the labour has been long or if it is in the middle of the night.
>
> (*Choices in Childbirth*)

Without suggesting that every woman wants to have an orgasm during labour, the Stanways reveal an aspect of the birth experience that most Westerners deny. They also explore the sexuality that underlies breastfeeding – symbiotic breastfeeding that is, and not the restricted method which brings pain to the mother as the infant takes every gulp.

A mother who is constantly suckling her child may find that breastfeeding has a mixed effect on her sexual libido. Prolactin, the hormone that controls milk production, sometimes prevents sexual arousal. But the Stanways show that many women find that the gentle stimulation of the breast during feeding arouses them:

> Breastfeeding is widely experienced by many women as pleasurable, yet this is a largely undiscussed or taboo subject. In a survey we made of 300 women, 64 per cent said that breastfeeding was 'sexually pleasant' or 'sensual' , and many said they had orgasms during breastfeeding ... Several women have told us that they felt guilty feeling 'so sexy' during breastfeeding and some have even given up because of guilt over this: this applies especially if the baby is a boy.
>
> (*Choices in Childbirth*)

Perhaps breastfeeding is meant to be a satisfaction in itself, soothing and stimulating the woman who may not be ready for full sexual intercourse.

We are so deprived of the joys of human touch, that it is little wonder our sexual inclinations turn sour. For many, this means our sensual capacity is vastly underused, and desire becomes suppressed. For others, the need to satisfy the senses becomes an overwhelming sexual urge. Often, because of sexual conditioning, it is women who fall into the first category, and men who adopt the latter.

Jean Liedloff believes the overspilling of sexual desire in our society is connected to our infant desire for mother-love. She says we carry our unfulfilled needs with us from babyhood into adulthood:

> ... the confusion between the need for sex and the need for affection, a maternal kind of physical contact, the confusion that gives rise to phrases like 'red-hot mama', is important to resolve ... The vast reservoir of longing for physical comforting might be significantly reduced if it became socially acceptable to hold hands with a walking companion of either sex, to sit touching, not just near, talking companions, to sit on people's laps in public as well as in private, to stroke a tempting head of hair when the mood takes one, to hug more freely and more publicly, and in

general not to curb one's affectionate impulses unless they would be unwelcome.

(The Continuum Concept)

In answer to *The Sun*'s correspondent, it is clear that her problem lies in her feelings about her own sexuality. Many adults are simply not ready to have their babies with them all the time.

An innocent question about wriggling (which could have been answered easily and modestly to the satisfaction of the three-year-old observer), was enough to put this mother 'right off' sex. This is not intimacy based on mutual love, self-confidence and respect – it is a guilt-ridden, closet activity, maintained only under the delusion that no one else knows it is going on.

Such attitudes are at the root of our current problem with child sex abuse. Some parents, still looking for comfort in their old age, mistakenly interpret the sensuality and passivity of a child as a sexual signal. Some severely emotionally deprived individuals are so unused to experiencing innocent physical intimacy, that they become sexually aroused when they find it. Sex may be the only way they know of expressing deep emotion. It may even be their way of loving their own children.

In all the literature written about the victims of sex abuse, I have read very little from the perspective of the abuser. He – or she – must have been a victim in his or her turn, rejected and unfulfilled as a baby, when touch was not only acceptable, but a necessity for proper growth. All that desire has been forced underground, and emerges warped.

One newspaper article written during the Cleveland crisis of 1988 made this comment:

> ... psychiatrists and therapists ... who are studying the problem are increasingly finding patients – both as adults and children – whose feelings of affection, fear, love, violence and intimacy have been hopelessly confused.

(The Sunday Times, 19 July 1988)

This confusion is the result of unresolved mothering. The child who has been excluded from his parents' affections may grow up to be a victim or a bully in his turn. The parent who rapes his child is stealing many things from him: the child's right to choose, the child's physical privacy, the child's peace of mind. And as we know, many sexually abused children take that secret into adulthood, with the danger of becoming sexual abusers themselves.

Vera Diamond, a psychotherapist for twenty-three years, confirmed this finding: 'Of the thousands who have come to me and my colleagues for therapy, seventy-five per cent turn out to have been sexually abused in childhood.'[6] As Jean Liedloff says, 'No one wins in such a game; no one is the villain. All one can discover from horizon to horizon are victims of victims.'[7]

But there is a way out of the downward spiral, and I do not believe it lies merely in the hands of the courts and social services and lobby groups. We desperately need to restore the balance between mother and child – to bring our babies back into our arms, to welcome them into our presence at night – as a first step towards ending the daily damage we do to them.

If a person has been convicted or is suspected of raping a child, then clearly it would be unthinkable to allow the two to sleep in the same bed. The success of bedsharing depends on the adult being mature enough, responsible for his or her actions, and happy enough in his or her own sexuality not to endanger someone else's.

But since the Cleveland crisis, the panic button has been pressed, and there will be many who believe that sexual abuse results from *too much* intimacy with our babies, rather than a lack of it. They will not sense the crucial difference between types of closeness: one type which is essential for the infant, the other which is a violation. As one nurse put it:

> ... it seems that problems encountered in sleep in child rearing would perhaps be best solved by bedsharing. However in the present climate of interest in incest in this country it seems ludicrous to mention it.
> (Kathryn Conder, *Midwife, HV and Community Nurse*, April 1988)

Some critics believe that even the desire to sleep next to your child may be abnormal. One of these detractors is Dr Richard Ferber, director of the Sleep Laboratory and of the Center for Paediatric Sleep Disorders at the Children's Hospital in Boston, Massachusetts. He writes:

If you find that you actually prefer to have your child in your bed, you should examine your own feelings very carefully ... If there is tension between parents, then taking a child into their bed may help them avoid confrontation and sexual intimacy. If any of this applies to you, then instead of helping your child you are using him to avoid facing and solving your own problems. As long as such a pattern continues, not only your child but your whole family will suffer.

(*Solve Your Child's Sleep Problems*)

While I was examining my own feelings very carefully, I stumbled on a suitable reply from Dr David Haslam's book, *Sleepless Children*.

Occasionally claims are also made that only couples with sexual or marital problems share their bed with a child. For example, a writer in the journal of the American Medical Association in 1980 went so far as to state that because most children in our society do not sleep with their parents, 'the physician should consider exploring underlying motives with the parents, as to whose needs are being served by this arrangement.'

Thankfully a few weeks later another paediatrician wrote to express an opposite opinion. An American study in 1974 claimed that bedsharing is an indicator of a disturbed parental relationship. This much-quoted study suggested that the mother often used the child's presence as a shield against her husband's sexual demands. However, a 1982 study from Sweden disagreed with this; it did not reveal any increase in divorce rates in families who shared beds with four- to eight-year-olds. As the Swedes concluded, 'The habit is too widespread among ordinary families for it to serve as a sign that the parents are in the process of separating.

Parents all over the world use their children as pawns in the games they play. No doubt, some use their baby as a physical barrier. But the best barriers are not made of flesh and blood. A baby between two people is more likely to be the greatest bond they will ever know. And even if parents were to use their baby as a cover-up for their marital tensions, the baby would come out the winner, with all his emotional and physical needs being so obviously met.

Many of the criticisms about baby bedsharing are rooted in fear. People are afraid the balance of their old lives will be upset. Sex will not be as it was. Touching a baby may be the kind of physical intimacy they have been avoiding all their lives. Either they can give in to these fears, or they can rediscover sensuality through the child.

In his book *Primal Health*, Michel Odent connects the well-being of a species with its ability to love (form attachments), reproduce (fulfil all the requirements of the sexual act, the gestation period and the birth) and nurture (feed its young). Our society manifests problems in all three areas. We have trouble making lasting relationships, both sexes suffer from infertility and lapses in sexual desire, and after mechanistic and painful childbirth, we suffer immense distress when we try to suckle our babies. The obvious crisis in our reproductive lives is a sure sign that we are on the wrong track.

'Difficulties in breastfeeding, just as difficulties in childbirth and sexual difficulties, are diseases of civilization,' writes Odent. 'And each in their turn is creating disease. Love; sexuality; health. These are words which only our Western analytical brain can consider as separate entities.'

The problem is not whether or not our babies are beside us when we make love. It is that society does not know where to draw the line between 'healthy' loving, constructive, reproductive relationships – and violent, abusive, uncontrolled desire.

Once again, we need to look back at our own infancy, when all we needed was our mother's loving touch. That is where a healthy sex education begins.

9 | TIME FOR BED

> The world is ruled by letting things take their course. It cannot be ruled by interfering.
>
> *(Tao Te Ching)*

Before setting out, many people want to know where their adventure is likely to end. When will the baby leave the bed? Should the child find his own way to independence, or should he be shown the door? Can parents do anything to speed up the process?

These are questions that encompass all our notions about independence and clinginess, strictness and permissiveness, weaning, spoiling and training our children.

Since doctors began to analyse the stages of childhood development, parents have been able to keep track of their babies' progress. Thanks to Freud, they can note the oral, anal and genital stages. They can look out for the first smile, encourage their children to sit up, egg them on to crawl, and help them walk their first few steps.

There are mechanical devices to 'aid' the child to do these things – cradles for sitting in, baby walkers to walk in and so on. The well-informed and well-equipped parent is expected to be aware of the phases of childhood, to anticipate them, and to help steer the child through them.

Before the last World War, childrens' playthings were few and mostly hand-made. These days, toys tend to be educative and sold in toyshops with names like the Early Learning Centre. It is not enough for a toy to be a diversion. It must be instructive, so that even the smallest baby can be 'taught' to discover colour, texture and sound.

Toy manufacturers tend to take themselves rather seriously. Here, for instance, is a blurb from one American company making plastic see-through roly-poly tubes with Disney characters on them (any grammatical error is theirs, not mine).

Shelcore's Promise

Baby's are wonderful people. That's why we try so hard to satisfy, stimulate, soothe and delight them with toys and baby care items that are the ultimate in safety, function and fun ... So, you know you're getting the best for your baby. After all, parents are wonderful people, too.

Most babies are more interested in the cardboard packaging than the lovingly mass-produced item that is meant to satisfy, stimulate, soothe and delight. It's not that toys are inappropriate in a baby's small life, but that he doesn't need them in the way most of us assume. As any baby will tell you, there's only one 'best' for him in the early months, and that's his mother. Libby Purves, author of *How Not to be a Perfect Mother*, writes:

> People forget that newborns are a race apart; reciting old nursery wisdoms, they get confused about babies' actual needs at the very beginning ... Infants have no prejudices, no preconceptions, no rituals. Their wants are fierce but few: a warm basket, a clean nappy, and an unreasonable amount of sucking at the breast.
>
> ('Babies Born to Travel', *Sunday Times*, 14 August 1988)

Even the basket is an unnecessary accessory, when a mother is prepared to hold her baby in her arms.

Similarly, older children do not need all the toys and stimulants we offer them. Sometimes it must seem to them as if all objects divide into two categories: tools and toys. The first are what life is about, the second are the items they are told to run away and play with, especially when parents are busy. But in the interest of furthering a child's motor skills and starting him on a good education, the parent feels compelled to spend, spend, spend on babycare items.

I believe we do this because we belong to a weaning society – using the word 'wean' in its broadest sense to denote the enforced transition from one stage to another.[1] We are a culture unable to enjoy fully the moment, to accept that change is inevitable, and to look neither forward nor back. We are programmed to interfere – we want a part in the action. Because we are so aware of the various phases through which a baby passes on the route to adulthood, we tend to urge him towards the next stage, weaning him hurriedly out of the last.

The weaning impulse affects every aspect of a baby's life. 'Can he sit/crawl/walk yet?' we ask other mothers. 'When are you going to take him off the breast?' Doctors tell us to go gently on the weaning process, but we can't help worrying about it. Will he ever be potty-trained? When will he tie his own shoe laces?

Every parental attempt to steer a baby in one direction inevitably has an effect on his overall development. I met one mother who was proud that her little boy was able to stand – with a little help – at five months. 'We didn't want him to crawl,' she told me, 'so we bought him a baby walker from the beginning and always put him in it.'

Unfortunately, prolonged periods strapped in the artificially upright position had made the poor lad very stiff. He was 'early' in walking, but was unable to fall over without hurting himself. His mother spent many months chasing after him to stop him doing himself severe damage.

The annual report of the Chartered Society of Physiotherapists published in 1988 confirms that baby walkers may not be as useful to motor development as parents expect:

> ... far too many babies are put into walkers from the age of four months. At this age, muscles are not strong enough to bear the weight, and may cause toes to turn inwards or outwards. Parents often believe that baby walkers will encourage their infant to walk earlier but, says physiotherapist Jill Breckon, the reverse is often true.
>
> (Liz Hodgkinson, *Early Days*, Summer 1988)

We interfere at our children's peril. By rushing them through the natural stages of development, we may alter the processes a baby goes through, the way he learns things, and even the order in which they come. Nurse Kathryn Conder reports:

> Babies who are constantly carried around, as South Indians do in Gopalur for example, acquire language and social skills before motor development.
>
> (*Midwife, HV and Community Nurse*, April 1988)

Why are Ugandan babies more advanced[2] than our own? Could it be because they spend their infancy in their mothers' arms, crawling in their own time, and walking only when they are ready? Observers working in rural villages in Malawi report that the African children there are more advanced than Western babies at every stage. Such babies sleep with the whole family in mud and straw huts, and are carried on their mothers' backs by day.

Different peoples have radically different approaches to the weaning process. The trend has changed drastically in our own culture, from infant training in the 1890s to permissiveness in the 1960s. Among primitive groups, we find the full range of weaning procedures, from the most gradual to the most sudden. The G/wi bushmen of the Kalahari Desert take it slowly:

> It appears to be a fundamental tenet of G/wi philosophy that man is an essentially reasonable being and is well disposed towards his fellows. This belief is consistent with the form that the processes of child training and socialisation take...
>
> The weaning process is described as 'the child's growing tired of the breast.' Solids are introduced into the infant's diet at an early stage as supplementary feeding and as material on which to cut emerging teeth. The supplementary component is gradually increased until, before his third year, the child is feeding himself and is given the breast only at fairly long intervals or when he needs comforting. The diminishing nutritional dependence on breast feeding and the desire to imitate older, weaned colleagues are probably the main factors terminating a child's desire for breast feeding. The initiative appears to come as much from the child as from the mother.
>
> (*Hunters and Gatherers*)

This is an arrangement whereby the needs of the mother and of the baby are considered, and whereby things are allowed to take their course. In fact, it does not resemble weaning at all, for it requires no effort or struggle from either the child or the parent. It only takes time and patience, neither of which is conspicuously available in our society.

In the West, the initiatives of mother and baby are suppressed by the expectations of professionals, and other mothers who are following modern advice. Just because we know when a baby crawls, does not mean we should anticipate that stage and hurry it on, or save him the trouble of bothering with it. We do not know – professionals do not know – the many ways in which the body and mind are connected. It is dangerous to assume that we completely understand early human development, and it is foolish to interfere.

> ... deprivation of any well precedented detail of experience will cost the individual some degree of well-being, perhaps one too subtle for us to notice, perhaps one so commonly lost that we do not recognise it as a loss. Research has already shown ... that deprivation of the experience of creeping about on hands and knees has deleterious effects upon verbal abilities when they develop at a later stage.
>
> *(The Continuum Concept)*

If not being allowed to crawl can leave a baby speech-impaired, there may be enormous consequences for babies who are not allowed their fill of sleeping by their mother's side. For all we know, co-sleeping may enable a baby to be more supple, or to see further. There might be many minute differences between a child who sleeps with others, and one who sleeps alone. Yet our society considers it reasonable to deprive a baby of that essential experience.

Many of the professionals who agree with the principles of bed-sharing insist that there will be difficulties in weaning the child away. The assumption again is that the child *must* be weaned, whether from the bottle or from the bed.[3] Weaning can be problematic, so is it entirely necessary?

Some of the more obvious effects of hurried weaning from one physical stage to the next are already well known to the childcare experts. Neurosis – the inability to take a rational hold on life – is one of these. Psychologists detail the effects of emotional disturbance on the child during Freud's 'oral period' – the first year or so:

> What happens if these needs [for the mother and her nurture] are frustrated severely or unnecessarily? ... This may result in the child's being unable to progress adequately to the next stage of development ... He becomes fixated at the oral stage, and under the influence of his biologically determined course of development, he progresses only weakly to the next stage.
>
> (English and Pearson, *Emotional Problems of Living*)

One very common sign of weak progression towards independence is a child's reliance on a transitional object. Most Western doctors believe the comfort toy is a normal phase of development, and some actively promote its use:

> Better than lying with your toddler or young child until he falls asleep at night is for him to fall asleep with a 'transitional object' – a stuffed animal, a doll, a toy, a special blanket.
>
> (Ferber, *Solve Your Child's Sleep Problems*)

Stuffed animals and special blankets are easy to come by in our society, and once a child becomes attached to a comforter, a mother is advised to buy two or more of the beloved article, in case one gets lost. But in primitive cultures, an entire family's belongings may not extend beyond a sleeping mat. Needless to say, in such groups the use of a transitional object is unknown.

> In many cultures where bed-sharing is the norm notably less sleep problems are found. There is no evidence either that it causes the child psychological harm. In fact in non-literate societies where because of bed-sharing the children have much more tactile stimulation, the use of transitional objects such as pieces of blanket, etc, is almost unknown.
>
> (Conder, *Midwifery, HV and Community Nurse*)

Michel Odent has conducted his own research among mothers who had home deliveries – an atypical group in London. Babies who were breastfed at night for more than a year did not resort to transitional objects for comfort. At the other end of the scale, it has been shown that children who are severely deprived of love and affection (for instance those kept in old-style children's homes) do not seek transitional objects either. He concludes that 'the need for a transitional object is the healthy reaction of a normal child to a special situation.'

One obvious example of a child's difficulty in becoming independent is when he displays shyness, or fear of strangers. It is a trait so common in our society that we almost expect it in some measure from our children – especially from the girls, according to a five-year study from Cambridge.[4]

Psychologist Joan Stevenson-Hyde assessed a group of children aged between two-and-a-half and seven years when separated from their mothers. She found that the children's security was affected by parental problems. Children were more prone to shyness, for instance, after the arrival of a new brother or sister:

> Anything that might make the mother less responsive, such as the demands of a new baby, which suddenly make her a different mother to the child, may affect how secure the child feels.
>
> (*The Independent*, 12 July 1988)

A tendency to shyness may be inherited, said the report, but Dr Stevenson-Hyde confirmed that the child's experiences were by far the most crucial factor:

> $2\frac{1}{2}$-year-olds who were warmly and confidently attached to their mothers showed only low or moderate fear of strangers, never high fear. These children cope with a noisy new environment such as a playgroup, given time and encouragement...
>
> In her unselected sample ... about one child in ten remained shy, causing difficulties at the transition to nursery or primary school.
>
> (Gillian Mercer, *The Independent*, 12 July 1988)

The South American Yequana baby, with all his needs fulfilled, has progressed to a stable level of independence by the time he crawls out of his mother's arms. In fact, the movement away from the mother is the child's own statement about his personal confidence. If he is unsure, he returns to the safety of the maternal zone. She does not push him in any direction, knowing instinctively that this will warp his behaviour, either to rebel against her, or to please her and thereby win her attention.

Likewise G/wi and Paliyan children do not develop patterns of shyness. However, the Paliyan people change their tactics when a child reaches two years of age. Noted for their extreme individualism, and the lack of co-operation between adults, the Paliyans fulfil a child's needs for his first two years, and then precipitously abandon him to his own devices:

> The comforting world of the child undergoes a series of rapid changes at the time of weaning at about two and a half years of age. The mother not only denies the child her breast or deters it

with bitter paste on the nipples, but she puts it down now for increasingly long periods ... Facing situations without continuous maternal guidance for the first time, the child is suddenly introduced to new kinds of experiences – misbehaviour and punishment ...

Although the punishment will not go beyond an angry word or at most a mild slap, this is a distinct change of tone, especially if it comes from the mother. During this period the mother frequently attempts to ignore her child's demands ... If the child is not already crying, it becomes enraged at its mother's lack of response; it cries spasmodically, pulls its hair, and stamps its feet ... it seldom calms down in less than ten to twenty minutes. Such tantrums continue until the child is four or five; in one case the episodes persisted until ten years of age.

(*Hunters and Gatherers Today*)

This portrait of an Indian people provides an excellent example of the effects of sudden weaning. It is easy to see why the child becomes enraged at such an uncompromising withdrawal of affection. This translates into the fierce independence of adult tribe members.

Another society noted for the temper tantrums of its toddlers is the modern, industrialized world. Current thinking is that babies need to be educated, and that parents should put down their collective foot to stop any nonsense. Failure to do this, say the professionals, will result in households being ruled by the whims of two-year-old tyrants. Here is a typical assessment from American Leo Madow, in his book entitled *Anger*:

... as the child grows older and is no longer considered completely helpless, demands begin to be made on him. One of the first of these is weaning.

Thus mother, by insisting that he do things for himself and restricting the total freedom he had enjoyed, frustrates him. The result is anger that he cannot fully express and that begins to accumulate. The process is normal; mother must frustrate the child, if he is to grow up and become acceptable to society. You might ask, 'Do little babies really have so much feeling?' Have you ever seen a baby have a temper tantrum, or hold its breath, or bang its head against the wall?

... This is only the beginning in the frustration taking place in the process known as 'growing up'. Growing up consists of increasing limitations of direct, immediate satisfaction of needs, which the child must learn to satisfy in what he feels is a less pleasant way, or to put off satisfying for a while.

In America and Europe, babies begin to have tantrums at about eighteen months old, and this behaviour may continue for four or five years. Child and parent are reduced to behaving like animal and trainer, in order to continue the battle which began at birth.

Some types of autism, a debilitating mental condition which prevents children making the proper responses to their environment, may be a product of that battle. The causes of autism are not entirely understood, and of course the parents are not to blame for their children's condition. However, cures are being made in certain cases, by bringing mother and child back into physical touch with each other.

Jasmine Bayley is one of three British teachers of holding therapy, which treats autistic children by asking mothers to take their children forcibly into their arms. After half an hour of holding, a severely damaged child emerges smiling and able to communicate. In up to thirty per cent of cases, a complete recovery is obtained. Ms Bayley explains autism in terms of the vicious circle of misunderstanding that exists between parent and child:

Whatever the cause of autism, it makes the child totally withdrawn from the mother, who goes after him and is rejected, building up a cycle of anger, frustration and despair on both sides. Holding brings the mother and child back in touch so that they can communicate.

(*The Independent*, 23 August 1988)

Holding therapy is one of the few techniques that brings the mother and baby closer, in an attempt to repair the bond that has been damaged by Western mothering practices. Who knows what symptoms of autism might be prevented if mothers held their babies in their arms from the beginning?

In an attempt to capture the maximum amount of a parent's attention – the result of basic needs not being fulfilled – the desperate child sometimes holds his breath. It's a classic warning sign, like the adult who threatens suicide. Here is a common example from the problem page of a parents' magazine:

> I'm having a real battle of wills with my very stubborn 18-month-
> old daughter. If she decides she doesn't want to do something,
> she stiffens, refuses to move and holds her breath until she turns
> blue.
>
> (*Young Additions*, Autumn 1987)

The doctor replies that 'breath holding is a common symptom in toddlers and is a version of "tantruming". She won't come to any harm doing this, so your best approach is to ignore it. It is important however, to talk to her about it afterwards and to try to find out if there is anything that's upsetting her.'

He offers useful interim advice, but it would clearly be preferable to avoid this level of conflict altogether. If we accept tantrums as a normal phase of growing up, they are not going to disappear. Most parents blame themselves ('She's got her dad's temper'), or the child for these regular outbursts. But we should remember that tantrums are unknown in societies where weaning is not imposed on the child.

Furthermore, by laying the blame for bad behaviour on genetics, and refusing to listen to the urgent message of a baby who is head-banging, thumb-sucking or throwing tantrums, we imprint the child with negative ideas for the future. Family therapist Steve Biddulph, author of *The Secret of Happy Children*, has written at length on the dangers of negative programming. This is the sort of thing he warns against:

> 'You're hopeless.' 'God, you're a nuisance.' 'You'll be sorry, just you see.' 'You're as bad as your Uncle Tom' (*who's just been in jail*). 'You're just like your Auntie Eve' (*who's fond of a drink*).
>
> This is the kind of programming many youngsters grow up with; it is passed on unwittingly by overwrought parents and continues a kind of family curse down the generations...
> What we have discovered is that comments such as these don't only have the effect of making the child feel bad momentarily. They also have a hypnotic effect and act unconsciously, like seeds in the mind, seeds which will grow and shape the person's self-image, eventually becoming true facts about his personality.[5]

Weaning is all about training, and training is preparation for competition. Though she may make desperate attempts to avoid the trap, every mother finds herself making comparisons between her child and the next. It is easy to become obsessed with 'norms' as laid down by paediatricians in the 1950s and 1960s, and to chart our children's development according to them: she's talking early, he's walking late, and so on.

Regular development checks by the health visitor reinforce the feeling that we should somehow encourage progress in our children. But this has not always been so. Older generations criticize the young for 'over-stimulating' the child, a phrase that was fashionable in the 'no-nonsense' 1920s. They also say our children grow up too quickly.

In sixty years, we have passed from deliberate isolation of the baby, to an American-style hot-house treatment, whereby children are forced into early brilliance like seedlings for a show. Forcing the child on enables him to attain excellence in his specialization (hence headlines, like 'Boy, 9, is new maths genius'[6]). But this narrow education may be achieved at the expense of the development of many other aspects of the personality and overall capabilities.

On the one hand, there was great-grandma who left her new-born child for hours alone in the cot or pram to get used to his own company, and on the other, there is the mother who plays Mozart to her four-month-old foetus, and wields a pack of flash-cards in her nappy bag. Our practice in recent decades has been the result of fashions dictated by various authorities. The need is to restore authority to the instincts of mothers; then books like this will no longer be required. I do not wish to add to the clutter of conflicting advice, but to point to a way out of it.

Parents in America – and latterly in Britain – talk of 'quality time' with their children. This means not getting on with the washing up, or mowing the lawn, but sitting in a room with the child, poring over books and toys, trying to 'teach' him something. If a child's early experience consists of playing in a room while adults sit and stare at him, then he is getting an extremely warped view of the world. At the very least, he is likely to grow up self-centred.

It is better to educate a child – literally, lead him out – by example rather than say-so. But this method requires participation, and parents are often frightened to allow their children to participate in the real world, because of its apparent dangers. Yet experience in many other cultures shows us that children are well-equipped with their own safety mechanisms, and will not readily fall downstairs or cut themselves if left to their own devices. Among the Paliyans, for instance:

> Nobody pays attention to a two- or three-year-old who runs about with a razor-sharp billhook or who climbs on a house top. A five-year-old is permitted to make fires for preparing food.
>
> (*Hunters and Gatherers Today*)

If a Paliyan child is capable of doing these things without hurting himself, then so can any other. But stories of domestic accidents with kettles and scissors are the stuff of consumer programmes. They set us worrying. And the more household gadgets we invent, the more reason parents feel they have to be protective.

In our own house, we have noticed that Frances is far more likely to hurt herself if an adult interferes with her activity, than if she is allowed to explore her world by herself. It took us a long time and a lot of tongue-biting to discover that she could crawl downstairs backwards on her own. It was only when we made a fuss of the event, or waited at the bottom to catch her, that she tended to abdicate her own responsibility and launch herself into mid-air.

If a child finds a sharp knife, there is no need to make any reaction, or snatch it from his hands. If seeing his infant toying with the garden shears is too much for the parent, he may quietly ask for their return, and distract the child with something else. I have often found Frances playing with sharp things, but she has never once hurt herself.

Children do not need protecting in a well-ordered home. If there is visible physical danger around, they can cope with it. Often, they will choose not to confront it until ready. If the danger is invisible, such as electricity, parents need only cover the plug socket. We merely confuse and anger our children by shouting 'no!' at every opportunity. It is also a sure sign to him that the danger point is extremely interesting, and that returning to it will excite the attention of grown-ups.

Musician and Suzuki teacher Ron Colyer made this point in a talk addressed to the conference of teachers of the Alexander Technique in 1988. 'Children like to do what they can do,' he said.[7] 'They develop the ability to say "no" inside themselves.'

How will a child learn that the oven door is hot? As he approaches it, he will feel the heat, and he will not repeat the action if left to learn that fact for himself. If mum is screaming 'don't touch it!' every time, it becomes a game – the very important game of getting mum as heated as the oven. In the excitement, he is also more likely to get burnt.

Mothers throw their hands up in horror at the idea of letting their babies loose in the kitchen, or the garden. But when they try it, and allow themselves to trust in the extraordinary ability of the baby to cope, they are always amazed at the results. A child used to his mother's alarmist approach will, however, take time to adjust to taking responsibility for himself.

What about the street? Surely I don't expect my child to learn about cars by getting run over? Clearly not, but neither is it sensible to test a two-year-old's assessment of the situation by instructing him 'not to go out of my sight.' A parent needs only to judge when his child's hand needs to be held. By running after your child, you can be sure he will run away from you – another wonderful game.

Steve Biddulph follows negative programming down this path, and discovers children who are not given the chance to fail. Before they can demonstrate their ability to cope in the world, many children are told they cannot cope. Some parents lack the patience to let youngsters learn for themselves:

> Take children playing in the woods, climbing trees. 'You'll fall! Look out! You'll slip!' cries the mother, anxiously watching. And, in a million sitting rooms and kitchens, parents' voices:
>
> *'God, you're lazy.' 'You're so selfish.' 'You silly idiot, stop that.' 'Give it to me, fumble fingers.' 'Don't be such a pest.'*[5]

Restricting a child's freedom goes hand in hand with urging him to perform. Both interfere with his natural inclination to explore his world at his own pace, and to fit in. Children are forced into an unnatural pattern – either one of attempting to please their parents for the rewards that brings, or one of rebelling against them, and achieving some sort of freedom that way. This is why so many people are unable, even as adults, to have reasonable relationships with their parents. Every action is charged with emotional content.

We need to reverse the current practice of putting down young babies and interfering with older ones. Infants require open access to adult company, but little else in the way of active education. 'Good boy' and 'naughty boy' are unnecessary tags which confuse a child's natural motivation.

The fulfilled baby is one who accompanies his mother on her usual daily round, meeting all the hazards she does, and learning about life from her arms. When he crawls away, she lets him go, neither watching nor cajoling him, neither urging him to perform various tricks, nor warning him of obvious dangers. She prepares the house so that he cannot break things she does not want him to break, or injure himself with gadgets he cannot be expected to handle. She does not follow him out of the room, he follows her. He wants to be where the action is. The emotionally secure baby will make brief forays into new territory and swiftly return to his mother.

If he does fall and scrape himself slightly, his mother calmly waits, and the child will come to her. More often than not, the crying stops in a matter of seconds, not a matter of minutes, as is usual when parents offer excessive sympathy. Whenever a child does come to be picked up, the mother takes him as a matter of course, not with undue delight or excessive attention, and not with sighs or groans.

If a child does something his mother considers to be 'naughty' (though a child cannot be naughty unless you give him rules and a means of breaking them), she does not have to withdraw her affection. As he gets older, she can explain that such a thing is out of bounds, or not to be done – but she does not need to punish him in any way. The desire to belong, conform, behave – survive – is what makes the human baby an innately social creature.

The average small child, when told off by his parents, will react with screaming, a tantrum or a sulk. It is as if his whole world has been shattered. In fact, this is exactly how the child sees it. Criticism goes to the very core of him: his sense of self is not strong enough to withstand a comment about his misdeed.

We see the same pattern in adults. Many of us are so brittle, that we take any criticism of our acts as an insult to ourselves. Because we were pushed into independence before our tender egos were ready, and prevented from taking responsibility for ourselves at an early age, our happiness is easily crushed.

Most of us have grown up believing that we will only be loved if we do right. All we needed was someone to accept us uncon-ditionally – and that someone, ideally, should have been our mother. A child needs neither punishment, nor praise – but information.

Instead of growing up constituting a 'series of frustrations' – to use Leo Madow's phrase – it could constitute a series of explorations. A child does not distinguish between work and play, and the longer we can put off that distinction, the better. Sorting out the washing basket with your baby can be a game of rough and tumble, peep-bo and tickles among the sheets. The task takes longer than it would if you were folding linen on your own – but it is also twice as much fun. Meanwhile, the baby has learnt something about domestic work.

After Frances was born, I began to enjoy ordinary, everyday jobs for the first time. I did not scoot round cleaning up while she was asleep, but took her with me while I mowed the lawn, dried the cutlery (her favourite game), and even washed the car. She showed me how to enjoy the things I always grumbled about.

I started when she was born – and by the time she was six months old, she was joining in with most activities. The number of accidents was negligible (a French teenage visitor broke more crockery in two months than Frances did in a year). The level of amusement was high. The quality of my life had vastly improved, and she was an extremely happy child.

We adopted Jean Liedloff's golden rule: 'Never do anything for a child that he can do for himself.' You could call it minimalist mothering.

Parenting, like giving birth or dying, may be more helpfully described as a non-activity. Growing up happens anyway, whatever stimulants, proddings or encouragement we give our children. Despite our interference, many children grow up not too badly damaged. That is the best we can say about the effect of intensive Western parenting.

We restrain and push our children at the same time. They are unwelcome in shops and restaurants, but yet they are the centre of attention wherever they go. We hate our children so much, we batter them – and we love them so much that they are spoiled by the age of two. It would be better to let them be.

'You don't have to go on being baby-centred,' Jean Liedloff told me. 'If you keep saying to a baby "what would you like to do now? Would you like this, or would you rather have that?" you drive them up the wall, and their response is anger. They can't express to you that you're not supposed to be doing this.

'By the age of four, they should actually be contributing more help in the house than they are costing, believe it or not. It sounds impossible, but that's exactly true. Not some fifteen-year-old spotty monster you have to clear up after. By the time they're eight, they should be helping you with the cooking and taking care of the next baby, and all this kind of thing.'

Maturity will emerge naturally if unhindered by parental pressure, which returns us to the question of weaning baby from the bed.

Every child has a capacity for independence. If pushed too hurriedly into leaving his mother's side, he is likely to cling to her skirts for longer. Putting a baby down to sleep in another room is the best way to create a rift, and to ensure that he comes running back for more.

So when should a baby leave the parental bed? When he and his co-sleepers are ready. It's a question that can only be answered after the event. And if you are doing it right, it really won't matter to you when the baby graduates to his own space at night.

Paediatrician Dr Hugh Jolly had a lot of experience with parents who slept with their children, as he came in later years to recommend the practice. He describes the usual pattern:

Children brought up in the family bed decide to leave it at a variable age. Some are ready to take to their own bed around the age of two years but others want longer. Sometimes they decide to vary the pattern, choosing their own bed some nights and the family bed on others. Sometimes they decide to share with an older sibling who has already left the family bed. Knowing that they can come into their parents' bed in the middle of the night makes the transition easier. It is all so natural that many parents cannot remember exactly when each child decided to make the change.

(Book of Child Care)

If a mother can accept her child, be available but not intrusive, let go and nurture at the same time, she will be a 'good enough' mother.[8] Then the baby is free to be independent. When that time comes, he will make the move to sleep in his own bed.

A healthy, happy child does not always want to cling to his parents. Once he knows he is unconditionally accepted by them, and he has his fill of their presence at night, he will go away. The move may happen at two years old – less likely at ten – but any attempts to rush the process are certain to set it back. This is why you occasionally hear of nine-year-olds still sharing bedspace with their parents. Our problem is that we have neither the faith to believe they will leave, nor the patience to see the process through.

As a baby, Frances always went to sleep on the breast, a practice warned against by experts like Dr Spock. Yet at eight months, quite suddenly, she started to find her own space to sleep in, and would turn over, away from the breast to go to sleep. She did not need to be pushed into this experience by me, but naturally altered her habit in her own good time.

At thirteen months, Frances was even more independent. On one memorable night, she actually put herself to bed. After her evening sleep, we all went upstairs together as usual, but Frances had woken up in transit to the bedroom, and started to play. Normally, she would go straight back to sleep once the lights were out, but on this occasion she was still lively. Paul and I went off to sleep on our mattress on the floor, while Frances amused herself quietly in our room. I opened my eyes about an hour later, to see that Frances had tucked herself up on her single mattress by the side of ours, without even bothering to come to me for a feed.

It is a pleasant feeling to see a baby progress, with no struggle at all, from one stage to another. It is an experience that many atricians and psychoanalysts have never known. Our experts, understandably, have been raised on the infant 'norms' of clinical trials in the 1950s, the only statistical evidence available to them. Their practical experience is often limited to babies who were born in hospital, who sleep apart from their mothers, and who are either bottle-fed or weaned from the breast by four months.

Perhaps it is time the 'norms' were re-evaluated, so that professionals would not express surprise or distaste when mothers say they sleep with their children, or breastfeed them beyond their first birthday. It is rare to hear a mother admit openly, and with pride:

> I breastfed my two children until they weaned themselves and it was such a lovely experience that seven years ago I became a counsellor to help others achieve it.
>
> (Mrs M. Goodall, *Parents*, April 1988)

Midwife Chloe Fisher, who advises mothers to let their babies decide the length of each feed, told me of the relief she feels to see a baby come off the breast of his own accord. It is so unusual in our society for us to allow the natural thing to happen, that we can scarcely believe it when it does. We start interfering from the moment a pregnancy is announced, and do not even trust a new-born baby to suckle according to the rules of instinct by which he is driven.

It seems an impossible dream to think of children moving into adulthood at their own pace; of teenagers who are not rebelling against family life, but contributing to the full; of parents who offer comfort to their children with no strings attached. Our adult relationships are so rarely based on mutual respect, that it is hard to envisage offering respect to our children.

Babies may leave the bed at any age from six months. The average age, if unhurried, is two years. A mother may decide she has had enough before he does, and some positive incentives to move may come in handy. (I explore these in the next chapter.) But any attempts to wean a child suddenly, before he is ready, are likely to have some detrimental effect.

Most parents who choose to sleep with their babies throughout each night enjoy the experience, and are in no hurry to push the baby out. Nature planned things that way. If we can give sleeping with our babies a fair chance, then our children's children will be strong enough to build on our attempts.

10 | PRACTICALLY SPEAKING

There is no established way of sleeping with a baby. Because the major civilizations of the world do not condone it, little has been written about its practicalities. In the past there has been no need for a method, just as there was no need to teach women how to breastfeed. But good tips are always useful, so here are some of mine – as from one mother to another.

WHAT PREPARATIONS SHOULD I MAKE?

Unlike all your friends, you will have no cot to buy. Some mothers may find this a strangely depressing experience, because our nesting instincts are closely tied to our passion for consumer goods. Others will delight in the financial saving. In any case, babies do not sleep in a full-sized cot for the first few months, so there's no need to buy one yet. Wait until after the birth, by which time you will have got used to the idea of a baby without bars.

Small babies do not take up much space at night. Frances slept in our ordinary double bed up to the age of one with no trouble. She and I have also slept in single beds together, and it wasn't a squeeze. You and your baby will probably cuddle up together for much of the night, and you soon get used to each other's presence.

If you have the money and the inclination, however, you may wish to invest in a king size bed, or two singles zipped together. Some families have beds specially made to share with older children. Michel Odent, Judy Graham and their three-year-old son Pascal sleep in a bed just six inches off the floor. Actress Jane Asher says parents may wish to construct their own bed from a simple wooden platform with two mattresses laid over it crossways. The La Leche League suggests removing the legs from a standard bed. Other families – like ourselves – simply put the mattress on the floor. Extra mattresses may then be added by the side as the children get older.

For those who intend to sleep in a bed of normal height, it is advisable to protect the edges, to stop the baby rolling out. This may be done by keeping the baby on the side next to a wall, by attaching cot sides to the bed, or simply by tucking the bedclothes under the mattress (Remember pre-duvet days?).

ISN'T BED-WETTING A PROBLEM?
A plastic mattress cover under the sheets is a good idea, to prevent any wetness getting through. When Frances was tiny, I used to lay an ordinary terry nappy under her, for added protection. After about three weeks, I found she did not wet the bed, because she wasn't waking up fully in the night.

The new 'ultra' brand of nappies are superb for the all-night stint. Even the Royal College of Midwives now recommend *not* changing a baby during the night unless absolutely necessary. They say:

> Minimal disturbance of a baby who has wakened only to be fed may result in the baby settling more quickly after the feed. It may also help the baby to begin to appreciate that night and day are different.
>
> (*Successful Breastfeeding*)

Third-time mum Janine Sternberg followed the same philosophy when she slept with her daughter Sarah: 'I think I'm less disturbed by Sarah than by the other children,' she said, 'because I'm not constantly getting out of bed. Unless I can actually smell or hear that there's a dirty nappy, I don't change the nappy in the middle of the night. I reckon that if it's been changed in the late evening it can last till morning, because the whole act of changing wakes them up.'

EVERY MOTHER NEEDS SUPPORT – OR DOES SHE?
Most mothering magazines advise women to wear a bra during the day and night during and after pregnancy, advice which I followed for a few weeks until the ludicrousness of having to refix a dozen hooks and eyes by moonlight finally got to me. Frances also preferred not to have the wings of a D cup flapping in her face as she fed. I remembered the words of Barbara Henry, chairman of the National Childbirth Trust's breastfeeding promotion group, whom I had interviewed during my pregnancy: 'I think the main reason for wearing a bra is for comfort's sake. My personal view is that it's not necessary.

There's no hard and fast rule about wearing a bra during pregnancy or afterwards.'

It was advice, incidentally, which the babycare magazine I was working for refused to print. It did not fit in with current thinking, I was told. Neither, presumably, did it go well with consumer features on 'choosing the right bra for you'.

So my night nursing bra was hurriedly dispatched. It was a weight off my chest. A year later, I cannot say that discarding my bra has caused me to sag unduly. If, after the sixth baby the story is different, it will still be preferable to bags under my eyes.

HOW WILL I SEE TO FEED THE BABY?
It took me a long time to perfect this one. You need just enough light in the room to breastfeed by, but not so much that you or your partner are kept awake. Michel Odent says the baby uses his sense of smell to find the nipple in the dark, but it was some months before I let Frances find her own position on the breast. As any breastfeeding mother will know, the pain experienced when the baby misses the nipple altogether can send you screaming to the ceiling.

I tried leaving the door of the bedroom ajar (rather cold, especially in winter), or draping scarves over standard lamps (fire hazard), and settled finally on the solution of a night light. These come in a variety of fancy shapes for fancy nurseries, but the most practical type are just glow-boxes that plug straight into the electric socket on the wall. Some are fitted with a fifteen-watt bulb, but mine takes ten watts, and I find that's ample to see by. After all, you only need to squint in the direction of the breast once or twice a night. The baby does the rest. By six months or so, Frances helped herself anyway, and I did not need to open my eyes at all.

WHAT CAN I EXPECT ON THE FIRST NIGHT?
The first night with a first baby will probably be in hospital, where it is harder to do what you want. You must decide whether to inform the hospital of your plans to sleep with the baby, in which case, be prepared to shop around for a maternity unit which agrees to this unorthodox practice. I gave birth at the University Hospital in Cardiff, where babies were not supposed to sleep with their mothers. However, since feeding the baby in the bed *was* allowed, I just stretched the feeds into all-night sessions, and nobody was too worried.

Chairs along the side of the bed will also do the trick. Midwives with experience of mothers sleeping with their babies in hospital say it makes for a better, not a worse, night's sleep all round:

> A mother is more likely to sleep soundly in hospital if she has her baby beside her, as she will be confident that if her own baby wakes, she will hear him. She is then less likely to be disturbed by the sound of other babies in the night.
>
> (*Successful Breastfeeding*)

London's Charing Cross Hospital allowed bedsharing when Dr Hugh Jolly was consultant paediatrician there. Dr Jolly warmly advocated keeping mother and baby together. But, as the Royal College of Midwives reports, bedsharing is more common in hospitals in developing countries than it is in the West:

> In the Nair Charitable Hospital in Bombay, for example, where bedding in is, and has been, common for many years, there have been no 'accidents' as a result of babies sharing their mothers' bed.
>
> (*Successful Breastfeeding*)

At a hospital in Chiang Mai, Thailand, researchers observed mothers and babies sleeping in standard hospital beds.[1] The infants, none of whom fell out in the night, occupied the well-worn hollow in the middle of the bed. Mothers slept to one side, with their arms around the babies.

If you are planning a home delivery, there is nothing easier than cuddling straight up in bed with your new-born child – and any other member of the family who wants to join in.

WILL MY CHILD REALLY BE SAFE IN THE BED?

Many people are frightened of smothering the baby. Their fear is unfounded. After a week or so, it will be obvious to you that you and your baby are well equipped to sleep through the night together, and that no harm is going to befall him while the two of you are healthy and acting sensibly. Dr Michel Odent writes in *Primal Health*:

> People warn [young mothers] that there is a risk of smothering the baby at night, but this simply does not happen, mothers always seem to be aware of their babies even while they are asleep.

Believe it, and you'll see how the rest fits into place.

I would always arrange the pillows so they could not fall on top of Frances in the night. Babies, of course, should not be allowed to sleep with their heads on a pillow before the age of one. After you have ensured that the pillows are straight, and that the baby cannot roll out of the bed, the only other precautions refer to the people sleeping together. Co-sleepers should observe a few important rules.

Never sleep with your baby if you or your partner are:

SMOKING
DRUNK OR DRUGGED
TOO ILL TO TAKES RESPONSIBLITY FOR YOUR BABY
VASTLY OVERWEIGHT
SLEEPING IN A WATER BED

Or if your baby is:

VERY ILL (Though constant human contact and feeding may be just what your baby needs. Seek professional advice on this.)
IN A SPLINT
SWADDLED (i.e. tightly bound in sheets or other clothing so that he cannot move.)

The reasons for these precautions are fairly obvious. A healthy adult body is attuned to the needs of a baby even while asleep, but this natural mechanism may not work if the mind is sedated, or if movement otherwise is impaired. Common sense will tell you what is appropriate.

WHAT SHOULD THE BABY WEAR?

A baby sleeping with his parents does not need to be wrapped up ready for an Arctic winter. In fact, there is no need for anything but a nappy to come between you and your child, because the benefits of skin-to-skin contact are all he needs for a cosy night's sleep. But I usually put Frances into a thin vest or baby suit as well, because she often kicks her end of the duvet off during the night. Also, the older she gets, the less body contact she seeks, so she spends the greater part of the night sleeping alone.

IS A BEDTIME ROUTINE IMPORTANT?

Consistency *is* important to a child: the consistency of being always with his mother or care-giver. His own patterns will evolve in whatever circumstances he finds himself, so long as she is there.

"Sleep with baby between you, it says"

Observe a child who has been allowed to find his own rhythm of sleeping and waking. His day will have its own regularity, though it may not conform to anything in the books. Frances would sleep every hour when she was first born, then every hour and a half, and so on. The distance between sleeps lengthened until she finally took only one sleep in the day. Watching her by the clock was of no value, as her sleep shifted according to the rhythm of her waking, not according to the hour.

People often ask me whether I put Frances to bed at night with a proper routine. The answer is that there is a definite pattern to her bedtimes, but not an imposed 'routine' as most sleep advisers understand the word. Every family is bound to have its own preference for the evening pattern, and the tea-bath-lullaby-lights-out sequence is not the only way of leading up to bedtime.

We make very few efforts to get Frances off to sleep. She has no need to fight sleep, because the aim is not to put her down as soon as she drops off. So she plays near us while we read, watch television, chat to friends, or eat out in a restaurant. Most often, she will come to either her father or to me when she is ready, and a quick walk in fresh air or a suckle at the breast sees her off. There is no fighting, crying or playing up.

Frances' average nodding-off time since she was three months old has been between 8 p.m. and 9 p.m. She wakes in the mornings some twelve hours later. Every child will need different amounts of sleep and will go through phases of taking more or less. But even if Frances slept only eight hours in a night, this would be oriented around our sleeping patterns. In other words, she tends to sleep when we sleep, and wake when we wake. Even in the summer, she sleeps through day-break, undisturbed by the light as long as I am nearby.

When Frances went off to sleep as a baby, we held her until it was our bedtime, too. Sometimes we took it in turns to hold her all evening. At other times, she rolled out of my arms and onto the settee, and I left her there by my side. Later, she went off to sleep in the big bed upstairs, and I came back down. But there are few domestic occasions when a sleeping baby is unwelcome, and background noise does not disturb her once she is off. If she does wake, it is often with a smile, and she goes back to sleep easily.

Our routine was not aimed at tucking a baby into bed upstairs. Every evening was open to change, and designed to suit the whole family.

In many countries, children may be observed playing on the beach or in the street at night, while their parents enjoy themselves in a taverna or bar near by. It is a practice the British often condemn, because it does not fit in with our traditional ideas of children being seen and not heard. However, while the child of India, the Mediterranean or the Middle East causes no trouble during the evening, the British infant can be both seen and heard invading his parents' privacy because he doesn't want to go to bed. Either that, or he rises a little before dawn every morning.

CAN WE GO OUT WITHOUT HIM?

Sometimes we go out without Frances, although I enjoy myself more when she's nearby. Friends appreciate our desire to bring her out with us. But if we have to leave Frances behind, it is always with someone she knows well, and who is happy to hold her.

As Jean Leidloff said, 'Babysitters, hired for an evening, can be asked to sit the baby, not just the television set. They can hold the baby on their laps as they watch the television or do their homework. The noise and light will not disturb or harm him, but being left alone will.'[2]

I started writing this book when Frances was seven months old, and she went to a child-minder for a couple of hours each week-day. This suited all of us very well, as the minder became her extended family, and I was able to exercise my brain a little. It would, of course, be preferable if the child could join the mother at her work – but seven-month-old babies are fairly incompatible with word processors.

All I required of my child-minder was that she should love babies and have time for them. Ours is a kind of proxy aunt, as all the real relatives live too far away to be involved. I have never left Frances for longer than she could go between breastfeeds, and she adores her brief morning outings to her friends down the road.

WON'T THE BABY IN THE BED RUIN OUR SEX LIFE?

Where there is desire, ways will be found for partners to make love, and desire is likely to be higher if you are both getting a good night's sleep.

New parents might like to act like young lovers again: finding places to rendezvous where the baby will not be disturbed. Inventiveness is important when there are toddlers around – especially if you feel like this harassed mother:

> It is very hard to have free, open, joyous, harmonious, adventurous sexual relations if they are interrupted invariably by the patter of tiny feet.
>
> (Quoted in *Sleeping Children*)

If you take your baby into bed from the beginning, then he'll grow into a toddler who can be safely tucked up in his own room without a murmur. A tiny infant needs instant care, an adult can wait a little while, knowing he is still loved. There will be plenty of times for making love, without disturbing you or your child.

WHAT DO I NEED TO KNOW ABOUT NIGHT-FEEDING?

Feeding and sleeping happen coincidentally for the mother who shares the bed with her baby. She will soon learn to feed on her back or side, and realize that there is no need to be particularly delicate as she shifts position in the night.

In the early weeks, I gave myself an extra pillow in the bed, not for my head, but to support my back as I fed Frances. We had a bouncy brass bed at the time, and I tended to roll away from her as I fed. Things improved vastly when we put the mattress on the floor.

The easiest position for me was the classic 'recovery' position, taught to all students of first aid. You simply lie on your side with your upper knee raised, so leaning in towards the baby. Your lower arm either goes under your pillow, or under the baby's head, and your upper arm is free to guide the breast, or to stroke the baby. Consult a breastfeeding book for the post-Caesarian feeding position.

Dr Penny Stanway told me that it was a good idea for the baby's head to be in the crook of the arm, as this made it very unlikely that he would choke on vomit – a potential cause of death in small infants. She also suggests an ingenious way of turning over in the night:

> ... it's easy if you leave your sleeping baby lying by the breast he was at last. When he next wants to be at the breast, roll over with him in your arms close to your chest so that he is lying by your other side by your full breast. Some mothers manage to feed their baby from the opposite breast by leaning towards him.
>
> (*Breast is Best*)

I found no problem leaning towards Frances to feed her as Dr Stanway describes. However, I do like to change position in the night, and I did prefer always to sleep facing Frances, not with my back to her (even though a time-lapse film made by Julian Aston showed that he and his wife rolled away from their three-month-old son in their sleep[3]). So I simply used to change sides, moving Frances along the bed as I did so. This woke neither her – nor me, as I learnt how to do it with my eyes closed.

Frequently, I have fed Frances lying on my back, she on her tummy, flopped across me and connected to one breast or the other. Fathers, too, often enjoy sleeping with a tiny baby across their chest.

The last thing I worried about at night was which breast Frances fed from. She suckled so extensively from each breast at all times, that there was no danger of becoming engorged. If, in the morning, I had the feeling that one side was heavier than the other, I merely offered it to her for breakfast.

I should add that it is completely normal for a baby to suckle on and off all night.[4] It is not an over-indulgence of the child to allow this. In fact, night feeding is essential to relieve the breast of heaviness and encourage long-term milk production (see Chapter 6). The baby takes instinctively all he needs.

Bottle-feeding mothers can make life as simple as possible for themselves by preparing any night-feeds beforehand. One of the aims of the exercise, after all, is to avoid having to wake up too much during the night. However, bottle feeding is likely to be more disruptive than breastfeeding, as the parent has to get out of bed to warm the feed. Mothers who have weaned their babies on to the bottle during the day may prefer to continue breastfeeding at night.

HOW CAN I DEMAND-FEED IF MY BABY IS DROWSY?

Many babies born under epidural spend their first days asleep in a hospital cot, scarcely waking to feed. Some babies are simply drowsier than others.

The benefit of night-feeding is that the sleepy baby maximizes his intake, by suckling through the night. He also stimulates milk production during the crucial night period, when the release of pro-lactin is greatest. So even if he does not take much during the day, he is creating demand for later on.

Many mothers complain of wakeful babies, but fewer see the dangers of an excessively sleepy infant. Night-feeding ensures that all babies, sleepy or not, get the optimum amount of nourishment.

WHAT IF THE BABY WAKES UP DURING THE NIGHT?

At first, your baby may wake up at all hours wanting to play. For a new-born baby this is to be expected, and the natural response should be warm, but minimal, if you want to encourage him to go back to sleep. Change the baby's nappy if that is what he needs, smile at him if he's smiling at you, and offer him the breast. I used to play with Frances in a quiet sort of way, because I was getting plenty of sleep during the day as well as at night, and I could not help responding to her. New babies are often at their happiest in the relaxed atmosphere of the bed.

Very soon, however, the baby gets the message that night-time is sleep-time, because that is what mother does. I would close my eyes to show Frances what was required. When I opened them again, she would be looking up at me, and would quickly close her eyes, as if I hadn't seen her. This game delighted both of us for a few minutes until eventually we both fell asleep.

Now, Frances only cries in the night if she has a pain. This happened just once in her first twelve months, and we had to call the doctor after she had cried for ten minutes or so. I knew she was suffering, because there was simply no other reason for her to cry. She does not worry us with false alarms.

WHERE SHOULD MY BABY TAKE HIS AFTERNOON NAP?

At first, I needed almost as much sleep as Frances did, feeling quite exhausted from the birth. I would take my sleep when she did, in the big bed alongside her. Apart from that, Frances did a lot of her daytime sleeping in the sling.

The sling I bought was, unfortunately, not really designed for new-borns, so I found it extremely difficult to get on with my normal life as my hands were tied up. I have since discovered the excellent Wilkinet Baby Carrier, which is suitable for all sizes of baby, and available by mail order.[5]

It is a good idea to get a baby used to the sling as early as possible, because it involves a particularly tight closeness of adult and baby, which youngsters may struggle against if it's introduced later on.

Other cultures have a variety of sling arrangements that range from tying the baby to the back (Turkey), to the hip slings of the Wodaabe (central Africa), the swag straps made of pounded bark of Maori mothers (New Zealand), and the traditional Welsh shawl, which young women learn how to tie from their grandmothers. The people of South Wales have a special phrase for snuggling close to a baby: 'cutching up'. There's nothing to stop a mother experimenting for herself with an old sheet and a few safety pins.

As a baby gets older, he may more easily be left to sleep by himself for a while, with the mother close at hand. When he wakes, the first thing he sees is her face, welcoming him back into the world. He does not need to scream for her attention, causing her to drop everything and come running. During the day, Frances sleeps wherever I am: in the bedroom, the lounge or the car.

WHAT HAPPENS WHEN A SECOND BABY COMES ALONG?

This is very often the natural time for the older child to graduate to his own bed. If he has had his fill of your company at night, he will not be jealous of the new arrival. But if – quite reasonably – your child protests at the usurping of his place in the big bed, then space may have to be made for him, too. This may be a chance for the first child to sleep alongside dad, or another partner, while mother is breastfeeding. Every family comes to their own arrangement.

If your first child has always slept alongside you, there should be no problem about sleeping as a family foursome. What, however, do you do if you want to take a toddler into bed for the first time?

IS IT TOO LATE TO TAKE A TODDLER INTO BED?

If you decide to sleep with an older baby, you take on a different set of challenges. The baby who sleeps with his parents from birth knows no other way and will not fight against the experience. The child who is used to solitary nights may not always take kindly to enforced company in the bed. He may struggle and whine at first.

The only answer is to persevere. At only a few months old, the child's experience tells him that his parents do not always want him around, so he suspects their motives when they suddenly do. 'What are they trying to trick me into this time?' He will have an emotional reaction to the physical change.

Of course, the earlier the habits change, the easier it is. Many parents do not have the patience to put this into practice. Jean Liedloff reports on parents Anthea and Brian, who decided to share a bed with their four-year-old son, Trevor:

For the first few nights none of them had much sleep. Trevor would wiggle and whine. There were toes up noses, elbows in ears. Glasses of water were called for at ungodly hours. Once Trevor jockeyed himself into position perpendicular, instead of parallel, to his parents, resulting in their clinging to the edges of the mattress on either side. More than once Brian stomped off to his office in the morning red-eyed and irritable. But they persevered, unlike others who would say to me, after three or four night trials, 'It doesn't work; we couldn't sleep,' and give up.

After three months, Anthea reported, there were no more disturbances; all three slept blissfully through the nights. And not only did the relationships of Anthea with Trevor and Brian with Trevor improve markedly, but so did Anthea's and Brian's. 'And,' she said at the end of her report, mentioning the topic for the first time, 'Trevor stopped being aggressive at school!'

Trevor moved back into his own bed some months later of his own accord, having had his fill of what would have been infant sleeping experience. His new sister was, of course, in their parents' bed too, and even after he had moved on Trevor knew he was welcome there whenever he felt the need.

(*The Continuum Concept*)

While some parents may choose willingly to take their toddlers into bed, others find themselves bullied into bedsharing. When a three-year-old refuses to sleep any other way, this is often the first time parents really question the practice of keeping the child out. They are unable to deal cold heartedly with a frightened youngster.

Despite the efforts of modern sleep advisers, there are still thousands of two-year-olds in the West who refuse to sleep alone at bedtime, or who wake in the night, begging to be with their parents. The parents are encouraged to believe that their sleepless children are either difficult or abnormal, but this is not so.[4] They are merely in tune with children the world over, who need food and the comfort of another human being at night.

Any child up to the age of three or four will benefit from a few months in the parents' bed.

To coerce a toddler into sleeping with you, patience may be required. Put him in your bed to sleep, and lie by his side. Neither withdraw, nor offer excessive affection, but let him take the lead. Reading books together in the big bed can be a great treat. Let him go to bed later than usual, if necessary, so you can all fall asleep together.

IS THERE ANY HARM IN SLEEPING WITH THE BABY OCCASIONALLY, RATHER THAN EVERY NIGHT?

Although many British children do sleep with their parents at night, theirs is a part-time arrangement – a reaction to sickness, crying or sleeping problems. Their parents only take them into bed when they (the children) are upset or ill.

One drawback with this method is that you are sleeping with the child at his worst. A baby screaming in pain is a poor companion. After a sleepless night calming a crying child, parents conclude that they have given co-sleeping a fair test, and it is not for them.

It is important to be consistent with the child. Ideally, a baby should sleep with his parents right through from the beginning, not just when he is ill or when he is naughty. Otherwise he will be ill or naughty in order to achieve the end result.

This is contrary to the advice of Dr Christopher Green, author of *Toddler Taming*, who suggests that illness is the *only* excuse for taking a child into bed during the night:

> A sick child on the other hand, has a rightful place in his parents' bed, although it is sometimes hard to evict him once his health has returned to normal. And all children are entitled to that enjoyable, early morning romp in their parents' bed – just as long as the cock has crowed and the tea has been made!

I am not suggesting that parents who bar the bed to their children continue the ban when the baby is sick. But they should be aware that in allowing sickness to be a ticket to their company at night, they are making an emotional statement about illness that will stay with the child. At the very least, he will grow up expecting extra emotional support when he is ill. He may even fabricate illness in order to receive that support.

Until the age of six, I used to have a nightmare almost every night, and trot along to my parents' bed to sleep with them. The nightmares were my passport to the big bed, and of course they ceased once my parents were sleeping by my side. But I remember the nightly fear of going to sleep by myself.

According to most authorities, nightmares are a 'normal' part of child development. Two paediatricians state:

> Nightmares occur almost universally in children from three to six years of age.
>
> (Snead and Bruch, *Pediatrics*, 1983)

But many parents whose children sleep with them say that the frequency and impact of nightmares are greatly reduced. Desmond Morris, for instance, tells me his son Jason does not suffer from nightmares, or any other sleep disturbance. Jason slept next to his parents until he chose to move out of their bedroom. Nightmares could be yet another product of the child's fear and lack of self-confidence when he is forced to sleep alone.

Maternal separation has been linked to bed-wetting problems in older children.[6] Sleepwalking and night terrors[7] may also be connected with children's unspoken fears. The more security we offer our infants, the less likely they are to associate bedtime with trauma.

ARE THERE ANY PREPARATIONS TO MAKE FOR TRAVELLING AWAY FROM HOME?

A child who sleeps with his parents at home can sleep with his parents anywhere. Strange surroundings do not prevent him dozing off, because his parents are not strange, and they are the most important constant in his life.

Travelling in a plane, boat or car is easy when your baby goes to sleep in your arms. The only difficulty I ever had, was reconciling the need for safety with the child's need for freedom in a car. Once she was mobile, Frances did not always enjoy being strapped into her safety seat, and I don't blame her. She wanted to be off, exploring. I limited the number of journeys we made on our own in the car, choosing whenever possible to take the bus, or to hold her in the back while someone else did the driving.

A note on breastfeeding in hot climates: the baby needs no supplements of water or juice if he is being breastfed. On holiday with Frances at ten weeks old, I was told I should be giving her water to stop her dehydrating in the heat. In fact, all that was needed was for me to drink more water, not the baby.

On British holidays, the problem is more likely to be hypothermia than dehydration. This is the traditional wisdom: 'However cold you find the weather,' writes Kim Sullivan in *Mother* magazine (February 1988), 'remember that your baby will become colder even quicker than you when you go out of doors because you're moving around and she can't.' Ms Sullivan lists the necessary accessories for keeping a baby warm: thick blankets, hot water bottles, natural fibres, cardigan, jacket and hat, mittens, bootees and a shawl. Then put the pram hood up to keep the cold out.

On the other hand, you could put the baby on a sling, and wrap him up in your own coat and arms. A baby can and should move around as much as possible – next to your body, not on a set of four wheels.

WHAT IF IT'S SIX IN THE BED?
Parents with two or more children may find themselves sharing bedspace with the whole brood once in a while. It is likely that even the oldest child will occasionally require the extra comfort of his parents at night – especially if the baby is still in with them.

Sometimes one parent finds it all too much and skulks off to sleep elsewhere. Others thoroughly enjoy the pell-mell of the family bed – so long as it is big enough to house everyone. It's the way thousands of families used to sleep in the days before central heating. Some call it 'spooning'.

The only practical advice here is to make sure that everyone has enough space to sleep in. One solution might be to put all the beds in one room, so that older children are near their parents, but not on top of them. Another simple suggestion is to allow all the children to sleep in one bed in their own room. Mothers have told me that brothers and sisters who sleep together are closer, and tend to row less, than the average siblings.

WHAT IF MY PARTNER DOESN'T LIKE THE IDEA?
Amazing, but true: a mothers' group in Manchester discussing the pros and cons of bringing baby into bed agreed that they couldn't

because their husbands wouldn't like the idea. At least, they had the idea that their husbands wouldn't like the idea.

If this is indeed the case, and not just a polite way of passing the buck, then it implies that the average man would rather risk years of disturbed nights than cuddle up with his children. Perhaps it is a matter of sexual roles: men feeling endangered by the threat to their machoism, and women reinforcing that image, with statements like this:

> Many husbands would be very unhappy at the idea of a third member of the family in the marital bed and if it is going to cause any friction then it is obviously not worth it.
>
> (Jane Asher, *Silent Nights*)

Of course, it is not only the men who object. The La Leche League recite a story of cross-cultural conflict in their book on breastfeeding . . .

> In the Zavari household, husband Hassan was born in the Middle East, where a baby sleeping with his parents is a natural part of life. Joan Zavari tells of her reaction to some of the ideas:
> 'When Hassan suggested breastfeeding, I didn't hesitate. Natural childbirth was even considered and agreed upon. However, being of a conservative nature, I had put my foot down when he suggested putting two beds together and sleeping family style. How would I make the beds? I found lots of excuses. When Stevie was born, I soon found out that some babies wake up five or six times in the night. Hassan didn't even say "I told you so," when I suggested putting the two beds together.'
>
> (*The Art of Breastfeeding*)

In my experience, if a mother really wants something for her child, no power on earth will prevent her from providing it. So if your partner, male or female, doesn't like the idea of bedsharing and you do, let them at least try it. It's refreshing to be woken up by a ten-month-old baby planting a kiss on your nose. Ask my husband.

DOES THE FATHER HAVE A SPECIAL ROLE TO PLAY?

I have often referred to maternal rather than paternal care, but this is for clarity rather than from any notion that only mothers can do the job. Sometimes it is impossible for the mother to feed and care for her child. Some fathers choose to look after the children while the mother goes to work.

As far as we know, the major drawback with paternal care is that dad cannot breastfeed. It may also be that the mother's biorhythms are important for her baby, in helping him to breathe regularly and develop into a healthy, well-adjusted child.[8] It is the mother who carried him in the womb, and she who may be best able to provide the sensory stimulation he needs after birth.

However, sleeping with the baby could give a new emphasis to paternal care. Some parents choose to bottle-feed their babies so that dad can get a look in. Fathers often enjoy the closeness that feeding involves.

But if a baby sleeps with you in the bed, dad gets all the closeness he wants in a full eight-hour stint. What's more, nobody has to be disturbed for the night-feeds. No one has to do shifts on the landing, warm bottles or prepare feeds.

Fathers will be able to bond with their babies as nature had intended them to – as they sleep. Even if dad is away all day, he need not become a distant figure, appearing only at bath-times and weekends.

Many mothers told me how much their partners enjoyed having the baby in the bed. Soon after the birth of her daughter, one friend wrote to say: 'She's sleeping well in our bed – half the night on Serge's chest and the rest snuggled up to me.'

It's a new way to share the care.

WHAT IF I'M AT WORK ALL DAY?

The mother who works may have problems getting to know her baby. One mother I interviewed confessed:

> You do feel you have to prove yourself. It's as though you should be performing all the time, in spite of the fact that you have children and all the extra duties they bring ... You're juggling three things, your job, your children and your home, and something has to go.

> (*She* magazine, August 1988)

It's much easier to be Supermum if you're doing part of your mothering in the night.

The mother who cannot be with her baby during the day has greater need to be near him when she gets home. Otherwise, the only physical contact she gets is the brief encounter between tea and lights-out. Why take on the hassles of routine, when you could be enjoying more cuddles? And all those peaceful nights' sleep are perfect preparation for another day's work.

SHOULD SINGLE PARENTS SLEEP WITH THEIR CHILDREN?

Many lonely mothers, whether alone because their husband is away on business or because of a marriage break-up, subtly encourage their children to come to bed with them each night as company. It is then difficult, when life returns to normal, to persuade the child to discontinue the practice.

(Toddler Taming)

Dr Green implies that using someone for company is a negative and underhand practice. I don't see why. People *are* company, and they love to be used as such. He also takes the rather narrow view that a lone mother is an abnormal occurrence, making no mention of lonely fathers, and rejects the way in which the parent 'subtly' lures the child into bed.

There are many thousands of single-parent families in civilized society, whether permanently or temporarily so, and each has its own reasons for living in this way. Many single parents choose to be single, and do not therefore sleep with their babies because of loneliness.

It is true that following divorce, death or separation, the adult is likely to be as much in need of company as the child. Holding someone at night is one way of expressing deep emotional need. Touch is a valuable means of communication to both adult and child. It should not be despised.

Film-maker Julian Aston told me he slept with his son after his first marriage ended in divorce. 'I used to say to him, "Why don't you sleep on your own?" He would say "You want company as much as I do," which I did.'

The single parent is not a selfish creature, using the child at a moment of crisis, and discarding him as soon as there is someone else to cling to. To many parents, single or not, the suggestion of hurriedly pushing the child out of bed when a partner comes along is incredible.

The needs of the new partner and the needs of the child have to be weighed up. Why should anybody be left out of the equation?

If a parent does accept a new partner into the family bed, then initially there might be a negative reaction from the child (although even this is unlikely if the baby is secure enough). But look at it another way: sleeping with your step-mother or step-father is a quick way to get to know and accept them. It is, for instance, a superb way of cementing the bond between an adoptive parent and a young child.

One mother, Judith Joseph from Glasgow, slept not only with her own daughter Lisa, but also with thirty foster children over a period of fifteen years. 'A lot of the babies come to me with sleep problems,' she said, 'especially when there have been difficulties at home. I don't breastfeed them, but they love the physical contact. As soon as they feel the warmth of your body, it sends them to sleep. I always try it. Their sleep problems usually go away.'

CAN I SLEEP WITH MY HANDICAPPED CHILD?

The handicapped baby has special needs, which may make sleeping with his parents an even more important part of his daily care. A blind or deaf baby will need increased parental contact at all times, not just at night. A baby with a disability will have a need to experience more of the world for himself, in order to participate in it. Andrina McCormack writes:

> Because of neonatal problems, illness, or prematurity, many handicapped children do not begin to get to know their parents until they are days, weeks or even months old. Therefore the natural mechanisms for establishing a bond are disturbed, and have to be closely and intensively worked on. Parents of very quiet passive babies may be tempted to leave the baby even when he or she is awake because they are relieved to have time to themselves. Parents of very grumpy babies may be only too glad to have a respite from the tension and stress that constant crying can engender. However, good parent-child bonding is essential for emotional health later on, and parents of handicapped children should recognise that they have to work a bit harder than others on this.
>
> (*Coping with your Handicapped Child*)

Intensive bonding goes on at night as well as during the day. It is also a more relaxing time for the disabled child, when he does not have to cope with all the physical obstacles of daily living.

The disabled child may be more obviously needy than the able-bodied child, but we should treat all our children with special care.

Down's Syndrome children may reap great benefits from bodily contact at night, since they have poor control of their body temperature. These children sleep restlessly, often kicking off bedclothes and quickly becoming cold. Chest and throat infections frequently result. One way of solving this problem would be to sleep with your Down's Syndrome baby, thus providing a human thermostat for the infant. But parents should beware – there will be plenty of contrary advice:

> The practice of bedsharing is almost certainly not a good idea with these children. The habit of being in bed with a parent, not to mention the attraction of the warmth they enjoy compared to the cold when they leave it, can be very difficult to break. The director of the UK National Centre for Down's Syndrome told me of a 30-year-old man who was still sleeping with his brother and step-sister.
>
> (*Sleepless Children*)

The disabled parent, like the child, may derive great satisfaction from cuddling up to a baby during the night. It certainly makes feeding the baby much easier. But sleeping with the baby may be impossible for someone with severe physical handicap. Every situation will be different, and people should be encouraged to find their own practical solutions to our universal needs.

WHEN CAN WE EXPECT THE CHILD TO LEAVE THE BED?

Eventually, it's time for the child to move on. He may be ten months or ten years old, and the sooner you start treating him as he wants and needs to be treated, the sooner it will all be over. You may be longing for the moment, or dreading it – but ideally, it should be just another, normal phase in the pattern of growing up. You should not attempt to push the child into it too hurriedly, or hinder him from going.

Two years old is about the age when children are independent enough to sleep alone, if they started early in their parents' bed. Some toddlers join their parents for a few months, and then proclaim they have had enough.

One parent asked me 'What earthly reason has the child for wanting to leave the bed?' In primitive societies, the child sees other children move away from their parents, and he knows that this is the natural thing to do. In our families, the first child has no example to follow, and therefore may cling to the parental bed for longer.

I do not see any harm in creating a positive choice for the child to move out of the bed. When Frances was exactly a year old, we gave her her own mattress by the side of ours, and from the first night, she moved between us and her new terrain. Such a mattress can be moved slowly away from the main bed, until it represents the child's own sleeping place.

Some parents redecorate the child's nursery, and indicate that moving in there is a step towards growing up. Little friends may come to stay the night, to help initiate the new room.

The way to know if a child needs comfort, is to allow him to come to you. Similarly, he will indicate when he wants to move away by doing so. Parents should not offer more comfort than is required, nor reject any reasonable appeal. They then can be sure of supplying a child's needs, and not his whims. As the psychologists put it:

If the infant has had parents on whom he can depend, he has experienced the inevitable frustrations in gradual small doses. He develops a feeling of social trust which he demonstrates by the ease of his feeding, the depth of his sleep, the relaxation of his bowels, and by his being interested and appearing happy and comfortable during the greater part of his waking hours.

(English and Pearson, *Emotional Problems of Living*)

Whatever way you choose to handle the weaning process, be aware that any attempt to hasten it unduly may end in conflict, or in the child returning to the bed for longer. The move towards independence needs to come from the child, or it will not be genuine. Independence is something we can only take for ourselves.

No one is in the running for the title of Perfect Parent. There are too many factors at play in our stress-ridden, polluted, competitive world for us to set up Utopia at home. But we can try.

11 | YES, BUT....

When we first told people that we slept with our baby, they gave us that look. The 'good-grief-I-knew-she-was-mad-but-don't-say-anything' look. Our strange nocturnal behaviour caused more whispering among friends and acquaintances than anything we had done before. Wear a wig, be convicted of insider dealing, but don't take your baby into bed – not if you prefer the quiet life.

I have been challenged with just about every objection our cot-bound society could come up with, so here is a list of the strongest – with some brief responses. Many of the topics are tackled at greater length elsewhere in the book, but you may be glad of some quick-fire ammunition to keep great-aunts and health visitors at bay....

● I couldn't possibly sleep with my baby, I'd be far too afraid of smothering her in the night.

(A mother)

Julian Aston, film-maker, took a camera into his bedroom, to film himself and his wife sleeping alongside Luke, their three-month-old baby boy. 'What is showed very dramatically,' said Julian, 'was that the parents rolled about all over the place and didn't touch the baby.'

Anyone who sleeps with a smaller creature will discover the same phenomenon. Fears of squashing or smothering the baby are completely unfounded. There is far more real danger in leaving a baby to sleep on his own, than there is in staying with him through the night. The mother is his lifeline and protector, and nature did not design him to survive without her. Any fears she feels in this respect are fostered by social practice, and pressures to conform.

● When the older baby gets used to attention every time he cries a little, he will soon come to want and demand it. Being rocked

back to sleep, taken downstairs or into your bed can all become
habits; bad because the baby's sleep is constantly interrupted and
because you can never relax. The odd occasion can do no harm,
but remember that it is easier to prevent a habit forming than to
break it later on.

(*The Bounty Baby Book*, (23rd edition, revised), 1987)

Forming habits – what a dreadful thought. Why do professionals get
so worked up about some childhood practices and not others? We
put our babies in nappies, knowing they'll be toilet-trained by the
time they're thirty-five. Yet babies who are given the security of being
rocked to sleep, or the welcome of the parents' bed, will, we are told,
be forever dependent. Please don't love them too much or they'll
come to expect it.

Sometimes it's not the baby who is accused of bad habits, but the
mother herself. Michel Odent says critics use this argument merely
as a way of defending the rules about feeding and routine that were
doled out in the first half of this century:

> Mothers of previous generations like to respect what they
> themselves were taught. What they call 'bad habits' are in fact
> normal and natural ways of meeting a baby's fundamental needs.
> Being accused of 'bad habits' is something which can frighten
> young mothers who would like to listen to their instincts.
>
> (*Primal Health*)

Let's indulge our instincts, while we can still hear them prompting
us.

- All this talk of not separating mother and baby has worried me
  more than ever. I'm frightened to put my baby down.

  (A mother)

The more evidence we discover that shows how much a new-born
baby needs its mother, the more disturbed we should feel about
modern mothering practices. Either we decide we are going to do
something about the situation, or we do not. There is no point using
this or any other book as fuel for your neurosis.

Sleep with your baby, if you feel up to it. The baby knows what he is doing, and maybe some of his natural confidence will rub off on you.

- You can't be with your baby 24 hours a day. Baby Link can. The Electronic Baby Link Nursery monitor lets you get on with your life while your baby's asleep, because it's so sensitive, you can even hear your baby breathing ... The Electronic Baby Link Nursery Monitor from Tomy. It's as good as being with your baby 24 hours a day.

(Advertisement)

Yes you can, and no it isn't. A mother and baby are programmed to be together twenty-four hours – as they put it – a day. Humans are a 'carrying' species – not a 'cache' species, like birds or reptiles, which put their babies in nests and leave them there while they forage for food.

Primitive humans, like apes and certain other mammals, traditionally carried their young as they worked. For at least three million years, women slept with, and carried, their babies. With the aid of a sling, the modern mother can do the same. No machine yet invented can simulate the physical contact of her body or the comfort of her constant presence. All an invention can do is to act as a warning device to assure already nervous parents that their offspring has not stopped breathing.

- This led many timid parents, in avoiding overwhelming their children with the demands of habit-training, to the opposite extreme of inviting the baby to tyrannize over the family with a whim of iron. This submissive and frightened version of self-conscious parenthood ('permissiveness') was reinforced by misunderstandings of other findings as well. Many, without comprehending the inter-relationships among all the ways of behaving which make up a culture, advocated the adoption of child-rearing practices of one or another primitive society.

(*Childhood and Adolescence*)

The examples of primitive culture quoted in this book are not models of perfection for Westerners to adopt. But the study of other peoples can lead us to a greater understanding of human nature, and give us ideas for change.

If, for instance, many children in all parts of the world suffered from sleep difficulties, in the same way that they all have finger-nails, we might conclude that such problems were physiologically normal. But a brief look at other societies shows us that some are more harmonious and less aggressive than our own, and that their children do not suffer in the way ours do.

We can usefully take a practice such as co-sleeping and adapt it to our own way of life without compromising our own culture, or the history that got us here. In the words of Frances Moore Lappé, author of *Diet for a Small Planet*, we should be looking for 'lessons, not models.'[1] Lessons we can learn from other people, and not from model societies that we can copy for good or ill.

• You give in to Frances on everything, don't you?

(An aunt)

To an outsider it can often appear that Frances gets her own way in all things. This is because there is no apparent conflict between herself and us.

If she does not want to do something relatively unimportant (sit in a high chair, eat certain foods) we do not force her. We do not pose our will against hers, as there is no conceivable advantage in negative training. Discipline is being applied nevertheless.

The first rule of socializing is example – we expect her to behave as we do, and she usually does. If she behaves in an unacceptable way, we distract her, and explain to her that such and such a thing is not done.

We do not withdraw affection, or punish her, but neither do we give in. If I say 'no' I say it once only, always with an explanation, and I make it impossible for the activity to continue (e.g. remove her from the television where she has been playing with the controls, and interest her in a book). I do not give her the chance to be naughty, which is only another way of saying that the child breaks rules.

Some see this as harsh, others as permissive. But if I want Frances to learn anything, it is this: while her actions may not always be acceptable, she always is.

• Many philosophers extol the virtues and joys of a family sleeping together in one giant, bed-bound commune. Although this may be a terrifically enjoyable state of affairs for those who are deep sleepers or lucky enough not to have children who behave all night like soccer stars at a goal-mouth, the vast majority of parents I see wish their bed to be a private, peaceful place. They greatly resent those little intruders making an appearance in the wee hours of the morning.

(Dr Christopher Green, *Toddler Taming*)

Dr Green is describing children who are normally not allowed in the big bed. In such a world, babies are often seen as intruders into the otherwise private and peaceful lives of their parents. But that does not mean that bedsharing parents are philosophers who get their kicks out of being kicked in the shins by a two-year-old in pyjamas.

The toddler who began life sleeping with his parents need never play this cat-and-mouse game of imprisonment and escape from his nursery. Always welcome wherever his parents may be, he chooses. instead to find his own space, first in the big bed, and later in his own room.

If, for whatever reason, he chooses to return to the parents' bed, he climbs in, already versed in night-time etiquette. Everyone else is sleeping, and he soon does, too. The child who rarely or never sleeps with his parents cannot be expected to behave in the same way. Perseverence is the only cure for his wriggling and squirming.

Parents who want to evict toddlers from their bed may wish to follow Dr Green's advice on that subject. He advocates trying this technique: 1. Put him straight back in his own bed; 2. Warn him; 3. Smack him and 'immobilise' various doors. You may, like an old-fashioned employer, wish to cut out the second stage, the doctor suggests. 'Most parents feel that this degree of civility is quite unwarranted at that time of night ... in which case, it's a sharp smack on the bottom and back to bed.'

Dr Green admits that he spent many years smacking, immobilizing doors and dodging his own children's efforts to be with him at night. I'm not surprised.

- Apart from these rare situations [illness and Sunday mornings], I believe that children should be excluded from their parents' bed at all other times. Peace and privacy are important to people, and that includes parents.

(*Toddler Taming*)

Peace and privacy are, believe it or not, important to children, too. But one vital quality of privacy is that we take it when we choose, otherwise it's called loneliness.

In making ourselves always available to our children, we enable them to find their own independence, to move towards solitary activities when they are ready for them, and to amuse themselves for reasonable periods of time. If we are always pushing the children away, they will return, clinging, for many years to come. As new parents, it is possible to make our children a welcome part of our private world – otherwise, we should ask, why have them?

Often, it is only a question of attitude that determines whether a mother sees her baby's demands as a chore or as a delight. In the words of American doctor, Gregory White: 'If a lazy, self-indulgent, old man like me can get out in the middle of the night to help people he hardly knows, certainly a mother can do this for her own child.'[2]

- Cosleeping, the practice of parents and children sleeping together, was routine in our own culture until the 20th century ... Concerns about potential ill effects are thoughtfully described by several prominent pediatricians and child psychotherapists and include the following: (1) cosleeping may interfere with a child's independence, (2) sleeping with parents may become a habit that is difficult to break or even an 'addiction', (3) children who sleep with parents may be more likely to witness sexual intercourse, a frightening experience for some, (4) the intimate body contact involved in cosleeping may be overstimulating to children, (5) cosleeping may reflect disturbances in the mother-child relationship or in the parents' relations with each other, and (6) children who sleep with parents may develop more sleep problems.

(Lozoff, Wolf and Davis, *Pediatrics*, August 1984)

Many of these objections are made by scientists who worked on the premise that co-sleeping with children was undesirable. Their conclusions are coloured by this belief. To answer them point by point:

(1) The more security you offer your baby, the more secure he will be. Co-sleeping can only enhance the child's eventual independence.
(2) Normal, healthy children will not become addicted to the parents' bed unless this is the only good thing in their lives. Their natural

inclination is to grow up and move away. (3) Children who sleep
with their parents are far less likely to be frightened by sexual
intercourse than children who sleep alone and stumble unexpectedly
on an interlude of love-making in the night. (4) Intimate body contact
enables the child to explore human touch in an uninhibited, non-
sexual way, and to grow up feeling at ease with his own body. (5)
Yes, some Westerners may take their children to bed as a shield for
their own problems. This does not invalidate the benefits of doing
so. (6) Children who sleep with their parents are likely to iron out
any sleep problems they may otherwise have had – unless, of course,
you count co-sleeping as a problem in itself.

- We know for a fact that people sleep better alone in bed. Studies
  have shown that the movements and arousals of one person during
  the night stimulate others in the same bed to have more frequent
  wakings and sleep-state changes, so they do not sleep as well.

  (Richard Ferber, *Solve Your Child's Sleep Problems*)

The assumption of many professionals is that the deeper and less
interrupted the sleep, the better. But as we can observe from primitive
cultures, disturbances need not ruin sleep. (Think of the Tauripan
people who wake in the night, enjoy a joke and then snooze off
again.[3]) The healthiest sleeper is the one who drifts lightly in and out
of the state, not bothering when he is woken up, and able to close
his eyes and sleep again at will.

Deep slumber is valued in our society, because we have lost the art
of flexible sleeping. When we are woken in the night, we are unable
to fall asleep again. We go to sleep with difficulty and we wake up
unrefreshed.

Factors such as diet, exercise and fresh air can play a large part in
relieving these symptoms. But we would all sleep more easily at night
if we slept alongside others from birth. Then we would learn to wake
and doze, to sleep and react at the same time. We would not be 'dead
to the world' when we dropped off, nor would we resent the inevitable
night-time intrusions that bother us all from time to time.

- I'm a very light sleeper. I couldn't take my baby into bed, because
  I would not get a whole night's rest.

  (A mother)

Light sleepers and heavy sleepers are both likely to find life easier with the baby *in* the bed. The light sleeper is often disturbed in the night by the sounds of the baby snuffling – is he awake, or isn't he? Is that the baby crying, or the wind in the trees? With the baby next to her, the mother knows he is all right, can react instantly to his needs, and go back to sleep with minimal disturbance. By the end of a few weeks, the baby is fast alseep for much of the night anyway, and the mother finds herself quite used to his presence in bed. Breastfeeding mothers are programmed to sleep lightly, to meet their baby's demands, and breastfeeding itself sends them dozing off again.

The heavy sleeper wakes up to find her tiny baby screaming in the night, because no one answered his initial whimpers five minutes earlier. With the baby sleeping by her side, the heavy sleeper will answer those cries more readily, before they become distressed.

- We're all different. Surely you don't think sleeping with the baby is going to suit every family in every situation?

  (A health visitor)

If tackled with the right attitude, when the baby is new-born, I see no reason why co-sleeping shouldn't work for every family. After all, before there were separate beds and bedrooms, our ancestors simply had no choice, and would not have questioned the practice. But generations of separate sleeping have passed, and many of us have lost the art of light and easy sleep. Most of us rapidly become accustomed to someone else in our bed – otherwise we would have difficulty forming adult relationships.

If you simply don't want to try, then fair enough, but let's not discourage those who decide to manage without the cot.

- Sleeping with my baby surely isn't going to solve all my baby's problems just like that. . . .

  (A mother)

There are many man-made factors that influence our babies' world, and we cannot control all of them – pollution, radiation and stress, poverty, diet and a sedentary lifestyle all take their toll. Under the threat of acid rain and nuclear fall-out, even the primitive Indian will live differently today from the way he did one hundred years ago.

But this should not stop us from giving our children the best possible start in life – and trying to improve things for the hassled mother at the same time. We can, for instance, encourage mother and baby to eat a wholefood diet. We can attempt to reduce stress, and take regular exercise. We can foster an environment where mothers may follow their own instincts.

One mother, Maggie, told me a story which illustrates how pressurized most women are when dealing with their children in a social situation. She was on holiday in France with her five-week-old baby, who was breastfeeding almost constantly. The friends she was staying with had read all the advice books, and every time the French mother fed her baby, dad was there watching the clock. They were trying to wean their four-month-old infant off the breast.

One day, the father went out and the two mothers spent the whole day together. Without saying anything, Maggie noticed that her friend took up her baby far more often to suckle, and did not wait until he cried before feeding him, as she had done before. Her manner became more relaxed, and the women were able to enjoy a day of uninterrupted mothering. The baby was far more contented.

The French mother's instincts were emerging, because no one was there to pressurize her, or to make her conform to the 'rules'.

I believe no mother would dream of putting her baby down to sleep on his own if authorities had not told her otherwise. Being left to sleep alone is not the only problem a new baby faces in the modern world, but it is one casualty of natural mothering that everybody assumes is normal. If mothers could see through this practice, they would be one more step along the way to restoring the power of parenting to their own hands.

- This is all very well, but what if I want my bed to myself, for whatever reason, after the infancy stage? Surely it's better not to start something you can't finish?

(A mother)

Give it a chance. Some mothers may feel frightened at the idea of a baby sleeping in the bed right through toddlerhood. They should be more frightened of the long-term effects of clinginess or shyness, of nightmares and irrational fears. But if a child must be weaned out of the bed forcefully, then so be it. Better to have a few months of good nurture, than to separate mother and child in the crucial first few weeks.

- By taking the baby into bed, aren't you smothering it with affection? Won't the baby be spoiled by all this extra attention, and isn't this just an attempt to keep him a baby for longer?

(A mother)

I neither want to keep Frances a baby, nor to encourage her to grow up. She sleeps with us because that is what she needs. I do not give her 'extra' attention. In fact, when she falls over and cries, we wait for her to come to us before we pick her up. We try never to do for her what she can do for herself.

Frances comes to us for all the love she needs, we offer her no more, no less. Spoiling comes with things you do when a baby is awake, not when he is curled up at night in your arms.

- Quite often, babies have become used to falling asleep only at the breast. They have thus no opportunity to be alone in their cot, half-awake, half-asleep, savouring the memory of a feed, and digesting the emotional experience along with the acutely physical nourishment. Emotional growth comes from digesting such an experience and, with this, the ability to start managing on one's own.

(Dilys Daws, *Journal of Child Psychotherapy*, 1985)

- Sleeping alone is an important part of his learning to be able to separate from you without anxiety and to see himself as an independent individual. This process is important to his early psychological development.

(Ferber, *Solve Your Child's Sleep Problems*)

- It is important that the baby is put down awake, then he has the opportunity of learning to settle himself.

(Dick and Pritchard, *Pampers First Years of Life*, 1988)

If a baby *needed* to be alone, he would not have been created such a helpless little creature. Talk of digestion and sweet dreams sounds delightful, but a baby knows nothing of this, when he is abandoned to lie in his cot. Staring through the bars or up at a dancing mobile, he only knows that his mother is not with him. Some babies voice the wrongness of the situation by crying, others resign themselves rapidly to hours in solitary. But none escape the inevitable psychological effects of being put to one side every night.

Learning to separate is, of course, crucial to the forming human ego, but this needs to come from a position of strength. The child will move away when he is ready, unless he is ill or disabled. Even then, the impetus is there, it might just require a little longer.

- It is a harsh life out there. All this mollycoddling won't prepare our children to face reality.

(A father)

The stronger our base position, the better we cope with what life throws at us. By allowing the child to claim independence when he is ready for it, and to take responsibility for himself, he will not keep making U-turns to his parents to get him out of trouble. He will have a greater self-awareness and self-confidence. Strength comes from within, not from the situations into which you are forced.

- Another reaction to be taken into account is the jealousy of the siblings. It may be hard enough to take the arrival of a new baby without discovering him in the parents' bed and some tactful transferring early in the morning may be necessary to avoid discovery. Alternatively be prepared for an invasion by the other child or children and to eventually all sleeping together in a true 'family bed'.

(Jane Asher, *Silent Nights*)

Identified first by Freud, sibling rivalry is one of the great topics of the twentieth century. It is considered normal for an older child to develop feelings of jealousy about the arrival of a new baby. But as Jean Liedloff says, 'Freud had no undeprived people in his acquaintance':

If he had had the opportunity to know the Yequana, he would have found that the idea of competing and winning, as an end in itself, is quite unknown to them. It cannot therefore be considered an intrinsic part of the human personality. When a baby has had all he needs of experience in his mother's arms and parts with her of his own free will, it makes him able to welcome with no difficulty the advent of a new baby in the place he has voluntarily left.

(The Continuum Concept)

The suggestion that a baby should be transferred to a cot to avoid offending his older brother or sister is ludicrous. Of course the infant is going to need more physical contact than the older child. Should we not breastfeed second babies, in case we upset number one? Far healthier for the toddler to witness his parents giving cuddles and intimacy to other people than only to himself. Why not accept the bigger children into bed in the morning, and encourage them all to sleep in their own bed at night when they're old enough?

● My two-year-old is far too naughty to deal with in this way. He doesn't listen to a word I say, and if I took him into our bed, he would just fight and keep us all awake.

(A father)

The 'naughty' toddler is an older version of the crying baby. He has learnt that breaking the rules gets him attention and the kind of involvement he requires from his mother. Tantrums and repeated bad behaviour are distress signals. He is getting too much interference from his care-givers, and not enough of what he really needs. The child does not understand this intellectually, but he does know how to protest.

If we expect our babies to misbehave, then they will. If we say, 'You'll get a smack if you climb up there,' then in all likelihood, the adventuring child will test our thesis to the full. He is not being given the chance to explore his world for himself. Instead, by disobeying, he has the promise of perverse satisfaction from a confrontation with his parents.

To welcome him into your bed would be a surprise to him. He is being treated like a sociable being – this is his chance to act like one. He may fight at first, but given a little patience and a wide berth, he should calm down in a matter of weeks.

● ... it seems that problems encountered in sleep in child rearing would perhaps be best solved by bedsharing. However in the present climate of interest in incest in this country it seems ludicrous to mention it.

(Kathryn Conder, *Midwife, HV and Community Nurse*, April 1988)

This objection was quoted earlier in chapter eight (Not in Front of the Children), and needs answering. Studies have shown that lack of touch in infancy relates to an increase in violence among adults. Sexual frustrations also mount up in people who do not know the joy and release of innocent touching.

Touch your children. Give them all the cuddles they crave. Teach them not to be frightened or guilty, or hung-up about their bodies. Do not drive their needs underground. It is the touch-deprived child who is most likely to be the tormented adult, unable to distinguish between proper and improper levels of intimacy. The child who gets his fill of human contact throughout his growing years will not abuse his own children.

We urgently need to feed our ancient hunger for physical contact. Otherwise, our children will grow up to associate sensuality merely with sex, and child abuse will become even more widespread than it is today.

- There can be few mothers who have not at some time felt the urge to lash out at their children, despite the intense love they may feel for them at other times.

    (Brigid McConville, *Mad to be a Mother*)

The media offer many warnings about baby blues and maternal ambivalence. I fully expected to have mixed feelings about my baby, and to reach that 'breaking point' that many mothers had warned me about. But of all the emotions I felt for Frances, the urge to lash out was not one of them. Along with many women in other cultures, I found I simply had no negative feelings towards my baby. I can only put this down to the effect her constant presence had on me.

One study reported that sixty-eight per cent of children with sleep problems were likely to get into bed with their parents for part of the night.[5] Researchers commented that 'the mothers of children with sleep problems could best be characterized as ambivalent, i.e. positive toward their babies but expressing resentment or hurt as well.' They concluded that taking the baby into bed was valuable for the ambivalent mother:

Sleeping with parents may occur in reaction to the child's sleep problem and/or to the mother's awareness of her partial emotional withdrawal from the child. Such bed-sharing may be one avenue via which an ambivalent, stressed mother expresses both her positive feelings towards her child and her own needfulness.

(Lozoff, Wolf and Davis, *Pediatrics*, March 1985)

If you have someone always in your arms, it is very difficult to hit them, or even to feel like it. Following my baby's interests turned out to be in my interest too.

12 | A MODEST PROPOSAL

I received my training as a Nursery Nurse more than 30 years ago and during that time I came into possession of a pamphlet entitled 'The Baby Who Does Not Conform to Rules'. I treasured it because there were many days when I felt that the author and myself were the only people who shared the belief that young children should be treated with respect, flexibility and love. This was especially so when I had the misfortune to work in a residential home where cleanliness, tidiness and the direction in which the cot wheels were facing was of paramount importance.

(Chloe Fisher, *Oxford Medical School Gazette*, 1982)

The management of mothering is entering a new phase at the end of the twentieth century. Professionals are better equipped than ever to bring accuracy and efficiency to their work. Incubators and drips, monitors and scales combine with new operational techniques to save babies' lives and to measure their progress. There have been many genuine advances in understanding in the past twenty years.

For the mother at home, convenience baby foods and disposable nappies make looking after baby a more civilized occupation. But somehow, her job does not seem to be getting any easier. Rather than becoming more confident, the mother is losing control. From the moment she books in at the antenatal clinic, she becomes a part of the Western mothering machine. By the time she takes her new baby home to care for him, her first impressions of motherhood may be very bleak.

Seeing the same woman pushing a pram down the street two months later, she is completely overwhelmed by the 'correct' way to look after her child. She will be counting the feeds, checking off his weight against a chart, and dreading the next meal because his bite is so painful to her cracked nipples. She envies everyone she sees around her, because they probably had a good night's sleep in the last fortnight. She is wondering whether to get pregnant again at the end of the year, to get it over with – or is one enough?

It may be another eighteen months before the woman realizes that her baby really wants to sleep with her at night. Even then, she probably will not let him – or if she does, it will be a guilty encounter at midnight: 'Oh all right, get in with us.' She wants to be a good mother, but she does not know how.

Two stories – one from Thailand and one from London – illustrate the extent of the growing powerlessness of mothers in the West.

Mike Woolridge, a lactation physiologist at the Department of Child Health, University of Bristol, went to northern Thailand to study the effects of breastfeeding management on new mothers. The routine policy at Suan Dok Hospital in Chaing Mai was based on American practices of fifteen years earlier. Babies were taken away from their mothers immediately after birth and not returned to them for between twenty-four and thirty-six hours.

The reasoning given for this policy was that the mothers were often in a poor state of health on arrival at the hospital. But when the mothers were finally allowed to have their babies, no rules were enforced:

> . . . demand feeding was universally practised, and once babies
> were returned to their mothers they remained with them, in their
> mother's bed, at all times, both day and night.
>
> (Woolridge et al., *Early Human Development*, 1985)

West meets East. Although the American doctors approached the arrival of the new-born with clinical caution, the Thai mothers knew what their infants really needed. As soon as they were allowed to sleep with their babies, they did so.

Antenatal care has since improved in Thailand, and mothers are healthier, but the hospital has not changed its rules on separation. Mothers at the Suan Dok and many other hospitals around the world are not allowed to see their babies for a day or more after the birth.

In July 1988, a consultant obstetrician, Pauline Bousquet, was suspended from the St Bartholomew's group of hospitals in London for refusing to use routine intervention in childbirth. Although Ms Bousquet was prepared to use drugs to induce labour, and to allow continuous fetal monitoring, she preferred to save these interventions for risky cases, rather than to prescribe them routinely. A letter to the district management describing Ms Bousquet's conduct said:

> ... there are no allegations of negligence, rather the reverse, of devoted care which is archaic and inept.
>
> (*The Sunday Times*, 10 July 1988)

Devoted care is out of date. Bring in 'the machine that goes "ping!" '.[1] It is ironic that in these days of high technology, a new mother is fobbed off with a list of rules that date back to the Victorians, from whom we have received our current taboos about co-sleeping. Not one good argument for the cot has emerged in a hundred years.

Now is the time to revise our outlook. We know what babies need, and we know how to provide it. All the professionals have to do is stand back and let the mothers get on with it. It is crucial that doctors and nurses, while making the best use of the machinery at their disposal, do not put more faith in the hardware than in the woman before them – otherwise there will be a chain of authority with a computer read-out at the top, and babies at the bottom.

Every child is different, but his needs are universal. All he wants is the nurture of a mother – and given in sufficient quantity, at an early enough age, he will grow up with security, and with responsibility for himself. This is the only prescription a doctor need give to a new mother and baby.

This is my modest proposal: hospitals should give courage to a new mother, by allowing her to sleep with her baby from the first night. Maternity ward beds should be low and large, rather than tall and narrow. Fathers should be welcome at all times, and even allowed to stay in hospital when there is space. Premature babies should be carried by their mothers as soon as they can survive out of the incubator.

Mothering classes should be designed to promote maternal confidence. Advice should be given only when it is sought. Mothers should be able to practise carrying and tying slings. Fashion magazines should write features on how cool it is to carry your baby on your hip. Research scientists should explore the value of co-sleeping, rather than enter the debate of which way up a baby should lie.

At clinics, less emphasis should be placed on a baby's weight gain in the early weeks, and more on the mother-baby relationship. Mothers should be encouraged to meet and talk without professionals on hand. Breastfeeding mothers should buy baggy jumpers and feed their babies anywhere.

If a baby has to go into hospital, a guardian should stay with him at all times. If this is not possible, he should be assigned a personal nurse to hold him and care for him. No institution should allow a baby to cry in a cot on his own.

If a mother wants to sleep with her baby at night, then no one should stop her. Taking her baby into bed may not solve all a mother's problems, but it may be the one thing that makes sense to her at the end of the day. At night, it is all her baby needs.

We are not the first society to separate mother and baby from the moment of birth. We are not the first to make our children unwelcome in our beds at night. We will not be the first to change our minds.

APPENDIX | BETWEEN YOU AND ME

One of the things that struck me when I interviewed parents, was that few of them knew what others were doing. Most were surprised to discover that thousands of families in Britain take their babies into bed, whether on a permanent or as an occasional basis. One study[1] reported that only eighteen per cent of parents who slept with their babies admitted the fact to their doctors. It's about time we had a coming-out party.

So here are the experiences of some parents who have slept with their babies, or who are sleeping with them right now. There are as many variations of method as there are families, and a few famous names are on the list.

I also include accounts of two women's different approaches to breastfeeding, which have implications for maternal separation and night-feeding. Let's begin with those:

JOY HENDERSON of Dumfries wrote this letter to *The Independent* (2 August 1988) in response to an article by Isabella Walker about the difficulties of breastfeeding. Many readers wrote in with advice on preparing the nipples for the onslaught of the infant gums. Joy concentrated on the relationship between mother and baby, and how desperately they needed to be together, alone:

> ... breastfeeding is instinctive, and can be easy and pleasurable. What makes it difficult and even impossible for many mothers is the well-meant but destructive help and advice of medical professionals.
> I have had considerable experience of breastfeeding, having fed each of my three children in this way until their first birthdays, and I learnt a lot during this time from my own experience and from watching other mothers. I feel that the most important

factor in the difficulties mothers experience with breastfeeding is that they are emotionally very vulnerable in those vital few weeks after the birth of their baby. At this point, in sweep busy overworked nurses, midwives and doctors whose main purpose is to get one mother ticked off their list and on to the next.

I'm sure Isabella Walker has experienced as I did the student nurse, who has never had a baby herself, who grabs the baby's head in one hand, the mother's nipple in the other (this alone was an embarrassing and tension-producing invasion of privacy for me) and tries to bring the two together by brute force, in the manner of fixing a shower attachment to a tap. After two days of this humiliating and fruitless procedure six or seven times a day, it's small wonder that so many mothers give up....

Small wonder that at this already difficult time of hormonal upheaval and bewildering new experiences, women are coerced into a state of child-like dependence and lose all confidence in their own ability to cope.

All it needs then is for the paternalistic forces of the medical profession to pronounce that breastfeeding is difficult and complex and has to be learned, the exact angle between baby and breast must be achieved, mothers must record on paper the precise length of time spent by the baby on each 'side'. I wonder how our forebears managed without these pieces of paper and this carefully researched 'knowledge'.

What is really required for successful breastfeeding is peace, relaxation, a mother's confidence in her ability to satisfy her own child, and protection from advice and interference...

None of the traditional and more modern lore about angles, the correct way to hold the baby, how much of the nipple to get in his mouth, is helpful – it only serves to add to the feeling that this is a difficult thing to get right. With my first baby I religiously, for the first few weeks, pressed the breast away from the baby's nose as advised by my midwife and Penelope Leach, for fear the baby would suffocate. Finally, after a few nights of falling asleep with the baby suckling in bed beside me, and a little private experimentation, I discovered that this was unnecessary. The nature of breast tissue and the shape of the baby's nose ensure that there is always a little space for air; and even if this were not the case, it is well-known that a baby who cannot breathe will stop feeding to take a breath through his mouth. This little procedure is simply another device for complicating the mother's life and making her feel guilty and inadequate if she doesn't follow the rules.

ANGELA MORRISON, from Bristol, did her own experimenting at night, though this involved keeping the baby *out* of the bed. She followed the advice of Mabel Liddiard, whose counsel in the 1920s caused many British women to deny nightly feeds to their infants. Angela's article details the hours of crying a baby has to go through before he learns his needs will not be met. Harry was eventually educated to 'sleep through':

I have always been interested in childbirth, and somewhere along the years I acquired *The Mothercraft Manual*. When I became pregnant with Harry at 33, and with a good deal of experience with other people's babies, I turned to this book to see what Mabel Liddiard, the author, had to say about breastfeeding. The first edition of her book was published in 1923, in a climate where most working-class women bottle-fed so that they could return to work – often after only 10 days' laying-in. Her method was to instil regular feeding to enable these mothers to breastfeed without giving up their livelihood. The regime she encouraged was five four-hourly feeds a day, with an eight-hour gap during the night. In this way, the baby and the mother (and the father) have a good rest so that the baby's digestion can have a break and the mother's milk has a chance to build up again. This sounded eminently sensible to me, and I decided to try it.

I was given a good start by having a short, straightforward home delivery, a baby who was not eager to suckle, and the confidence (stubbornness!) to do my own thing. I had noticed that most families went through nights on end of baby crying when they tried to drop the night feed, so I thought: 'Why not have it now, with a tiny baby who does not know what he is missing, rather than a strong-willed one later on?' I settled on aiming for my long gap between midnight and 8am, because this suited our usual late bedtime. As soon as my milk came in, I moved Harry into his own room and fed him at four-hourly intervals during the day. He has always been woken for the midnight feed and bedded down soon after 12.30. For the first seven weeks we would wake again around 5am about four nights out of five. I went through a whole range of techniques to cope when he cried, but I never fed him before 7am. Mostly he could be rocked to sleep, and for the last couple of weeks before he started sleeping through he just needed turning to lie on his tummy, but there were a couple of nights when he cried for an hour in my arms, and a couple when I left him to cry himself to sleep.

If it sounds cruel, I can only say that it has been worth it. He is now six months old, and rarely wakes before 9am. He sucks his thumb for comfort, and beds down with ease. He is still fully breastfed, five feeds a day, three to four hours apart. We all appreciate our uninterrupted nights, and I have not had any problems with engorged breasts or lack of milk.

Zoologist and anthropologist DESMOND MORRIS looked beyond human example when deciding his own parenting methods twenty years ago. He observed the sleeping habits of chimpanzees and gorillas, and felt inspired to borrow their practice of keeping in touch with their offspring at night. The Morrises did not take their son, Jason, into the parental bed, but kept him in a cot by the side of them for an extended period. One or other parent would dangle an arm out of the bed during the night, for touch-comfort. It was Jason who finally made the decision to sleep in his own room, with no pleadings from his parents:

Gorillas and chimps are nomadic. They don't reoccupy the same beds – this has to do with hygiene. At the end of the day, they take a scoop of grass or straw and make a sort of nest to lie on, chimps in trees and gorillas on the ground. I noticed that the babies shared the mother's bed for the early part of their lives. At a certain point when they grow older, they will make their own bed a little way from the mother. It's the infant that makes the decision to do this. It gives the young a sense of security.

One of the things I noticed in human families, is that toddlers don't like going to bed in their own room. They object rather strongly to being isolated in this way. I started to ask basic questions about our practice of separating children at night. This was probably never done in a million years of early human nest building.

Babies during the very early stage do seem to benefit from being within reaching distance of the mother. Instead of having to cry its heart out in the next room, the baby can be comforted by a hand reaching out. It's the initial contact and intimacy that's important.

Jason made the decision to leave our room himself. I can't remember how long he slept with us. Much, much longer than the typical family arrangement.

He's 17 now, and he has never to my knowledge had any of the sleeping problems that so many children have. He is capable of sleeping everywhere – which I have witnessed, as he has travelled round the world twice with me. I have never seen him show any sense of what I would call nocturnal anxieties, or any irrational fears of the dark or place of sleep. He has no nightmares.

It's at a later stage that children are frightened of sleeping alone. I wonder to what extent this is caused by premature separation at bedtime. This might be one of the causes in later life of bad dreams, insomnia and fear of the dark.

It worries me that we always seem to know better than the child. It's like the ritual of slapping a baby to make it breathe – these things are enshrined in medical practice. If left, a baby will breathe by itself, thank you very much. What we are doing is rushing the child to the next stage, even from the moment of birth.

Child psychotherapist JANINE STERNBERG from London discovered bedsharing with her third child, Sarah. She fed all her babies in bed, but realized that the transfer to the cot afterwards was likely to wake them up. I talked to Janine when her new baby was only a few weeks old:

I slept with Sarah on her first night. Luckily she was born early after lunch, and I had a six-hour discharge from the hospital. We came home at six in the evening, and that was lovely, because Mike came in with the older children, and we all came home together. I got straight into bed with Sarah next to me.

I had this excuse, if you want, which was that the swinging crib which we'd had for the other children was broken by Daniel, who's five, while I was in hospital having Sarah. Although the cot got tied up with string, I said, 'Oh no, far too dangerous to put my baby in there.' It wasn't true – I didn't want to put her in there, and that was that!

In the night, she doesn't wake up very much. I don't want her to, this is the aim of the exercise. I can hear her snuffling and turning rather than crying. If she's clearly being restless, I plug her in and she can be back to sleep again in ten minutes. Quite often in the night she'll only take one breast. She doesn't seem to want both sides.

I could be wrong in physical terms, but it seems to me that she can't co-ordinate herself enough to get to the breast and help herself yet. But she can fall asleep, and if I'm in the right position I can go back to sleep that way too.

I wouldn't want to isolate the effects of sleeping with your baby from all other factors. After all, I suppose you could sleep with your baby at night, but neglect it during the day. Although I expect that's unlikely. It's a way of responding to your baby's emotional needs quickly.

If the baby gets enough of what he needs when he needs it, he won't look for it later on. If you don't supply those needs, he won't have the strength to go on exploring. It's from a firm base that individuality comes.

The child may grow up to like lots of cuddles. But nobody objects to that.

Childcare expert MIRIAM STOPPARD says in her *Baby Care Book* that she is in favour of bedsharing. However, like many other Western parents raised on strict ideas of bedtime etiquette, she would try many strategies before finally taking her children into bed. This meant that she and her husband Tom went through years of cot-side vigils trying to coax their babies to sleep.

I'm very sympathetic to parents with sleepless children having had two myself, one of whom was sick if he wasn't reached within a minute or two of starting to cry. I would like to give the parents of such children a hopeful message. Neither my husband nor I enjoyed an unbroken night's sleep for six years and on many days we were almost too tired to drag ourselves around; but we got through it and we've forgotten the dawn vigils. . . .

We decided to do anything to ensure a full night's sleep, at least now and then. I had never believed that taking the baby into our bed could do him or us any harm. . . .

We gave the child fifteen minutes to settle to any of our

strategies, then we tried taking him into our bed – a sure fire success.

Tears before bedtime were an everyday occurrence in the Manchester household of WENDY GOODWIN and family. Her story shows the struggle many parents have in 'training' their babies to sleep sociable hours. Wendy eventually became national co-ordinator of CRY-SIS, the support network for families with crying babies. This account of her own 'sleepless' children was given at the 1988 CRY-SIS conference, which took infant sleeping problems as its theme:

When Lucy was born $7\frac{1}{2}$ years ago, things got off to a very bad start. She was a difficult breech delivery, screamed constantly from day one and slept only for half-hour snatches.

Things got gradually worse until, at six weeks, we were finally told that she had colic. More bad news – there was nothing much we could do about it, and that it would last until she was about three months old. Lucy cried for 18 out of any 24 hours for the next two months, and still only slept for very short periods.

My husband and myself took it in turns to stay up all night – it was the only way we could get any sleep. We both felt dreadful – guilty, upset, let-down, alone, unhappy and exhausted.

Lucy's colic subsided when she was four months old and from then we tried desperately to get into some sort of normal waking and sleeping routine. But Lucy did not know the difference between day and night. All life had revolved around her screaming for four long months and she still demanded a lot of attention. The only way she slept for any length of time was in bed next to us.

It took two long years finally to get her to sleep all night in her own bed ... By the time Lucy was sleeping normally I was expecting baby number two. It had been a huge decision to have another baby – as I'm sure you'll understand. But I was determined that this time things would go according to plan.

Pregnancy and birth went extremely well and Stuart was a beautiful, healthy-looking baby. He did scream the labour ward down when 20 minutes old, but after that he was very quiet, and was the perfect new-born baby.

At two weeks, he developed evening colic. We spent four hours each night pacing the floor with him. Instead of getting gradually better, as Lucy had, he got slowly worse. I spent the next 12 months trying to find some cause of his disturbance, cutting out cows' milk, additives, colourings, eggs etc., with little result.

Stuart eventually peaked at 18 months when he whinged most of the day and cried most of the night. By this time I had tried every trick in the book. I had asked for advice at the doctor's and clinic, but was never treated seriously. I asked friends whose children slept like logs, but there was no clue why their kids slept and mine didn't.

One really bad night, I broke down and sobbed my heart out at the injustice of it all. I felt very sorry for myself – how could this happen to me twice? I was a useless mother; I shouldn't have bothered with another baby. . . .

My husband ushered me into Stuart's bed and put Stuart into bed with him. He fell asleep immediately and I slept undisturbed for the rest of the night.

And so it continues. Stuart is now three and a half and still gets up each night. But at least now he only gets up once, gets into our bed and goes back to sleep. I get out and get into his – musical beds, I think it's called. I have tried from time to time to break the waking habit, but each time it has ended in tears and frustration. I have now decided that I didn't have children to fight constantly with them – and it seemed like a fight to me.

We are quite happy with the way things are now. At least everyone gets a good – if a little disturbed – night's sleep.

A prominent London journalist tells of the importance he attaches to having slept alongside his daughter when she was young. He has asked for his name to be withheld.

In the case of our first daughter, I think I was a helpful father. I was involved, and did things with the baby, but with our second daughter I played a much greater part. For one thing, I was present at the birth of our second girl, and that involved me right from the beginning.

There was just 18 months between the two girls, and my wife was very tired and rather poorly, and suffered from postnatal depression because of this. So I found myself taking over the care of the younger baby to some extent, winding her and looking after her when she cried. I was at work during the day, but I helped particularly at night, so my wife could sleep and wasn't disturbed.

I would sit over the cot and put my finger in the baby's mouth. She would fall asleep like that, but sure enough in an hour's time she would wake up again. I would be falling asleep over the cot! So I found the best way of coping with this was to take the baby into bed with me.

The baby was warmer, I could cuddle her, and often she could go through to the morning that way. From when she was really quite tiny, almost the time when she was born, I took her into bed. At the beginning I was worried about rolling over on top of her, but I found that if I put my arms round her to cuddle her, that didn't happen.

After a while, she used to call out to me in the middle of the night from her cot. It wasn't really a distressed cry, just a 'come on and get me, then,' and I would wake up and go to the cot. I didn't bother to fiddle around, I would just pick her up and put her straight in our bed.

You could say we had a system going. And then when she reached the age of one and could walk, I thought 'I'm going to train her to come to us. If she wants me, she can come and get me.' So I put the side of the cot down, and when she called me the next night, I called 'Darling, come along here!' She stopped crying, all went quiet, and pad, pad, pad along the corridor she came. It worked the very first time I tried it.

My wife and I had two separate duvets on our double bed. By now my daughter was not hungry in the night, so she would tend to come to me rather than her mother. And that pattern was established until she was round about ten or eleven.

I didn't mind her coming in to us at all. It didn't bother me. This was before we had heard so much about sex abuse, and it was all innocent cuddles. She naturally wanted to stop that when she reached puberty. My daughter is 16 now, and she is very relaxed about her body, and has a happy, steady relationship with a boy. I wish I had been that relaxed at her age.

Her sister never came into bed with us, except in the morning when we were all cuddling and shouting together. My relationship with the two girls is completely different. My wife and I were divorced, and neither she nor my elder daughter have spoken to me for two years. But I still have a very strong bond with my younger daughter, although she has been under a great deal of pressure to have nothing to do with me.

In fact, my relationship with my younger daughter couldn't be better, and it has survived this great challenge of the divorce and break-up of the family. I'm only sorry I didn't have the same relationship with the older one. Now I realise why I'm so much closer to my younger daughter. It would have been better to have treated them both in the same way.

WENDY ROSE-NEIL became Family Writer at *Woman's Realm* in 1988, and her first letter to mothers was about her own experience of bedsharing. Wendy is a founder member of The Parent Network, a national family support group.

Like most parents, I found bringing up two small children great fun and completely exhausting. I don't think I ever worked so hard in my life as I did when my daughters were under five. And, like about one third of all families, we had sleep problems with our first baby. Part of it was due to the fact that she had colic during the first two months and she spent much of her time screaming, while I felt more and more like a complete failure.

So peaceful nights were out of the question – she refused to sleep in her cot and we grew bleary-eyed walking her around the house in the small hours, trying to get her somehow – anyhow – to fall asleep. Then one day, being incapable of sitting up with her any more, I took her into bed that night. She finished feeding and then blissfully, magically fell asleep snuggled up close to me, and we heard not a sound until the next morning.

After that we never looked back. Since then, I've been an advocate of bedsharing with babies and small children for sleeping problems, although some parents swear that taking a restless child into bed is a recipe for a disastrous night. Some parents worry they'll injure or suffocate their youngster in bed. In fact, unless you're drugged or drunk this is almost impossible – although of course, pillows should be kept away from tiny babies.

And before too long, most children do grow out of wanting to sleep in their parents' bed. Parents who want privacy find that taking their children to bed for feeding or for comfort, and then putting them back in their own bed, is a useful compromise.

So if your baby or toddler has been keeping you awake at night, you could do worse than to try this method. It might work wonders!

Actress and author JANE ASHER recommends co-sleeping in her book *Silent Nights*. But she concludes that long-term bedsharing may not be appropriate in our society, 'where one is expected to keep going for most of the day.' However busy the modern mother may be, I cannot imagine she keeps going any more than a Malawi mother who pounds maize for hours at a time, with a baby strapped to her back, before sleeping at night with her brood on a mat on the floor. The answer lies not in putting baby back in his cot, but in learning to relax and sleep through the feeds.

... we expect a great deal of a new born baby when we banish him to a separate, silent room all on his own after he has spent nine months in the warmth and security of his mother's womb ... It's a lovely feeling to have a warm snuggly baby next to you in bed to cuddle....

There are of course some disadvantages to having the baby in bed with you. Theoretically he should space out his feeds naturally so that after a few months he is only waking once or twice in the night [this is in fact what Frances did at around eight months], but I found with Alexander this didn't really happen. He slept in bed with us from birth, as I found it much more trouble to keep getting out of bed to feed him, and also of course it had the enormous advantage that instead of the sometimes impossible business of getting him back to sleep after a feed by rocking, singing, patting and so on, he would just drift off peacefully next to me, with no effort on my part at all. For the first few months it worked very well, and I got much more sleep than I had with Katie who had slept in a cradle.

Alexander was a large baby who needed to feed very often but as he got bigger he did indeed start to sleep longer between feeds. Then however he started gradually to return to the frequent feeds, and eventually couldn't sleep at all unless constantly at the breast. This I began to find very tiring and when I did decide to move him to his own bed it was a long and difficult process ...

I have no doubt that having the baby next to you is the natural way and that frequent small feeds are as nature intended but in our society where one is expected to keep going for most of the day then obviously a certain amount of uninterrupted sleep at night is essential. As with so many aspects of baby care the success of sharing the bed depends on the temperaments of both mother, father and baby and must remain an individual decision.

DR DAVID HASLAM explores many ways of solving infant sleep problems in his book *Sleepless Children*, but states that he 'received more letters quoting bedsharing as a success story than any other solution.' This was his own experience:

When it came to bedtime the books were wrong too. Katy woke every single night until she was two years old, with only one glorious exception. When she wouldn't settle at bedtime and screamed, it became pointless to leave her there as the books suggested. A healthy child can scream for an incredibly long time....

On occasions when she woke in the night and we were both exhausted we would take her into our bed. She usually slept wonderfully, but her wriggling kept my wife awake and so was a less than perfect answer. In fact, the solitary occasion when she slept right through the night without waking was when we spent a night camping in Scotland when she was seven months old. It was bitterly cold, but she had a warm sleeping suit and did not move all night. It was so unusual that Barbara and I lay awake wondering what was wrong. Had she died? Was she still breathing? Whatever had happened?

Eventually she woke happy and bright at 8 o'clock. For a long time I assumed it was the clean Scottish air, or the novelty of camping. Could it have been the closeness to her parents that our tiny tent made inevitable?

MAGGIE STRATFORD and her partner Serge, from Leeds, are unusual, in that they decided to sleep with their baby as a matter of principle. The inspiration for this came not from primates, but from accounts of primitive cultures, in particular the Yequana tribe of Venezuela. Maia Rosa had a difficult birth, but Maggie managed to keep her baby near her from the beginning:

Before the birth I was determined to sleep with my baby in hospital, but after 24 hours of labour I was exhausted and worried that this, together with the various drips I'd been given, would affect the natural alertness I knew I would otherwise have towards my baby should she wake. So I spent the first few hours of that night staring at her in her little hospital cot, holding her hand and unable to sleep with her at all.

As soon as she woke, however, in the middle of the night, I whisked her into bed with me and fed her – and couldn't put her back again! It just felt so right for us to be snuggled up together. The night staff didn't seem to notice, or assumed I was feeding her and so said nothing. As I'd arranged to leave hospital the next day I avoided what I thought might be the inevitable battle with the nursing staff.

For a few weeks our sleeping arrangements followed a pattern. When we took her to bed with us, Maia slept on my Serge's chest until she woke to be fed, then spent the rest of the night in the crook of my arm, where she could easily feed if and when she wanted to. Now at nine weeks, and having doubled her birthweight of 5lb 12oz, Maia is too heavy to sleep on us, so snuggles down either between us or on my side of the bed.

Though she does wake once or twice during the night to be fed, I wake up as soon as she does, and she has never woken up crying. Her need for food is met immediately.

I'd recommend it to anyone: a) you *won't* squash your baby; b) your baby won't have to wait to be fed, so won't cry and feeding is calm; c) you won't spend anxious moments listening out for your baby crying in another room, or rushing in every few minutes to check she's still breathing; d) most important of all – it's enjoyable, and it feels *right*.

NOTES

PREFACE

1 'One-star rating only for Dr Hugh Jolly, late Consultant Paediatrician at Charing Cross Hospital, who has now gone out of fashion, and whose Book of Child Care displays a robust common sense now decried by modern authorities. His one note of eccentricity is his passion for the family bed ...' Jane Ellison, 'Mums brought to book', *The Guardian*, 27 October 1988.

CHAPTER 1

1 Benjamin Spock and Michael B. Rothenberg, *Dr Spock's Baby and Child Care*.

2 Quoted in *Woman's Realm*, 2 April 1988.

3 Bob Mullen, *Are Mothers Really Necessary?*

4 Ronald V. Snead and William M. Bruch, *Pediatrics*, 1983.

CHAPTER 2

1 'In the actual clinical work I undertake myself I see families where there is a feeling of not being able to manage a particular state of a baby's or small child's development. The most pressing of these are ofen presented as sleeping problems.' Dilys Daws, *Journal of Child Psychotherapy*, 1985.

2 '... reduced sleep is not as harmful as is commonly believed ... Unfortunately, however, a lifetime's upbringing that one needs eight hours' sleep a night is difficult to combat, especially since popular magazines, information supplied to the medical profession by pharmaceutical companies and many doctors actively promote this belief.' Jim Horne, *The Practitioner*, October 1985.

3 *ibid*.

4 Jim Horne, 'Quality Matters', *The Guardian*, 5 April 1988.

5 '... the clinical picture of the normative development of infant sleep behaviour is derived from studies of infants sleeping alone in sleep laboratories.' James McKenna, *Medical Anthropology*, 1986.

CHAPTER 3

1 *Letters to a Mother on the Management of Herself and Her Children in Health and Disease ... with Remarks upon Chloroform* (new edn), Longman, London, 1848.

2 'Smiles Bull and Combe all agreed [that the mother's bosom was the baby's natural pillow] – the new baby had a low body temperature and could not generate much heat itself. After six or eight weeks, it might be

moved to a cot or cradle. Chavasse originally left the baby on its "natural pillow" until it was weaned at nine months; but he changed his mind. The seventh edition of *Advice to Mothers* altered that nine to "a few", and a lengthy warning of the dangers of suffocating was added. "Careless, heavy-sleeping girls" were partly to blame – as were mothers who allowed the baby to suckle while they slept.' Christina Hardyment, *Dream Babies*.

3 'All we desire to prove is that a child *can* be brought up as well on a spoonfed dietary as the best example to be found of those reared on the breast; having more strength, indeed, from the more nutritious food on which it lives.' Mrs Isabella Beeton, *Household Management*, 1861.

4 Christina Hardyment, *Dream Babies*.

5 See chapter 4, p. 64.

6 *Toddler Taming*.

7 The Kangaroo Mother Studies are described by James McKenna: '... this method applies only to preterm infants who no longer require life-saving technology and involves the infant's being strapped to its mother's chest under her blouse. Using this human incubator method, mother and infant stay together 24 hours a day and, according to one description, this procedure has led to decreases in mortality, morbidity, and parental abandonment.' *Medical Anthropology*, 1986.

CHAPTER 4

1 Ref. 'Anxiety States, A Preliminary Report on the Value of Connective Tissue Massage', *Psychosomatic Research*, vol. 27 no. 2.

2 'A 10-year study of 150 middle-aged men, reported in the *Journal of the American Medical Association*, has revealed that heart attack risk was higher for men with irregularly beating hearts and also for those who were socially isolated ... Dr Orth-Gomer believes that it may be linked to other hormonal and biochemical activity in the body, and that lonely people are not stimulated to produce certain substances which keep the cardiovascular system functioning.' 'Why socialising is good for you', *The Independent*, 12 July 1988.

3 Kattwinkel, 1977, cited by James McKenna, *Medical Anthropology*, 1986.

4 McGinty, 1984, quoted by James McKenna.

5 'What is certain is the REM stage is essential. If for some reason – say, the use of sleeping tablets – the amount of REM sleep is reduced, when the tablets are stopped there will be a compensatory increase of REM sleep for a while. Experimental work which has deprived people – volunteers, naturally – of certain phases of sleep shows that if the sufferer is deprived of stage 4 sleep only, he will tend to be lethargic and run down the next day, but if the REM sleep is lost then more complex skills such as learning and memory will be interfered with.' Dr David Haslam, *Sleepless Children*.

6 'McKenna's study monitored the breathing patterns of both parent and child, first in separate rooms, then in the same room, and then finally in the same bed. Preliminary evidence from the first mother and baby tested shows that the baby's breathing rhythms followed the mother's. This closeness may serve to remind the baby to breathe.' *Genesis*, June/July 1985.

7 'That both prenatal and postnatal vestibular stimuli may help develop the infant's motor skills has been documented. Masi (1979) found that the vestibular stimulation of preterm infants improved their sensorimotor functioning relative to those of unstimulated controls.' James McKenna, *Medical Anthropology*, 1986.

8 '... it is well known that ventilation depends on environmental (ambient) and body temperature (Lahiri and Delaney 1975); in fact, temperature is also one of the most important external modulators of sleep, especially REM sleep (McGinty 1984).' James McKenna.

9 Foundation for the Study of Infant Deaths newsletter 30, projects 53 and 66, August 1986.

10 'Studies conducted in the labs of Hofer, Reite, and Levine ... most especially, have shown that in order to understand the form and consequences of separation (primarily mother from infant) for the infant, we must know how the infant's body changes physiologically after separation and, thus, how through contact the mother physiologically regulates her infant's temperature, metabolic rate, hormone levels, antibody titer, sleep cycle, heart rate, and respiration so as to promote her infant's health and survival.' James McKenna.

11 T. F. Anders, *Pediatrics*, vol. 63, pp. 860–4, 1979.

12 Ref. Jim Horne, *New Scientist*, 12 December 1985.

13 Dr David Haslam, *Sleepless Children*, p. 36.

14 Michel Odent, *Primal Health*, p. 148.

15 Price quoted in 1988.

CHAPTER 5

1 Indidences of SIDS decreased to 1.44 per 1,000 live births in 1992, from 2.3 per 1,000 in 1988.

2 'Every year in the United Kingdom about 2,000 babies between the ages of one week and two years die suddenly and unexpectedly for no obvious reason, 90% before the age of eight months. These unexpected deaths account for half of all deaths in this age group ... In some cases the cause is evident at post mortem; but in many others ... the cause of death is not found.' FSID leaflet for bereaved parents, September 1983.

3 The Back To Sleep campaign in Britain has dramatically reduced the rate of SIDS. Co-sleeping babies sleep-feed on the side.

4 'Cot death ... remains a focus of concern, controversy, and speculation.

It closely follows congenital abnormalities and preterm birth as the most common single cause of infant death in many parts of the world, especially in western countries, with an average incidence of about 2–3 per 1000 live births.' D. P. Davies, *The Lancet*, 14 December 1985.

5 Gantley, Davies, Murcott, 'Sudden infant death syndrome = links with infant care practices.' British Medical Journal, January 2, 1933.

6 'Most interesting is that the human infant's vestibular system [touch-response] is functioning at its 'highest level of reactivity' after the first few months of life [Ornitz 1983:527], the very time period when infants are at greatest risk of dying from SIDS. In other words, at the time their respiratory [breathing] control system is the most vulnerable, infants may be most sensitive to respiratory augmentation [help with breathing] through external vestibular and auditory stimuli [touching and noise] – cues readily available in the infant's expected microenvironment [near him] if parents and infants sleep together throughout the night.' James McKenna, *Medical Anthropology*, 1986.

7 C. Templeman, 1892, *Edinburgh Medical Journal*, vol. 38, pp. 322–9.

8 Julian Aston Productions, London.

9 'Mr J. P. Nicholl and Miss A. O'Cathain (Sheffield, Project 80) have completed a further analysis of 304 SIDS infants from the Multicentre Study of Post Neonatal Mortality ... They also looked at evidence for some recent claims about factors associated with SIDS. They found no evidence for 'overlaying' as the cause of death in the very small number of babies who had died in their parents' beds.' FSID newsletter 34, August 1988.

10 Faroooqui, Perry, Beevers, 'Ethnic differences in sleeping position and in risk of cot death,' *The Lancet*, 1991, vol. 338. No cot deaths reported in two years at only hospital in Zimbabwe town, pop. 300,000.

CHAPTER 6

1 'Present Day Practice in Infant Feeding', 3rd report, HMSO, February 1988.

2 Chloe Fisher, *Oxford Medical School Gazette*, 1982.

3 Jane Ellen Panton, *The Way They Should Go*, London, 1896.

4 *Mother*, September 1988.

5 DTW (direct test weighing) involves putting the baby on scales after every feed. ITW, the indirect method, is a complex calculation involving measurements of urine and evaporated water-loss, but it allows mother and baby to sleep uninterrupted through the night. DTW is believed to cause a reduction in nocturnal milk intake. ITW, being non-intrusive, does not.

(Ref: Stella M. Imong et al., *Journal of Pediatric Gastroenterology and Nutrition*, 1988.)

6 '... over 24h post-delivery, a mother ... might be expected to give up to 8 breastfeeds, which, based on an average values, may amount to a total of 3h of suckling.' M. W. Woolridge et al., *Early Human Development*, 1985.

7 *Concise Oxford Dictionary*.

8 Edmund Owen, *Baby*, 1888. See chapter 6, page 96.

9 Comparisons of hospital management in Sweden (where mothers were only allowed contact with their babies at feeding times) and Thailand, (where mothers fed their babies freely through the night) showed that mothers' milk flowed regardless of differences in policy. (Ref: Woolridge et al., *Early Human Development*.)

10 e.g. Valerie Fildes, *Wet Nursing: A History from Antiquity to the Present*.

11 Norman Tindale, chapter in *Hunters and Gatherers Today*.

12 P. W. Howie et al., *British Medical Journal*, 1981.

13 Ref: Máire Messinger Davies, *The Breastfeeding Book*, page 13.

14 'Breast feeding of first babies drops', *The Independent*, 28 July 1988.

CHAPTER 7

1 Barry and Paxson, 1971, quoted by James McKenna in *Medical Anthropology*, 1986.

2 James Prescott, *Bulletin of the Atomic Scientists*, November 1975.

3 Quoted in M. Dorothy George, *London Life in the Eighteenth Century*.

4 Quoted in Sarah Helm, 'When children were chattels', *The Independent*, 5 July 1988.

5 Lozoff, Wolf and Davis, *Pediatrics*, August 1984.

6 C. C. Hanks and E. G. Rebelsky, *Psychiatry*, 1977.

7 'The most suggestive feature of the relationship of mother and son is their extreme physical intimacy. Elvis slept in the same bed with Gladys until he was at the threshold of puberty.' Albert Goldman, *Elvis*.

CHAPTER 8

1 'Rise in cases may be levelling off', *The Independent*, 5 July 1988.

2 *Mother*, October 1987. Statistical analysis supplied by Andy Coasby.

3 '... a staggering 60 per cent either make love for their partner's sake or because they can't tell him they don't want to.' *Mother*, October 1987.

4 The Maori, Mbuti pygmies and many other peoples expect the husband to refrain from sexual advances towards his wife for some time after the birth of a baby. Some cultures allow the man to have an affair or a second wife, where the period of abstinence is more than a few months.

5 The Andamanese, islanders from the Bay of Bengal, are typical of most non-industrial people living in primitive conditions. They 'perform the

sexual act with little privacy, owing to the flimsy construction of their huts around the dance floor and to the dangers, real and imagined, of the dense jungle'. Carleton S. Coon, *The Hunting Peoples*.

6 *The Sunday Times*, 19 July 1988.

7 Jean Liedloff, *The Continuum Concept*.

CHAPTER 9

1 '(figurative) disengage or cure (*away*) *from* habit, specified company, etc., by enforced abstinence or counter-attractions.' *Concise Oxford Dictionary*.

2 Michel Odent, *Primal Health*. See chapter 1, p. 22.

3 'No matter how carefully the child is cared for he has to experience one major frustration in his early life – he has to be weaned from the breast and later from the bottle.' English and Pearson, *Emotional Problems of Living*.

4 Reported by Gillian Mercer, 'Shyness is a family problem', *The Independent*, 12 July 1988.

5 Quoted in *Family Circle*, 27 November 1988.

6 *The Independent*, 19 August 1988.

7 'Making Links with Children's Education', a pamphlet for the 2nd International Conference on the F. M. Alexander Technique, Brighton, 1988.

8 'Winnicott ... says about the good enough mother that the infant, as he looks into her face, sees there himself – or one might say, finds there himself – because the good enough mother, because of her deep empathy with her infant, reflects in her face *his* feelings ... The not good enough mother fails to reflect the infant's feeling in her face because she is too preoccupied with her own concerns, such as her worries over whether she is doing right by her child, her anxiety that she might fail him.' Bruno Bettelheim, *A Good Enough Parent*.

CHAPTER 10

1 Breastfeeding research by Mike Woolridge and a team from the Department of Child Health, University of Bristol. Report in *Early Human Development*, 1985.

2 Jean Liedloff, *The Continuum Concept*.

3 Julian Aston Productions, London.

4 'Norms for sleep/waking patterns in infancy were developed in the 1950s and 1960s, decades that marked the nadir of breast-feeding in the United States ... the norms do not apply to infants who continue to be nursed for many months.' Elias, Nicolson, Bora and Johnston, *Pediatrics*, March 1986.

A child of two, nursing and sleeping with his mother, typically sleeps for 4.8 hours at a stretch, compared with 6.9 hours for the breastfed child who sleeps alone. The child in a cot who does not nurse at night sleeps longer – an average of 9.5 hours in one go.

In other words, a child can sometimes be trained to sleep through the night alone, if he does not find the constant comfort he needs and expects. But the mother who is breastfeeding her baby can expect him to feed every two to four hours during the night (just as he does in the day).

5 The Wilkinet Baby Carrier is available from Penrallt, Pantyderi, Boncath, near Cardigan, Wales SA37 0JB (tel. 023 974 390).

6 'J. W. B. Douglas, in a review of the problem in 1967 [*BMJ* II, pp. 233–5] found that there was a correlation between bedwetting at four-and-a-half years and the number of stressful events which occurred when the child was two or three, such as illness, operation, and separations from the family.' Dr David Haslam, *Sleepless Children*.

7 'Many parents confuse night terrors with nightmares, but they are very different. A child with a night terror will be found screaming, sitting up, wide-eyed with dilated pupils, and very frightened and agitated. He doesn't recognise his parents during the attack and is disorientated ... These upsetting episodes last an average of two minutes ... Thankfully, the entire episode will not be recalled.' *ibid*.

8 'The discovery that external rhythmic breathing cues, in this case movement, influence infants' breathing patterns implies that there is continuity in the ways that mothers' biorhythms physiologically regulate their offspring both prenatally and postnatally ...' James McKenna, *Medical Anthropology*, 1986.

CHAPTER 11
1 Frances Moore Lappé in interview with Derek Cooper on BBC Radio Four, August 1988.
2 Quoted in La Leche League, *The Art of Breastfeeding*.
3 See chapter 2, p. 31.
4 Hormones regulate our sleep patterns: pregnant and breastfeeding mothers do not enter the fourth, or deepest, stage of sleep. (Michel Odent, *Primal Health*, p. 148.)
5 Lozoff, Wolf and Davis, *Pediatrics*, August 1984.

CHAPTER 12
1 'The machine that goes "ping!" ' featured in Monty Python's film *The Meaning of Life* (UK, Terry Jones, 1988).

APPENDIX
1 Hanks and Rebelsky, *Psychiatry*, 1977.

BIBLIOGRAPHY

Jane Asher, *Silent Nights: For You and Your Baby*. Pelham, 1984.

Norman Autton, *Pain: An Exploration*. Darton, Longman and Todd, 1986.

Bruno Bettelheim, *A Good Enough Parent: A Book on Childrearing*. Thames and Hudson, 1987.

M. G. Bicchieri (editor), *Hunters and Gatherers Today: A Socio-economic Study of Eleven Such Cultures in the Twentieth Century*. Holt, Rinehart and Winston, 1972.

Prof. Herbert Brant and Prof. Kenneth S. Holt (consultants), *The Complete Mothercare Manual: An Illustrated Guide to Pregnancy, Birth and Childcare*. Conran Octopus, 1986.

John Bowlby, *Childcare and the Growth of Love*. Pelican, 1953.

Carleton S. Coon, *The Hunting Peoples*. Cape, 1972.

Dr Richard Ferber, *Solve Your Child's Sleep Problems: The Complete Practical Guide for Parents*. (1985) Dorling Kindersley, 1986.

Valerie Fildes, *Wet Nursing: A History from Antiquity to the Present*. Blackwell, 1988.

M. Dorothy George, *London Life in the Eighteenth Century*. (1925) Penguin, 1965.

Albert Goldman, *Elvis*. (1981) Penguin, 1982.

Dr Christopher Green, *Toddler Taming: A Parent's Guide to the First Four Years*. Century, 1984.

Dr David Haslam, *Sleepless Children: A Handbook for Parents*. (1984) Futura, 1985.

Christina Hardyment, *Dream Babies*. (1983) Oxford University Press, 1984.

Sally Inch, *Birthrights: A Parent's Guide to Modern Childbirth*. (1982) Hutchinson, 1985.

Hugh Jolly, *Book of Child Care: The Complete Guide for Today's Parents*. Unwin, 1985.

Sheila Kitzinger, *Pregnancy and Childbirth*. Dorling Kindersley, 1980.

Penelope Leach, *Babyhood*. (1974) Penguin, 1980.

Frédérick Leboyer, *Birth Without Violence*. (1974) Fontana, 1987.

La Leche League International, *The Art of Breastfeeding: The Complete Guide for the Nursing Mother*. (1958) revised edn. Angus and Robertson, 1988.

Mary R. Lefkowitz and Maureen B. Fant, *Women's Life in Greece and Rome*. Duckworth, 1982.

Jean Liedloff, *The Continuum Concept*. (1975) Penguin, 1986.

Aidan Macfarlane, *The Psychology of Childbirth*. Fontana, 1977.

Leon Maidow, *Anger*. Unwin, 1972.

Brigid McConville, *Mad to be a Mother: Is There Life after Birth for Women Today?* Century Hutchinson, 1987.

Andrina E. McCormack, *Coping with Your Handicapped Child*. Chambers, 1985.

Máire Messinger Davies, *The Breastfeeding Book*. (1982) Century Hutchinson, 1986.

Daphne Metland, *Getting Ready for Baby*. Foulsham, 1987.

Bob Mullen, *Are Mothers Really Necessary?* Boxtree, 1987.

Michel Odent, *Entering the World: The Way to Gentle, Loving Birth*. (1976) Penguin, 1985; *Primal Health: A Blueprint for Our Survival*. Century Hutchinson, 1986.

Donald J. Olsen, *The Growth of Victorian London*. (1976) Penguin, 1976.

Maud Pember Reeves, *Round About a Pound a Week*. (1913) Virago, 1979.

Libby Purves, *How NOT to be a Perfect Mother*. Fontana, 1986.

Edith Rudinger (editor), *The Newborn Baby*. (1972) Consumers' Association, revised edn 1979.

Peter Saunders, *Birthwise: Having a Baby in the 80s*. Sidgwick and Jackson, 1985.

Dolly Scannell, *Mother Knew Best/An East End Childhood*. (1974) Pan, 1975.

Rudolf Schaffer, *Mothering*. Fontana, 1977.

André Singer with Leslie Woodhead, *Disappearing World*. Boxtree, 1988.

Joanna Smith, *Edwardian Children*. Hutchinson, 1983.

Benjamin Spock and Michael B. Rothenberg, *Dr Spock's Baby and Child Care*. (1945) W. H. Allen, 1985.

Margery Spring Rice, *Working-Class Wives*. (1939) Virago, 1981.

Royal College of Midwives, *Successful Breastfeeding: A Practical Guide for Midwives (and other supporting breastfeeding mothers)*. RCM, 1988.

O. Spurgeon English and Gerald H. Pearson, *Emotional Problems of Living: Avoiding the Neurotic Pattern*. Unwin, 1963.

Drs Penny and Andrew Stanway, *Breast is Best*. Pan, 1978; *Choices in Childbirth*. Pan, 1984.

L. Joseph Stone and Joseph Church, *Childhood and Adolescence: A Psychology of the Growing Person*. Random House, 1957.

Tine Thevenin, *The Family Bed: An Age-Old Concept in Child-Rearing*. Avery, 1987.

Peter Tinniswood, *A Touch of Daniel*. Arrow, 1983.

Jane Vosper, *Good Housekeeping's Baby Book*. (1944) National Magazine Co., 1969.

Peter Walker, *The Book of Baby Massage: For a Happier, Healthier Child*. Bloomsbury, 1988.

Annette B. Weiner, *The Trobrianders of Papua New Guinea*. Holt, Rinehart and Winston, 1988.

William Wharton, *Tidings*. Cape, 1988.

ARTICLES IN SPECIALIST JOURNALS

T. F. Anders, 'Night Waking in Infants during the First Year of Life', *Pediatrics*, 1979, vol. 69, pp. 860–4.

Kathryn Conder, 'Sleep in Child Rearing – A Cross Cultural Perspective', *Midwife, Health Visitor and Community Nurse*, April 1988, pp. 126–7.

Dilys Daws, 'Sleep Problems in Babies and Young Children', *Journal of Child Psychotherapy*, 1985, vol. 11 no. 2, pp. 87–95.

D. P. Davies, 'Cot Death in Hong Kong: A Rare Problem?', *The Lancet*, 14 December 1985, pp. 1346–8.

Marjorie F. Elias, Nancy A. Nicolson, Carolyn Bora and Johanna Johnston, 'Sleep/Wake Patterns of Breast-Fed Infants in the First 2 Years of Life', *Pediatrics*, March 1986, vol. 77 no. 3.

Chloë Fisher, 'Mythology in Midwifery – or "Making Breastfeeding Scientific and Exact"', *Oxford Medical School Gazette*, Trinity Term 1982, vol. XXXIII no. 2; 'How did we go wrong with breastfeeding?' *Midwifery*, 1985, vol. 1, pp. 48–51.

C. C. Hanks, and F. G. Rebelsky, 'Mommy and the midnight visitor: A study of occasional co-sleeping', *Psychiatry*, 1977, vol. 40, pp. 277–80.

Jim Horne, 'Insomnia; some facts and fiction', *The Practitioner*, October 1985, vol. 229; 'Snoring can Damage Your Health', *New Scientist*, 12 December 1985; 'The Substance of Sleep', *New Scientist*, 7 January 1988.

P. W. Howie et al., 'Effects of supplementary food on suckling patterns and ovarian activity during lactation', *British Medical Journal*, 1981, vol. 283, pp. 757–9.

Stella M. Imong et al., 'Measuring Night Time Breast Milk Intake – Why Bother?', *Proc. 5th Asian Congress of Nutrition*, October 1987; 'Indirect Test Weighing: A New Method for Measuring Overnight Breast Milk Intakes in the Field', *Journal of Pediatric Gastroenterology and Nutrition*, 1988.

Betsy Lozoff, Abraham Wolf and Nancy S. Davis, 'Cosleeping in Urban Families with Young Children in the United States', *Pediatrics*, August 1984, vol. 74 no. 2, pp. 171–82; 'Sleep Problems Seen in Pediatric Practice', *Pediatrics*, March 1985, vol. 75 no. 3, pp. 477–83.

Penny Mansfield, 'Getting Ready for Parenthood: attitudes to and expectations of having children of a group of newly-weds', *Journal of Sociology and Social Policy*, 1982, vol. 2 no. 1, pp. 28–39.

James J. McKenna, 'An Anthropological Perspective on SIDS', *Medical Anthropology*, 1985, vol. 10 no. 1.

James Prescott, 'Body Pleasure and the Origins of Violence', *Bulletin of the Atomic Scientists*, November 1975.

Ronald W. Snead and William M. Bruch, 'Social and Emotional Problems of Childhood', *Pediatrics*, 1983.

A. N. Stanton and J. R. Oakley, 'Pattern of illnesses before cot deaths', *Archives of Disease in Childhood*, 1983, vol. 58, pp. 878–81.

M. W. Woolridge, Vivienne Greasley and Suporn Silpisornkosol, 'The initiation of lactation: the effect of early versus delay contact for suckling on milk intake in the first week post partum. A study in Chiang Mai, Northern Thailand', *Early Human Development*, 1985, vol. 12, pp. 269–78.

INDEX